PENGUIN BOOKS

THE RISE OF BENEDICT XVI

John L. Allen is the Vatican correspondent for the *National Catholic Reporter* and a Vatican analyst for CNN and National Public Radio. He has also reported for the BBC and will appear in a BBC documentary on Opus Dei later this year. Considered by many as the best single source of insights on Vatican affairs in the English language, (particularly through his internet column 'The Word from Rome'), he is the author of four books on the Catholic Church, including *Conclave: The Politics, Personalities, and Processes of the Next Papal Election* (1992). His new book, *Opus Dei: Secrets and Power Inside the Catholic Church*, will be published this autumn. His work has appeared in *The New York Times*, *The Boston Globe*, and many other publications.

D0680223

The Rise

OF

BENEDICT XVI

THE INSIDE STORY OF
HOW THE POPE WAS ELECTED
AND WHAT IT MEANS
FOR THE WORLD

JOHN L. ALLEN, JR.

PENGUIN BOOKS

PENGUIN BOOKS

Published by the Penguin Group
Penguin Books Ltd, 80 Strand, London WC2R 0RL, England
Penguin Group (USA) Inc., 375 Hudson Street, New York, New York 10014, USA
Penguin Group (Canada), 90 Eglinton Avenue East, Suite 700, Toronto, Ontario,
Canada M4P 2Y3 (a division of Pearson Penguin Canada Inc.)
Penguin Ireland, 25 St Stephen's Green, Dublin 2, Ireland
(a division of Penguin Books Ltd)
Penguin Group (Australia), 250 Camberwell Road,
Camberwell, Victoria 3124, Australia (a division of Pearson Australia Group Pty Ltd)
Penguin Books India Pvt Ltd, 11 Community Centre,
Panchsheel Park, New Delhi – 110 017, India
Penguin Group (NZ), cnr Airborne and Rosedale Roads, Albany,
Auckland 1310, New Zealand (a division of Pearson New Zealand Ltd)
Penguin Books (South Africa) (Pty) Ltd, 24 Sturdee Avenue,
Rosebank 2196, South Africa

Penguin Books Ltd, Registered Offices: 80 Strand, London WC2R 0RL, England

www.penguin.com

First published in the United States of America by Doubleday 2005
First published in Great Britain in Penguin Books 2005
1

Printed in England by Clays Ltd, St Ives plc

CONTENTS

Preface   1

Part One

"AT THE WINDOW OF THE FATHER'S HOUSE"   15

1 The Final Days of Pope John Paul II   17

Part Two

"HABEMUS PAPAM"   45

2 The Funeral Effect   47

3 The Interregnum   74

4 The Conclave   105

Part Three

A PAPACY OF EPIC AMBITION   141

5 Who is Joseph Ratzinger?   143

6 Battling a "Dictatorship of Relativism"   165

7 Changing the Culture of the Church   199

8 Surprises and Challenges   227

PREFACE

Politics, it is often said, is the art of compromise. Because elections involve the clash of different interests, victory usually belongs to the candidate who can offer something to everyone, negotiating between competing visions and desires. The winning candidate is generally the one who seems most likely to appeal to all constituencies, or, at a minimum, to be the least disappointing to the majority. Political rhetoric is crafted with this in mind, offering a mixture of platitudes and banalities whose main aim seems to be to offend the fewest listeners possible.

Sometimes, however, the electorate is not in the mood to compromise. Sometimes, with an important historical crossroads looming in front of them, voters opt for a bold choice rather than a "least common denominator."

Such was the humor of the College of Cardinals of the Roman Catholic Church in April 2005, when it gathered to elect a successor to Pope John Paul II. Faced with a slew of potential compromise candidates, the cardinals opted instead for a clear, resounding choice, entrusting the Keys of the Kingdom, which Catholics believe were promised by Christ to St. Peter, to seventy-eight-year-old Cardinal Joseph Ratzinger, a man whose resolute views on the challenges facing the Church and the broader culture could not be more unambiguous.

Pope Benedict XVI is a man of epic ambition who hopes to do nothing less than challenge four centuries of intellectual development in the West toward subjectivity and relativism, producing what European intellectuals who share his view call a climate of "weak thought." Like St. Benedict sixteen centuries before, from whom the new pope took his name, Benedict XVI aims to inspire alternative models of Christian existence for a culture that, he believes, is too often in denial about the real meaning and purpose of human existence. Benedict is convinced, in a way that has to be nuanced in order to be understood, that there is a historical parallel between the collapse of the Roman Empire and the slide into the Dark Ages, and the era in which we live. Benedict XVI is too sophisticated to launch a crude jihad against secularism, but his pontificate will, nevertheless, be a tough, demanding one, and those who elected him certainly knew that. He will challenge the world to recover confidence in the power of the human intellect to find truth, and the moral and spiritual capacity of men and women to order their lives in the light of that truth. He will do so joyfully, in a spirit of service rather than power, but he will be uncompromising and crystal clear.

There are few jobs on earth more complex, and more consequential, than serving as the Supreme Pontiff of the 1.1 billion-strong Roman Catholic Church. The election of a pope is not just a colorful ritual cloaked in centuries-old mystery and romance, but the naming of an important global leader whose policies touch the lives not just of Catholics, but people of all faiths and of none. Try as one might, a pope cannot be ignored. Religion stirs the deepest passions of the human soul, so that a pope has the capacity to shape not just people's voting patterns or ideological self-interest, but their dreams and the best versions of themselves. The pope is a moral compass, a voice of conscience, and a cartographer of the soul, and because of all this, the pope is inevitably a major political force. A handful of other religious figures play a similar role, but none so prominently or so influentially as the head of the Roman Catholic Church. To put the point bluntly, a pope *matters*.

For Catholics, the pope is believed to be the Vicar of Christ on earth, the successor of St. Peter as the chief shepherd of the Christian community. Before all else, therefore, he is supposed to be a man of exemplary holiness, someone who can radiate a sense of God's love and the power of redemption, someone who can inspire and challenge and console, someone who can do all this while also governing and correcting members of the flock when they stray. It is, in many ways, an impossible and thankless job, imposing a bewildering cluster of demands—the mastering of any one of which would be a life's work.

All this went into the reflections of the members of the College of Cardinals, 115 of them under eighty years of age and healthy enough to participate, who arrived in Rome in April 2005 to face the daunting task of electing a new pope. Moreover, they were not just electing any new pontiff, but the successor to John Paul II, a titan who cut across his times in a way few popes of any era ever have. To invoke a tired cliché, John Paul II would be a very hard act to follow, and the cardinals knew they had to consider this choice carefully. Most cardinals who were already in their late sixties and seventies were also aware that they would likely have only one opportunity in their lifetime to cast a ballot for a pope, and so the responsibility wore even more heavily.

Catholics believe that the selection of the pope unfolds under the guidance of the Holy Spirit, so that it is not, in the first place, a political exercise but a process of spiritual discernment rooted in prayer. This idea was summed up on the eve of the conclave by the smiling, cheerful Cardinal Ennio Antonelli of Florence, considered by some to be a candidate himself, who said that God already knew who the new pope was, so it was simply up to the cardinals to figure out what God had already decided. Many longtime Vatican-watchers regarded the comment as pious sermonizing, but listening to cardinals after the fact, many seemed to have really experienced the process this way. At least some cardinals perceived a clash between their prayer and their politics; in their heart of hearts, many saw Joseph Ratzinger as the right man for the job, but worried that in some sectors of opinion, especially in western Europe and the United States, he might bring too much "baggage" because of twenty-four difficult, controversial years as the Church's top doctrinal watchdog. In the end, most voted their conscience rather than their fear, trying to be faithful to their vow, uttered aloud below Michelangelo's intimidating fresco of the Last Judgment during each round of balloting: "I call as my witness Christ the Lord, who will be my judge, that my vote is given the one who before God I think should be elected."

In doing so, many of the cardinals no doubt heard the words of John Paul's last poem, "Roman Tryptych", echoing in their memories. Meditating on the conclave that would elect his successor, the late Pope had written: "It is necessary that during the conclave, Michelangelo teach them . . . Michelangelo's vision must teach them." The idea was that the cardinals should be thinking not about political or careerist consequences when they cast their ballots, but the moment of judgment in the next life when they will have to account for their choice before God.

Whether God—or history—will eventually judge their choice to have been the correct one remains to be seen. At this stage the pontificate of Benedict XVI is very much an open book, the chapters of which are waiting to be written. Given the character of the man, however, the one thing we can say with certainty about the 265th papacy of the Roman Catholic Church is that it will not be dull. Dramatic, fascinating days lie ahead.

In electing Joseph Ratzinger, the cardinals managed to shatter several bits of conventional wisdom about conclaves: that he who goes in a pope, comes out a cardinal (now false in three of the last six papal elections); that someone too closely identified with the policies of the previous pope is usually not chosen; that the 76 percent of cardinals who come from dioceses around the world would not vote for a member of the Roman Curia; that the cardinals would not want to elect someone from Europe, where the faith is flagging; that seventy-eight years of age is too old to begin so awesome a ministry; that Ratzinger had been in power too long, made too many enemies as well as friends, to put together a two-thirds majority. All these handicapping tips turned out, at least this time around, to be hogwash. In addition, the widely held belief that the Italians would gang up to ensure that the papacy came back home also proved unfounded. In fact, several non-Italian cardinals said that their Italian colleagues by and large approached the election "objectively," concentrating on the person rather than the passport he happened to hold. For the most part, conventional political logic gave way to a genuine sense that Ratzinger was the most qualified and best prepared candidate, regardless of age, nationality, or career path.

On the other hand, it is also traditional Catholic theology that grace builds on nature, it doesn't cancel it out, so that the belief that God is involved in the selection of a pope does not make it any less a political process. As one cardinal put it to me afterward, "I was never whapped on the head by the Holy Spirit. I had to make the best choice I could based on the information available." Thus the election of Joseph Ratzinger was also a political drama whose outcome was uncertain until the curtain came up, and one that could have gone another way if a few variables had fallen into place differently. As obvious as the selection of a given pope may seem after the fact, it never feels that way going in. History, as they say, can only be understood backwards, but must be lived forwards.

In a sense, Pope John Paul had been dying for years by the time his death actually came, and one might expect that therefore the conclave of 2005 was a well-prepared, well-rehearsed event. In fact, however, most cardinals said the opposite was the case. Because John Paul had survived so many crises over the course of almost twenty-seven years, many had given up thinking about the succession, since the politics and personalities could shift many times before the moment actually arrived. (Indeed, had John Paul lived just three more months, he was expected to create a slew of new cardinals, once again recasting the drama.) Even in the final weeks of the Pope's life, when the end seemed painfully near, most cardinals were thinking in terms of issues and profiles of leadership, not actual candidates. When they gathered in Rome in early April, therefore, it was still very much anyone's game.

Perhaps the best expression of this idea belongs to none other than the new pope himself, Benedict XVI, who, as Cardinal Joseph Ratzinger, was asked on Bavarian television in 1997 if the Holy Spirit is responsible for who gets elected pope. This was his response:

> I would not say so, in the sense that the Holy Spirit picks out the Pope. . . . I would say that the Spirit does not exactly take control of the affair, but rather like a good educator, as it were, leaves us much space, much freedom, without entirely abandoning us. Thus the Spirit's role should be understood in a much more elastic sense, not that he dictates the candidate for whom one must vote. Probably the only assurance he offers is that the thing cannot be totally ruined.

Then the clincher:

> There are too many contrary instances of popes the Holy Spirit would obviously not have picked.

In attempting to piece together the story of the conclave, I have been primarily guided by after-the-fact conversations with eight cardinals, representing five nationalities (spanning three continents). Because the cardinals had taken vows of secrecy, these conversations were of necessity "on background," meaning they are not quoted here by name. None of the cardinals, in my view, came even close to violating his oath of secrecy in our conversations. No one revealed round-by-round voting totals, for example. They were, however, willing to offer me a window into the preconclave politics—the meetings over dinner at national colleges, the late-hour chats, the free-flowing conversations at the Roman residences of friends within the College of Cardinals. They were also willing in a general sense to talk about the drama within the conclave itself, and how in relatively short order a disparate group of 115 men, each with his own strong vision for the future of the Church, was able to come to consensus on a single candidate to lead them. To these cardinals, who understand that legitimate public curiosity will either be fed with accurate information or with gossip and innuendo, go my eternal thanks.

My rule in this process was that I trusted nothing that came from a secondary source. Until I had a point confirmed by at least two cardinals, I treated it as unreliable. There are all sorts of widely circulated rumors surrounding events inside the conclave that do not appear in this book, and with the passage of time it may even emerge that some are true. I want the reader to know, however, that whatever is in this book has undergone the most thorough process of verification possible.

Joseph Ratzinger's election as Pope Benedict XVI, the 265th pope in the official Vatican listing (though that counts Pope Benedict IX three times, who had three separate pontificates in the eleventh century), is of importance not just for Church historians and idly curious onlookers. The reasons he was elected, and the policies he is likely to pursue, will have decisive global consequences. Moreover, it would be foolish to interpret the election of this seventy-eight-year-old German as a vote for a do-nothing, "transitional" pontificate. To put the matter bluntly, there isn't a transitional bone in Joseph Ratzinger's body. Nor is this merely a vote for continuity with John Paul II, as if the College of Cardinals has simply reelected the previous pope. Though Benedict XVI will certainly continue the main lines of John Paul's papacy, since he was intimately involved in constructing the intellectual agenda of that pontificate, he will also bring his own style and sense of priorities to the job. He is an original thinker, and one can expect his papacy to be an original one.

At the outset, one should not shy away from adding the necessary adjunct to the above: Benedict's papacy is also likely to be contentious, especially for those Catholics of a more liberal bent, as well as secular centers of opinion that would prefer a pope whose opinions hew more closely to the editorial pages of the *New York Times* than to the *Catechism of the Catholic Church*. While Pope Benedict XVI will prove to be a more gracious figure than his previous public image suggests, there is no ducking the point that his will be a strong teaching papacy, and people may not always like what they hear—on issues ranging from human sexuality to religious pluralism to the exercise of ecclesiastical authority. There will be much to debate, much about which faithful Catholics, as well as men and women of all creeds, will disagree. The cardinals knew this as well, which makes the logic for their selection of Benedict XVI especially worthy of study.

This book tells the story of Pope John Paul II's last days, the behind-the-scenes dynamics within the College of Cardinals that led to the choice of Joseph Ratzinger as Pope Benedict XVI, and where the new pope is likely to lead the Catholic Church. Fortunately, this is not an exercise in speculation, because Ratzinger has perhaps the most extensive public track record of any member of the College of Cardinals, and is that rare Vatican official who has been a celebrity in his own time. He led the crackdown on liberation theology in Latin America in the 1980s, the strong defense of traditional positions on issues of sexual morality such as homosexuality, the insistence that respect for other religions not obscure the uniqueness of the salvation won by Christ, and the demand that Catholic theologians uphold magisterial teaching, thereby restricting the notion of "loyal opposition" or "dissent" as a legitimate theological option. It is hardly guesswork to expect that these views will continue to have force in his pontificate.

This record however, is not, the whole story about Joseph Ratzinger. Those who know him privately have long commented on the disjunction between his public reputation and his private persona. In intimate settings, Ratzinger has always come across as generous, humble, and gentle, never seeking to impress others with his razor-sharp mind, but always prepared for whatever discussion is at hand. He's known for a sly sense of humor, an impish smile, and the capacity to put people at ease.

In a book-length interview in 2002 titled *God and the World*, Ratzinger says that "God has a great sense of humor."

"Sometimes he gives you something like a nudge and says, 'Don't take yourself so seriously!'" Ratzinger said. "Humor is in fact an essential element in the mirth of creation. We can see how, in many matters in our lives, God wants to prod us into taking things a bit more lightly;

to see the funny side of it; to get down off our pedestal and not to forget our sense of fun."

This is not the Joseph Ratzinger that some people think they know.

The new pope is also regarded as a good listener. More than one bishop after an *ad limina* trip to Rome, the visit to the Pope and Vatican offices that all bishops are required to make every five years, has come away contrasting their experience in the Congregation for the Doctrine of the Faith with other offices in the Roman Curia. Elsewhere, they say, it is not uncommon for the head of the office to walk into a room, read a prepared speech to the bishops, and then exit, as if they were a group of college undergraduates. With Ratzinger, on the other hand, bishops report that he asks about their concerns and seems to genuinely listen to what they have to say. These are promising traits for a pope who inherits a College of Bishops often frustrated precisely by the sensation of not being heard in Rome.

Moreover, to focus entirely on the public controversies during Ratzinger's Vatican years risks obscuring the deeper concerns of the man that underlie those specific debates, as well as the more quiet activity of his office that never draws public attention. Fundamentally, Ratzinger has long been concerned that the Christian message, that God entered history in the person of Jesus Christ in order to mark out a path to salvation, one that does not vary with time or fashion, becomes jeopardized in a cultural environment that has largely abandoned the concept of objective truth. Collapse of confidence in truth, he believes, leads to disastrous consequences. He witnessed that in Nazi Germany, when mistaken ideas about human nature led to the disasters of the Second World War, including the horrors of the Holocaust. His concern for maintaining the truths of the faith is therefore not simply an authoritarian desire to police the limits of acceptable thought; it has much deeper roots.

The point is that one cannot automatically collapse Ratzinger's tenure at the Congregation for the Doctrine of the Faith into his new role as the Universal Pastor of the Catholic Church. The Pope, whatever one makes of his career as the Vatican's enforcer, realizes that in the first place people are not convinced of the Christian message on the basis of doctrinal debates. They want to see that Christianity is a joyful thing, a source of life and hope, that it lights fires of love and self-sacrifice. In the 1985 interview with Vittorio Messori that became *The Ratzinger Report*, he acknowledged precisely this: "The only really effective apologia for Christianity comes down to two arguments," he said, "namely, the saints the Church has produced and the art which has grown in her womb."

In the early days after his election, Pope Benedict attempted to strike just these notes. In his programmatic talk on Wednesday morning, April 20, following Mass with the cardinals in the Sistine Chapel, he talked about dialogue, ecumenism, interreligious outreach, the need for the Church to witness to authentic social development, and his desire to transmit joy and hope to the world. The Pope called for collaboration between the bishops and the Pope, a reference to collegiality in the Church. He committed himself to the Second Vatican Council (1962–65), an important signal for those who believe he has tried to "roll back the clock" on the reforms associated with the council. Benedict XVI also said he would reach out in a special way to the young, much in the style of his predecessor, John Paul II. (The Vatican later confirmed that the new pope will travel to Cologne in August for World Youth Day.) On Monday, April 25, in an audience with representatives of other religions, the Pope said: "At the beginning of my pontificate I address to you, believers in religious traditions who represent all those who seek the truth with a sincere heart, a strong invitation to become together artisans of peace in a reciprocal commitment of comprehension, respect and love."

All this suggests the pontificate of Benedict XVI may have surprises in store.

Because the new pope has been a highly public figure generating diverse reactions, the early response to his election was perhaps a bit overheated in some quarters. In progressive or liberal Catholic circles, the emotional reaction sometimes verged on despair. One well-known liberal commentator called the result a "disaster," and others had even worse things to say, well before the new pope had even opened his mouth. One leading leftist paper in Italy captured this sense of where the Pope would go, publishing a front-page editorial cartoon that was a parody of a famous moment from the pontificate of Pope John XXIII. "Good Pope John" once stood at his Vatican window on a moonlit night and, speaking to a crowd in St. Peter's Square, said, "Go home and kiss your children, and tell them that this kiss comes from the Pope." The cartoon showed Pope Benedict at the window saying, instead, "Go home and spank your children, and tell them that this spanking comes from the Pope." Another Italian paper dubbed the new pope *il pastore Tedesco*, "the German shepherd," a play on his nationality as well as his reputation for being a ferocious guard dog of doctrinal orthodoxy.

On the Catholic right, there were still uglier voices to be heard. Within hours of Benedict's election, for example, I received e-mails predicting that the newspaper for which I work, the *National Catholic Reporter*, would be eviscerated under his pontificate. Others began circulating enemies' lists, with the names of well-known Catholic liberals who would be purged on Benedict's watch. As we will see later in chapter five, one such prominent liberal did indeed fall shortly thereafter, though as a result of a process that had been under way long before Ratzinger became pope. Of course, it is entirely legitimate to discuss the positions one can take and still meaningfully refer to oneself as "Catholic," and it seems this pontificate will occasion such conversations. But to make your first reaction to the joyful news that the Church has a pope one of vengeance can suggest a worrying lack of Christian spirit.

In this regard, I am cheered by responses such as that of Stephen Hand, who edits a small on-line service called "Traditional Catholic Reflections and Reports." Hand would conventionally be described as a Catholic conservative, and a few years ago he wrote a blistering review, not entirely undeserved, of my 1999 biography entitled *Cardinal Ratzinger: The Vatican's Enforcer of the Faith*. In the aftermath of Benedict's election, Hand wrote to invite me to write an essay for his site, expressing his desire to make a new start: "Let's begin anew," he volunteered. "All any of us want is fair reporting, even if tensions in perspective exist. God knows we need to strive for true communion. The future can be very different."

Unfortunately, the need to finish the manuscript of this book prevented me from writing the piece Hand requested. Yet I want to take this opportunity to applaud the spirit in which he extended the invitation, which it seems to me synthesizes the best of the Catholic instinct— alive to the possibility of conversion, redemption, and new beginnings. One hopes that the spirit spreads as this new pontificate begins to take shape.

I would be negligent if I did not take this chance to offer thanks to several people without whose support this book would not exist. First of all, my deep thanks go to the board of directors at the *National Catholic Reporter*, whose decision to invest resources in Vatican coverage five years ago made everything possible. Without the support and vision of the board, I would not have experienced any of what followed. A similar note of gratitude goes to the staff of the *National Catholic Reporter*, especially those who made up our conclave coverage team: Sr. Rita Larivee, the publisher; Tom Roberts, the editor; Sr. Joan Chittister, providing analysis and commentary; and Stacy Meichtry, whose reporting was spectacular. If some major paper or news agency does not quickly offer Meichtry a job, there is something seriously flawed about the judgment of the American press. Dennis Coday also provided important editorial and technical support.

I would also like to thank everyone at CNN, the network that extended me the privilege of being part of their coverage team for the death of John Paul II, his funeral, the conclave and election of Benedict XVI, and the new pope's inaugural Mass. I was given the opportunity to work with some of the finest journalists, producers, and technical staff in television news, and the memories of that experience will last a lifetime. A special note of thanks to Gail Chalef, who set my schedule for a month and offered constant encouragement, and to Joy DiBenedetto, whose faith in me resulted in my contract. A word is in order here, too, about Delia Gallagher, my partner as a CNN Vatican analyst during this period. The experience would have been much more difficult, to say nothing of much less fun, without her good humor, support, and generosity. Jim Bitterman and Alessio Vinci, with whom I have been privileged to cover the Pope for years, were once again terrific colleagues. My thoughts also turn to Hada Messia, CNN's Rome producer, who endured unimaginable stress to make the network's coverage successful. She and I shared this experience from the beginning, more than five years ago. Her constant support, her friendship, and her trust will live in my memory.

Finally, I want to thank my wife, Shannon, though no words here can ever be equal to her sacrifice and support. Without her logistical backup, willingness to go anywhere and do anything to be of help, and her unflagging confidence in my capacities, this book would be unthinkable. Shannon is also by now one of the world's most sophisticated amateur Vaticanistas, so news agencies looking to beef up their Vatican coverage might take note! She also provided extremely useful feedback on the manuscript of this book.

I am convinced that the Roman Catholic Church, and especially the Vatican, is the best beat in journalism. It combines ritual, mystery, and romance with the deepest concerns of human life and religious faith and the real-world political impact of a major global institution. There is no region of human concern that is alien to the Holy See, from landmines and the Iraq war to genetic engineering to religious pluralism. I am deeply grateful to all who make it possible for me to watch the world through this particular window, and I hope something of my passion and fascination finds an echo in these pages.

Part One

"AT THE WINDOW OF
THE FATHER'S HOUSE"

Chapter One:

THE FINAL DAYS OF JOHN PAUL II

When Karol Wojtyla was elected to the Throne of Peter on October 16, 1978, the world was dazzled by his sheer physical force. He was, to invoke a tired expression, a "man's man"—rugged, handsome, brimming with energy and self-confidence. Fr. Andrew Greeley, the American novelist and sociologist, rightly observed that he looked like a linebacker in American football. Archbishop Michael Miller, today a senior Vatican official, who at the time of Wojtyla's election was a junior cleric in the Secretariat of State, said in a January 2005 reminiscence that from the moment John Paul II stepped out onto the central balcony of St. Peter's Basilica, "He simply dominated that space. He looked like he had been pope forever."

In the press coverage from those early years, the Pope was dubbed "God's athlete." He skied, climbed mountains, swam, and had an undying passion for the outdoors. The story of his nomination to be a bishop in Poland, when he had to interrupt a camping trip in order to accept and then went immediately back to kayaking after he had signed the paperwork, became the stuff of legend. At the table, the Pope had the hearty appetite of a man who once worked in the Solvay salt quarry outside Krakow; he could wolf down a plate of Polish sausage and potatoes, and a glass of beer, with obvious gusto. Even when he was wearing his pontifical vestments and saying Mass, he projected a raw physical energy. When he traveled, he kept up a brutal schedule that left his aides, as well as the journalists who traveled with him, exhausted. It seemed that he chafed against the very limits of time and space, so brimming was he with determination and drive. In 1979, for example, he took a nine-day trip to the United States and Ireland, and over the course of that time he delivered a staggering seventy-six speeches, which works out to roughly eight and a half speeches per day. Oral tradition in the press corps that followed the Pope has it that at one point, exhausted reporters tossed a message up to the front section of the papal plane asking for a day off, which produced a smile from John Paul II, as if to say, "I dare you to keep up."

This was a pope who understood the virtue of keeping in shape. Upon his election, he ordered a swimming pool installed at Castel Gandolfo, the pope's summer residence outside Rome. When some in the Roman Curia, the papal bureaucracy, objected to the expense, he replied, "It's cheaper than holding another conclave." Coming fast on the death of his predecessor, Pope John Paul I, after just thirty-three days, his point was well taken.

John Paul II's astounding drive did not, of course, come just from his physical strength. He also had a deep, unwavering confidence in divine providence, that God would not send him any burden that was not accompanied by the strength to bear it, and that everything that happened to him was according to cosmic design. It was his firm belief, for example, that on May 13, 1981, the Virgin Mary altered the flight path of would-be assassin Mohammed Ali Agca's bullet in order to save his life and prolong his papacy. May 13 is the Feast Day of Our Lady of Fatima, and on the first anniversary of the assassination attempt, John Paul II traveled to Fatima in Portugal in order to lay the bullet that doctors had removed from his body before the statue of the Virgin, thanking her for coming to his aide. The motto of his pontificate was *Totus tuus,* "totally yours," meaning that he had offered it to the Virgin Mary, and now he believed she had returned the favor.

It was in part that belief in providence that allowed John Paul II to bear the sufferings and ailments of his final years, not just with grim determination, but with serenity and good humor. Always the "great communicator," John Paul learned to use his growing physical limits—the Parkinson's disease, hip ailments, breathing problems, and arthritis—as another set of tools in his evangelizing toolbox, capitalizing on his infirmity as a "teaching moment" about the value and dignity of human life from the beginning to the end.

In one sense, John Paul's long winter, roughly dating from the mid-1990s to his death on April 2, 2005, illustrates the inhuman nature of the job he held. To be a pope is, in effect, a life sentence, and by the great Jubilee Year of 2000, the toll it had taken on John Paul II was unmistakable. His once-beaming, lively face had become frozen into a sort of Parkinsonian mask. His stooped frame and trembling hands spoke more eloquently than words ever could about the bone-crushing nature of the papacy. Yet the Pope's deep faith meant that it never even crossed his mind to abandon his post. Later, some would read his final will and testament, released days after his death, to indicate doubt on this question; John Paul wrote in 2000, "I hope [the Lord] will help me to recognize up to what point I must continue this service to which I was called on October 16, 1978." It seems clear, however, that John Paul was referring in this passage to the prospect of death, not resignation. He added in the very next line, "I ask him to call me back when He Himself wishes." As John Paul said on numerous occasions, "Christ did not come down off the Cross." John Paul was convinced that God had given him a mission, and God would decide when it was complete.

On what turned out to be one of his final apostolic voyages, to Christianity's premier healing shrine in Lourdes, France, in the summer of 2004, John Paul II declared himself a "sick man among the sick." By that stage, his transformation from corporate CEO to an icon of human suffering was complete. As I walked through the crowd of 200,000 people gathered for John Paul's Sunday morning Mass on August 15, I saw tens of thousands of people using canes and walkers and in wheelchairs. When the ailing, elderly John Paul II appeared, many in the crowd recognized one of their own, and the emotional response was electric.

"My mother had Parkinson's disease for thirty years, and I was with her," said Irish pilgrim Lyla Shakespeare. "When I looked at the Pope today, all I could see was my mother." But, she added, "I also saw Christ."

Cardinal Jean-Marie Lustiger of France put the theological reading of John Paul's physical decline this way: "The Pope, in his weakness, is living more than ever the role assigned to him of being the Vicar of Christ on earth, participating in the suffering of our Redeemer. Many times we have the idea that the head of the Church is like a super-manager of a great international company, a man of action who makes decisions and is judged on the basis of his effectiveness. But for believers the most effective action, the mystery of salvation, happens when Christ is on the cross and can't do or decide anything other than to accept the will of the Father."

Granted, not everyone saw it this way. Over the last years of John Paul's life, there were persistent calls on him to resign on the grounds that he was harming the Church by depriving it of the opportunity for more energetic leadership. Some saw his determination to continue not as heroic but as stubborn, even egotistical, as if Roman Catholicism could not go on without him. Others felt the images of the suffering Pope weren't so much inspiring as embarrassing, even pathetic. All this is a matter of legitimate discussion, and when the immediate outpouring of sorrow and respect that follows the death of any great figure subsides, no doubt that conversation will continue.

However one resolves those questions, it seems indisputable that in death, as in life, John Paul made us think. For all the ink that was spilled over nearly twenty-seven years about John Paul the politician or John Paul the globetrotter, in the long run it may be this final period of his papacy, John Paul the invalid, that leaves the deepest impression. He made us watch him slump and wince and become confused, and thereby forced us to confront the reality of decline and death—our own and that of our loved ones. One simply could not watch the Pope in his last days and not think about the final things, about the meaning and purpose of human life.

That, by itself, is a legacy.

THE FINAL DAYS

Looked at in reverse, it seems self-evident that from the hospitalization of February 1 forward we were on a papal "death watch," that the end of John Paul's long reign was in sight. Yet until the very end, the very night the Pope died, many Vatican officials, journalists, and ordinary Romans remained skeptical that it would actually happen. We had survived so many health scares before that it seemed part of the script that John Paul would defy predictions of his demise once more and pull through. Just days before his death, senior aides were telling reporters that the Pope still intended to travel to Cologne, Germany, in August for World Youth Day, and they were serious. One reason that St. Peter's Square did not swell with well-wishers until the very end was that Romans had seen it all before, and at some level had grown accustomed to thinking of John Paul II as virtually immortal.

Obviously, however, the end had to come for Karol Wojtyla as it does for all human beings, and that was the drama of February and March 2005 in Rome.

Tuesday, February 1

At approximately 10:50 p.m. Rome time, John Paul II was rushed from the papal apartments to the nearby Gemelli Polyclinic Hospital, where the tenth floor is permanently set aside for his use. Several hours later the Vatican reported that he had been suffering from respiratory problems complicated by spasms of the larynx, and that he had been placed under the care of the department of emergency medicine as a "precautionary move." Long into the night, speculation swirled in the city and throughout the world, that the Pope might be in mortal danger. While the Vatican minimized the seriousness of the episode, press reports would later claim that John Paul had actually been minutes away from death due to severe respiratory difficulties.

(One comic aside: Word of the hospitalization broke around 11:00 p.m. in Rome, at which time a substantial chunk of the city's journalistic community was at the Foreign Press Club at a gala dinner. I'm told that the buzzing of cell phones set on "vibrate" going off simultaneously produced an audible hum in the room, though I wasn't there to witness it. Instead, my cell phone jarred me from the early stages of a good night's sleep, which was obviously not to be.)

John Paul was no stranger to the Gemelli. He once jokingly referred to the hospital as the "third Vatican," after the Vatican itself and his summer residence at Castel Gandolfo, in the Alban hills outside Rome. This episode marked the ninth time the Pope had been hospitalized at the Gemelli over the course of his papacy, including the 1981 assassination attempt, though it was the first time it had happened in response to a crisis in the middle of the night. The Pope's inner circle had apparently hoped to hospitalize him without fanfare, and then make an announcement in the morning. How they expected to keep the news of an impromptu papal hospitalization under wraps for twelve hours is unclear, but in any event word leaked moments after the papal entourage pulled through the hospital gates, and from that point forward, it was off to the races for the world press.

The Pope's health crisis was not a complete bolt from the blue, since on the previous Sunday, January 30, during his regular Angelus address, his voice had seemed strikingly hoarse and weak. Yet his body language that day did not seem alarming; John Paul was flanked by a couple of small Italian children who helped him release two "peace doves," one of which flew back into the room, with John Paul laughing and playfully trying to bat it away. It was to be the last time the world saw John Paul II with the broad smile that was such a trademark of his public image.

Later that Sunday night, Vatican spokesperson Joaquin Navarro-Valls announced that due to a case of the flu, the Pope's appointments would be canceled for the next day. On Monday evening, word broke that the Pope's schedule for Tuesday and Wednesday had been scrubbed as well. Official confirmation of the cancellations came Tuesday morning. By midday Tuesday, however, the sense was that he was improving and would probably return to work on Thursday. That same day, I spoke by telephone with Navarro-Valls, who is also a medical doctor, who joked that "a flu given proper treatment lasts seven days, whereas the flu without care runs seven days." In other words, he expected the Pope was on his way to a normal recovery.

Obviously something dramatic transpired after dinner Tuesday night. Navarro-Valls later described it as "acute laryngeal tracheitis," meaning the Pope had throat problems that led to difficult breathing. Given his age and Parkinson's disease, the Pope has long struggled for breath, and thus his personal physician, Renato Buzzonetti, who was summoned to monitor the Pope's condition, decided not to gamble with the possibility of respiratory arrest. The Pope was placed in an ambulance and driven speedily through a Vatican side entrance to the Gemelli, about two and a half miles from St. Peter's Square.

Vatican spokespersons the next day attempted to calm fears by insisting that there was "nothing alarming." Wednesday morning, February 2, Navarro-Valls went to the Gemelli to see the Pope, and then told journalists that John Paul was in good spirits. The Pope's vital signs were normal, Navarro-Valls said, he slept during the night, and was under the care of the hospital's department of emergency medicine. In remarks to journalists, Navarro-Valls added that the Pope had a "slight fever," but had never lost consciousness, had not undergone a CAT scan (as had been initially reported in some Italian newspapers), and was preparing to say Mass with his private secretary, Archbishop Stanislaw Dziwisz. Later in the morning, Navarro-Valls told Vatican Radio that the Pope was expected to remain at Gemelli just for "a few days."

Reassuring bulletins were issued Thursday and Friday as well. In a briefing in the Vatican Press Office on Friday, Navarro-Valls told reporters that the Pope's condition had improved, and that there would be no further bulletins until Monday. Pushed by Alessio Vinci of CNN as to why the Vatican would, in effect, go silent about the Pope's condition for forty-eight hours, Navarro-Valls responded, "I can think of American situations where there's been less information than we've given. I can't feed your television station twenty-four hours a day." Navarro-Valls also said that the Pope would follow a ceremony scheduled for Saturday with Roman seminarians from a television monitor in his room, and that he wanted to lead his regular Sunday Angelus address, but the exact way in which it might happen was still to be determined. Navarro-Valls added that the Vatican had received a flood of phone calls and faxes wishing the Pope a speedy recovery, including a call from the Chief Rabbi of Rome, who wanted to tell the Pope that "we are praying for him."

Some Vatican officials attempted to project a testy "there they go again" air with respect to media sensationalism about the Pope's health. When Navarro-Valls was asked whether the Pope had ever lost consciousness, for example, his literal response in Italian was *per carità!*, which translates roughly as "for God's sake." No doubt there was over-interpretation involved. Yet journalists could be forgiven for jumping the gun, since it is not every day that the Pope is taken to the emergency room. Moreover, in the absence of swift and reliable information, speculation and worst-case scenarios are bound to take over. As things turned out, it was less a case of reporters making too much of a minor illness than the Vatican making too little of serious conditions that eventually snowballed and led to John Paul's final agony.

Sunday, February 6

As expected, John Paul appeared at the window of the tenth floor of the Gemelli Hospital on Sunday, February 6, for the Angelus. The text of his message was read by the *sostituto*, or "substitute," in the Secretariat of State, Archbishop Leonardo Sandri. John Paul spoke briefly, reciting two final invocations in the Angelus as well as the sign of the cross.

Though his voice was weak and raspy, the body language seemed relatively good. The Pope first appeared slumped over, but at a couple of points he straightened up and seemed in control of himself. Perhaps the most reassuring element of the event was that his doctors permitted him to sit for roughly ten minutes in front of an open window on a chilly Roman morning. Especially since spending time in front of a window in his study on January 30, an even colder day, was among the factors many people believe brought on his flu in the first place, this choice suggested that his doctors were not worried that another gust of cold air might send the Pope back into crisis.

Yet there were at least two elements of the Angelus appearance that triggered new controversy. First, a debate broke out over whether what the audience heard that morning was actually live or a recording. After the fact, some believed that the Vatican had the Pope lip-synch to a recording he had made earlier, out of fear that he would not be able to perform when the moment came. That theory was bolstered by the fact that observers standing in St. Peter's Square who planned to watch the Angelus on a big TV screen clearly heard a few words from the Pope over loudspeakers just before the broadcast began, which sounded to some like a tape being cued.

Listening carefully to the playback, there appears to be a clear shift from an exceptionally weak and soft voice on the initial invocation, to a stronger, louder, and deeper voice for the sign of the cross. Between the two there is a distinct "click" that some interpreted as the sound of switching on a tape recording. If the Vatican had used a tape recording, it would not be a complete surprise. In the past, when the Pope has been hospitalized, tape recordings have been made of his greetings in case he was not capable of delivering them live, and then his condition was analyzed shortly beforehand to determine if the tape was necessary. Some even believed that such a tape was triggered by accident halfway through the Pope's comments.

Yet by week's end, many seemed convinced that the comments were indeed live, and that the clicking and shift in voice quality were related to moving the microphone in his room.

At 5:30 p.m. Sunday afternoon, Navarro-Valls sent the following declaration to journalists via e-mail: "Naturally, the words of the Holy Father in the benediction this morning were pronounced by him in the same moment in which we heard them in a live broadcast. Thus the affirmation of a previous recording of those words transmitted in that moment doesn't make sense."

In any event, whether the Pope was live or Memorex almost didn't matter if the point was to get a reading on his physical state. People who were in the room Sunday morning all said, to the *National Catholic Reporter* and to other press outlets, that the Pope pronounced the words he was supposed to speak, and did so without obvious struggles. Whether they were broadcast live, or whether a tape kicked in at some point, was therefore perhaps irrelevant in terms of establishing his condition.

The second controversy stemming from the February 6 Angelus concerned why a papal aide held a piece of paper in front of John Paul's face, presumably with the lines of the Angelus and the sign of the cross. Some hypothesized that it was to disguise the use of a recording. Others, however, wondered why the Pope needed to be reminded of the words of a prayer he presumably knew by heart, fueling speculation about his mental state. Was he so out of it, some wondered, that he had to be coached on how to lead the sign of the cross?

The official answer, given to me by Vatican officials who deal with papal protocol, was that the Pope always has a sheet with the Angelus prayers in front of him, but usually we don't see it because it rests on a small lectern in front of the window in his studio. It's not because he can't remember the prayers, they say, but it's the same reason that priests always have a book with the prayers of the Mass in front of them: because exact recitation is important, and anybody can experience a "mental block." Indeed, one senior Vatican official later pointed out to me that if one looked closely at Sandri as he was leading the prayers on the Pope's behalf, an official was holding a paper with the words up for him, too.

Thursday, February 10

The Pope returned to the Vatican on Thursday, February 10, after spokesman Joaquin Navarro-Valls announced that his inflammation of the larynx was healed, that his general condition was continuing to improve, and that all diagnostic tests were clear. The mode of his return was classic John Paul, a brilliant piece of theater that captured the world's attention. He climbed into the Pope-mobile at the entrance to the Gemelli Hospital at around 7:30 p.m. and drove back to the Vatican, down the Via Gregorio VII, a broad street leading to the eastern entrance to the Vatican. Television covered the entire procession live, and all along the path well-wishers turned out to wave and cheer on the

Pope. The Pope seemed alert and engaged, obviously enjoying the scene. It was widely interpreted by commentators as a triumphant, emphatic way of saying "I'm back in business."

Despite the impressive display, the length of the Pope's stay at Rome's Gemelli Polyclinic Hospital, nine nights all told, suggested that his condition was far more serious than the reassuring tones from the Vatican implied. Sensing that there was concern in the air, Vatican sources supplied a logistical motive for the long convalescence: the annual Lenten Retreat in the Roman Curia began Sunday, February 13. By bringing the Pope back to the Apostolic Palace near the end of the week, the Vatican did not have to explain why he would not be seen for several more days. During the weeklong annual retreat, normal Vatican business is suspended and the Pope does not appear in public, so there was no need—at least for that week—to explain why John Paul was off the public stage. The retreat bought some time to monitor his condition and determine what level of activity he might be able to sustain.

(As a footnote, the Pope's return to the Vatican on the eve of February 11 was propitious, since it is both the anniversary of the Lateran Pacts of 1929, and therefore more or less Vatican Independence Day, as well as the Church's annual Day of the Sick.)

As the Pope appeared to have weathered the immediate crisis, public conversation shifted from whether he would survive to whether he should continue in office. There was a minitempest earlier in the week when the Vatican's secretary of state, Cardinal Angelo Sodano, answered a couple of questions from reporters on the sidelines of a book presentation. He expressed the hope that John Paul II would pass the record of papal longevity set by Pope Pius IX, who reigned thirty-two years and seven months, a milestone John Paul would not pass until 2010. Yet when asked about a possible resignation, Sodano did not seem to rule it out completely: "If there is a man who loves the Church more than anybody else, who is guided by the Holy Spirit, if there is a man who has marvelous wisdom, that's him. We must have great faith in the Pope. He knows what to do." In substance, what Sodano seemed to be saying was that, "it's up to the Pope." Nevertheless, the fact that Sodano was not more emphatic, along the lines of "never in a million years," became in some media retelling a subtle way of preparing the ground for papal abdication. The truth is, there was never any serious indication that John Paul might resign. In his Angelus message on Sunday he struck precisely this note: Even in the hospital, the Pope wrote in his message read by Sandri, "I continue to serve the Church and all of humanity."

Thursday, February 24

After a two-week lull on the papal health beat, news broke in the early afternoon Rome time that John Paul II had been taken back to the Gemelli Hospital, marking his second hospitalization in less than a month. It was obvious now, if it had not been before, that the Pope's condition was indeed serious, though it was not yet clear if the various conditions described in Vatican bulletins added up to anything fatal.

At 9:15 p.m. on the evening of February 24, Navarro-Valls released a statement to news agencies after John Paul II has exited the operating room and was still under the effects of anesthesia. It read, "The flu syndrome, which was the reason behind the Pope's admittance this morning to Gemelli Polyclinic, in recent days was complicated by new episodes of acute respiratory insufficiency, caused by a pre-existing functional restriction of the larynx. This clinical picture pointed to an elective tracheotomy to assure adequate breathing for the patient and to favor the resolution of the larynx pathology. The Holy Father, duly informed, gave his consent. The procedure, which began at 8:20 p.m. and ended at 8:50 p.m., was successfully completed. The immediate postoperative situation is regular."

The next day, at a 12:15 Vatican briefing, Navarro-Valls confirmed that John Paul II had undergone a tracheotomy the previous evening to relieve respiratory difficulties (a procedure described as "elective" rather than "emergency"). The Pope, he said, was now breathing more comfortably, and recovering some of his vocal capacity. Navarro-Valls indicated that the operation was finished "in a positive way" and lasted thirty minutes. Navarro-Valls also told the media that the morning after his operation, John Paul II ate a small breakfast of coffee, yogurt, and ten small cookies.

The account strained credibility, since it seemed unlikely that a patient with a tracheal tube could actually swallow cookies, but it was indicative of the Vatican's attempt to project an air of serenity and normality.

What made this hospitalization especially surprising was that John Paul had twice greeted pilgrims at the window of his studio at St. Peter's Square since his release from Gemelli on February 10, and, on both occasions, seemed clearly to be on the mend. On the previous Wednesday, February 23, John Paul had made his longest public appearance since falling ill. With each successive appearance, he seemed a little stronger, a little more alert, and his voice rang out with greater clarity. Both the press corps and most Vatican officials drew the conclusion that he was recovering, and began relaxing back into the patterns of business as usual. The impromptu rush to the Gemelli jolted them out of that complacency.

Later, physicians quietly said that John Paul's iron determination to get back to the Vatican after his hospitalization earlier in the month may have actually contributed to the second crisis. Dr. Corrado Manni, the Pope's former anesthesiologist, told the Italian newspaper *La Stampa* that John Paul should have "definitely" stayed hospitalized longer, but he added that the Pope had also been a "difficult" patient after the 1981 attempt on his life.

"He told me: 'The Pope is either well, and then he must leave, or he is not well, and then he must stay,'" Manni recalled. "I answered him: 'Your Holiness, there is a state of illness and of well-being, but in the middle there is a third state, that of convalescence.' Words spoken to the wind. I understand the difficulties his aides must have in dealing with such a situation. The Holy Father is difficult."

Early March 2005

On Tuesday, March 1, the Pope had a working meeting at Gemelli with Cardinal Joseph Ratzinger, after which Ratzinger said the Pope was engaged in the conversation and had spoken briefly in both Italian and German. It marked the first public indication that the Pope had recovered his capacity to speak, and optimism seemed to be in the air. A senior Vatican official told the *National Catholic Reporter* on March 2 that the Pope's progress was steady, and that there was every expectation that he would be able to resume his normal activity in relatively short order. Plans were being made for new documents and even new trips, on the assumption that John Paul would emerge from the hospital with a reduced vocal capacity but little else by way of wear and tear. Reports in the Italian press that John Paul II had been on a respirator following his emergency hospitalization were denied by spokesperson Navarro-Valls.

Even those disinclined to believe the Vatican's reassuring tones were more likely to speculate about scenarios involving permanent incapacitation rather than swift death. An endless series of television packages and newspaper articles aired in these days pointed out, for example, that there is no provision in the *Code of Canon Law* for declaring the papacy vacant if a pope were to remain alive but in a persistent vegetative state. Many speculated about what might happen in such a scenario, but everyone seemed in agreement that no clear answer existed. To some extent, these fears were perhaps exaggerated; in an interview just days before the Pope's death, Cardinal Francis Stafford from the United States, head of the Apostolic Penitentiary, a Vatican court that deals with matters of conscience, pointed out to the *National Catholic Reporter* that the prospect of death creates anxieties about worst-case scenarios that rarely come to pass. Still, several cardinals privately said during this period that one immediate task facing the next pope would be to convene a blue-ribbon panel of canon lawyers and other experts to come up with a solution to this scenario, given the capacity of medical science to sustain people, including popes, in life long beyond their ability to think or communicate.

On Thursday, March 3, Navarro-Valls told reporters that the Pope's health was in "progressive, continual improvement," that he was nourished regularly, that he was spending several hours every day in a chair, and that he also was spending time in the small chapel next to his hospital room. The Pope was receiving aides from the Vatican, Navarro-Valls said, and "follows the activity of the Holy See and the life of the Church daily." He was also continuing exercises to improve his breathing and speech, Navarro-Valls said. Navarro-Valls refused to be drawn into speculating about when the Pope might leave the Gemelli, saying only that "I will tell you when the doctors tell me." When asked if the Pope would come home before Easter, he said only, "It's possible."

Among both journalists and medical observers, it seemed odd that all the medical information concerning the Pope's condition was coming from the Vatican's spokesperson, and not from any of the physicians actually involved in his treatment. In the past, medical bulletins about the Pope's health had been signed by his doctors, whereas in this case it was all coming directly from Navarro-Valls. Sources at the Gemelli remained largely mum, explaining to reporters that word had gone out that leaking information to the media would cost them their jobs. This situation led some to wonder if a "filter" was being applied to the medical information, so that only what the Vatican wanted on the public record got out. During this period, I asked Navarro-Valls if reporters could have access to some of the physicians treating the Pope. He responded that this was up to the doctors, but they probably did not want to give interviews. Instead, Navarro-Valls gave me the following statement: "From the very beginning—that is, from the first recovery of the Holy Father in the Gemelli Hospital until now—all the clinical information that I have been releasing to the press was written by the group of physicians attending the Holy Father and was supervised by the personal physician of the Holy Father, Dr. Renato Buzzonetti."

Navarro-Valls also told reporters that the Pope was maintaining his sense of humor. John Paul had written a note on the night of his tracheotomy, Navarro-Valls said, asking in jest, "What did they do to me?" Navarro-Valls wasn't the only witness to the Pope's good humor. According to Italian politician Gianni Letta, who visited the Pope prior to the tracheotomy, doctors described to the Pope what they intended to do, saying the intervention would involve "a small hole" in his throat. "Small, it depends for whom," Letta recalled John Paul quipping.

John Paul also struck a more serious note, however, in reflecting on his illness. "I am always *totus tuus*," Navarro-Valls quoted the Pope as writing during this time. "*Totus tuus*" is John Paul's Latin motto translated by his spokesman as meaning "I am completely in your hands." The reference was to the Virgin Mary, whom John Paul always regarded as the patroness and protector of his pontificate. Even at what turned out to be just a month before the end finally came, John Paul's thoughts still turned to the Madonna, whose maternal love had been such a strong feature of his spirituality and worldview.

Sunday, March 13

John Paul returned home from the Gemelli Polyclinic Hospital for the second time in less than a month on Sunday, March 13, just hours after appearing at his window from the hospital's tenth floor and saying a few reassuring words in a raspy but comprehensible voice. "Dear brothers and sisters, thank you for your visit. To everyone, have a good Sunday and a good week," he said, reading from a sheet of paper. He singled out faithful from his hometown of Wadowice, Poland, who had gathered below his hospital window, for a special greeting. Though John Paul struggled to catch his breath, the overall impression once again was of a man recovering from an illness. It was his first public appearance since the February 24 tracheotomy.

John Paul's return was motivated in part by the fact that Holy Week began with Palm Sunday on March 20, and the Pope wanted to pass the holiest period of the Christian liturgical calendar in the Vatican. When John Paul was ready to go home, he exited the hospital, made the sign of the cross, and this time took a gray Mercedes minivan back to the Vatican. Cries of *Viva il Papa!* once again were heard along the route. In another bit of modern communications savvy, a Vatican television camera was actually positioned in the back of the Pope-mobile, so all along the route viewers saw the scene from John Paul II's point of view. The Pope's motorcade crossed the spectacularly floodlit square just as night fell, passed beneath the Arch of the Bells and disappeared inside the Vatican.

Late March 2005

Though not much news surfaced on the papal health front in the first three weeks of March, that doesn't mean these were quiet times in Rome. In fact, virtually every day brought fresh rumors—that the Pope was dead, that he had slipped into a coma, that Vatican officials were quietly preparing to declare the See of Peter vacant, even that John Paul was actually much better than reported and preparing to startle the world once more. Reporters were constrained to leave their cell phones on at all hours, which meant, among other things, that virtually no one got a decent night's sleep from February 1 through April 24, the date of the inaugural Mass of the new pope.

To take just one example, on Monday, March 21, at roughly 8:00 p.m. Rome time, rumors began to fly across town that John Paul II was dead. In this case, it seems the rumor first cropped up with an Italian TV channel. However such talk originated, once a journalist got hold of it, he or she began calling sources to try to find out what was going on. This being the Vatican, when those sources were unavailable or unresponsive, the journalist turned to colleagues to find out what they were hearing. Those journalists, in turn, started calling their own sources and colleagues, and so on. Pretty soon everyone in Rome was calling everyone else, recycling the same noninformation, hoping against hope to find that one person who actually knows something. It didn't take long for something like mass panic to set in.

The only "official" channel of information in such a situation was Vatican spokesperson Navarro-Valls, who at least initially was not taking calls Monday night. Beyond him, the only sources who could authoritatively confirm or deny the story, at least in the critical early moments, were the Pope's doctor, Buzzonetti, or his private secretary, Dziwisz, and neither were quickly reachable. For a half hour or so, there was no natural brake on people's imaginations, and virtually anything seemed believable.

The backdrop to this speculation was the clearly visible fact that the Pope's recovery was neither as speedy nor as full as his doctors had hoped. In his fleeting public appearances since coming home on March 13, he appeared gaunt, weak, and in discomfort, providing a context in which health speculation was certain to flourish. In the end, while such talk was premature, it was not far off the mark: John Paul II died just thirteen days after this particular rumor made the rounds.

Sunday, March 27

John Paul II delivered an Easter Sunday blessing to tens of thousands of people in St. Peter's Square, but the ailing pontiff was unable to speak and managed only to greet the saddened crowd with a sign of the cross, bringing tears to the eyes of many. Aides had readied a microphone, and the Pope tried repeatedly to utter a few words from his studio window overlooking the square. But after making a few sounds, he resigned himself to blessing the crowd with his hand and the microphone was taken away. At one point he lifted his hand to his throat, as if to indicate to the crowd that he wanted to speak but just couldn't manage because of his health difficulties. All told, John Paul spent twelve minutes and seventeen seconds at the window, and then was wheeled back inside.

There was a remarkable, if little noticed, dramatic arc to the scene. When Karol Wojtyla was elected pope on October 16, 1978, he stepped out onto the central balcony of St. Peter's Square to deliver the traditional *urbi et orbi* blessing, "to the city and to the world," and then ad-libbed a few lines to the assembled crowd. The papal Master of Ceremonies, now Cardinal Virgilio Noe, gently tried to steer him back after the blessing, as if to say that papal protocol did not allow anything else, but John Paul pushed him away. Once again, on this Easter day, John Paul would not allow his aides to come between him and the people who had gathered to be with him. Thus at the very beginning and at the very end, John Paul II was determined to be pope his own way, deepening that special rapport with the public that went over the heads of church bureaucrats, politicians, and the press, reaching straight into the hearts of those masses who knew that he loved them, and who loved him ferociously in return.

This marked the first Easter Sunday Mass that John Paul was unable to celebrate in his twenty-six-year pontificate, so Cardinal Angelo Sodano, the Secretary of State and the Vatican's number two official, led the Easter liturgy in St. Peter's Basilica. In fact, the Pope missed all the Holy Week liturgical celebrations, a sure sign that his condition was serious indeed. Yet senior aides told reporters that in private the Pope seemed stronger than in public. They insisted he was able to speak and remained fully lucid. Such comments led many to believe that John Paul might yet stage a recovery and be able to continue for months, if not longer.

Wednesday, March 30
On this date, the pattern of Vatican communications on John Paul's health took a sharp turn. Between March 10, two days prior to the Pope's second return from the Gemelli Hospital, and March 30, there had not been a single bulletin on the Pope's condition, despite the fact that his public appearances had been severely limited, and that he obviously seemed to be in a weakened and distressed state. That silence brought grumbling from journalists that the Vatican was hiding something, along with concern from the broader public. Beginning on March 30, however, the bulletins became much more regular and forthcoming, and the honesty of the information stood in stark contrast to the old Roman witticism that "the Pope is never sick until he's dead." Many longtime Vatican watchers believed these days were among Joaquin Navaro-Valls's finest hours, in that they exhibited the transparency and openness to the media that had always been John Paul's trademark, however much it contrasted with normal operating procedure in the Vatican.

On March 30, Navarro-Valls told the press that John Paul was now receiving nutrition through a tube in his nose, since he was unable to swallow and digest nutrients on his own. Navarro-Valls later told the *National Catholic Reporter* that the tube had first been inserted on Tuesday morning, March 29, and that it was used only intermittently—that is, when the Pope needed to be fed. Navarro-Valls stressed that the tube was used only to "boost the Pope's caloric intake," and was not a matter of a life-or-death intervention. Earlier in the morning of March 30, John Paul had appeared at his Vatican window in place of the normal Wednesday audience, and was not wearing the tube at that point. The March 30 statement also said that John Paul was spending "many hours" seated in an armchair, that he celebrated Mass in his private chapel, and had work contacts with his aides "following directly the activities of the Holy See and the life of the Church." It said the Pope continues "his slow and progressive convalescence," and that public audiences remain suspended.

Navarro-Valls's announcement created alarm in the American media, in part because the phrase "feeding tube" caused most Americans to think of Terry Schiavo, the Florida woman in a comalike state who was being kept alive only through the use of a surgically inserted feeding tube in her abdomen. In fact, there were three critical differences between the Pope's tube and Schiavo's. First, the tube used with John Paul II was not implanted surgically, and he did not have to wear it constantly. It was run down the nose and into the intestine when needed, then removed. Second, John Paul II remained conscious, and made decisions for himself about the course of his treatment. Navarro-Valls said that the doctors had explained to the Pope what they wanted to do on Tuesday morning, March 29, and he agreed. Third, in Schiavo's case, the tube was a matter of life or death. With the Pope, the tube was a tool intended to speed his recovery. He was able to consume food without it, though not enough to ensure that he didn't become lose weight. In the end, the Pope's condition turned out to be just as grave as Schiavo's, despite these differences in the feeding apparatus.

Some commentators were struck by the juxtaposition of the two highly public deaths, one which, at least to those on the front lines of the pro-life movement, seemed to illustrate the logic of a "culture of death"; the other, a stirring witness to the "culture of life." In that sense, in the eyes of some observers, John Paul's lifelong sense of dramatic timing was once again right on the money; even his death, against the backdrop of wide public fascination with end-of-life issues, turned out to be a much discussed teaching moment.

Thursday, March 31
In a terse statement issued at 10:15 p.m. Rome time, Navarro-Valls acknowledged that John Paul II had been struck with a high fever provoked by a urinary tract infection, and that treatment with antibiotics had been initiated. The statement also said that the Pope's condition "is being closely monitored by the Vatican medical team, which has him under their care." This latest health shock renewed speculation that John

Paul might once again have to go to the Gemelli Hospital, but Navarro-Valls repeatedly insisted that no such hospitalization was anticipated.

Medical experts around the world, who had been stressing that none of the Pope's problems were necessarily fatal and that recovery was still a realistic possibility, now began to grow much more pessimistic. Crowds began to swell in St. Peter's Square, as the realization dawned that this pope of nine lives, who had so often outlived predictions of his own demise, might not have another miracle up his sleeve. Around the world, Catholics began not so much to pray that John Paul would recover, but that his passing would be peaceful and happy.

Friday, April 1

During a noon briefing in the Vatican Press Office, Navarro-Valls released a detailed update on John Paul's condition. It called the Pope's condition "very grave," and said that the day before the Pope had suffered septic shock and cardio-circulatory collapse. Septic shock involves both bacteria in the blood and a consequent overrelaxing of the blood vessels, so that the vessels, which are normally narrow and taut, get floppy in reaction to the bacteria and can't sustain any pressure. That loss of blood pressure is usually catastrophic, making the heart work harder and harder to compensate for the collapse. Even the hearts of fit and healthy people struggle with septic shock, and given John Paul's general weakness, it seemed clear to everyone that hope was fading fast.

Navarro-Valls indicated that John Paul, informed of the gravity of his condition, had decided to remain in the Vatican rather than to return to the Gemelli, and that all possible medical interventions could be carried out just as well in his apartments as they could in the hospital. Navarro-Valls said that in the afternoon of March 31 there had been a temporary stabilization in the Pope's condition, followed by further deterioration. The Pope received the Sacrament of the Anointing of the Sick (which had been formerly known as The Last Rites), he said, and remained lucid. At 6:00 a.m. on April 1, he concelebrated Mass from his sickbed. Navarro-Valls described John Paul as "extraordinarily serene."

At 7:15 a.m., Navarro-Valls said, the Pope requested the reading of the fourteen Stations of the Cross, representing the steps Jesus took to death and burial in Jerusalem. "He crossed himself at the reading of each station," Navarro-Valls said.

Perhaps the most telling indication of the true gravity of the situation came at the end of the briefing, when Navarro-Valls choked back tears as he walked away from the platform where he spoke to reporters. Navarro-Valls is ordinarily a poised, highly composed man, a spokesperson who has learned over more than twenty years of service how to camouflage his emotions beneath a poker face. Reporters who have worked with him for more than twenty years struggled to recall another moment when he lost his cool in such a public fashion. The sight of him overcome with emotion, more than any of the words he spoke, communicated to longtime Vatican-watchers that the end was near.

"This is surely an image I have never seen in these twenty-six years," Navarro-Valls said of the Pope's condition, beginning to cry as he left the room.

In another sign of the extraordinary nature of the situation, Navarro-Valls announced that the Vatican Press Office would remain open all night for reporters awaiting the latest information. Given that the office normally closes each day at 3:00 p.m., this, too, was an obvious concession that the death of the Pope could come at any moment.

Later in the day, Navarro-Valls issued another bulletin. "The general conditions and cardiorespiratory conditions of the Holy Father have further worsened," he said. "A gradual worsening of arterial hypotension has been noted, and breathing has become shallow. The clinical picture indicates cardio-circulatory and renal insufficiency. . . . The biological parameters are notably compromised."

Once again, rumors swept Rome in this period. One had it that John Paul had actually died in the early morning on Friday, and that the Vatican was holding off on an official announcement until preparations were in place. That theory, dissipated when Navarro-Valls announced the names of several senior aides who had seen him and spoken with him in his room that morning, including Cardinal Edmund Szoka from the

United States, the former governor of the Vatican city-state, who re-called the minutes he spent with the Pope on American television.

"As soon as he saw me, he recognized me," Szoka told the "CBS Morning News" of his visit. "I blessed him, and as I did, he tried to make the sign of the cross. So he was perfectly lucid, perfectly conscious, but was having a great deal of trouble breathing."

Another rumor made the rounds at roughly 8:30 p.m. Rome time, when Italian media reports indicated that the Pope's electrocardiogram was flat, effectively meaning that he had died. SkyItalia, the Rupert Murdoch–owned Italian television news channel, reported that the Pope was dead, followed in short order by Fox News in the United States. CNN walked up to the brink of issuing the same report, but was pulled back by analyst Delia Gallagher, who insisted on-air that the network await official confirmation before reporting that the Pope was dead. In the end, the SkyItalia and Fox report, based on Italian wire services, turned out to be more than twenty-four hours premature.

Also on Friday, the Vatican released seventeen appointments of bishops and papal ambassadors, a clear signal that they wanted to move appointments already approved by the Pope through the pipeline while there was still time. These were not appointments made at the last minute, but rather appointments made some time prior that for one rea-son or another had been delayed. (Sometimes a new bishop will ask that his appointment be made on a particular day, such as the feast day of his patron saint, or a day with special importance in his nation or diocese.) Had John Paul died before the appointments were made public, they would have died with him, causing further delays in providing leader-ship for these dioceses or embassies.

Friday night, Cardinal Camillo Ruini, the Pope's vicar for the dio-cese of Rome and a longtime confidant, celebrated a Mass for John Paul II at St. John Lateran Basilica, the Pope's own diocesan church. Runi conceded that the end was not far away. "We pray for him," Ruini said of the pontiff, "as we, like him, trust ourselves to the will of God." In words that would prove fateful, Ruini then said: "The Holy Father can already touch and see the Lord." Archbishop Angelo Comastri, the pope's vicar for Vatican City, was equally candid: "This evening or this night, Christ opens the door to the Pope," he said.

Saturday, April 2

In a noontime briefing, Navarro-Valls reiterated that John Paul's condition remained "very grave," and offered the first hints that the Pope might be losing consciousness, though he insisted that he was not in a "coma."

"The Pope's overall condition, both cardiorespiratory and metabolic, remains basically unchanged and thus very serious," Navarro-Valls said. "At dawn today, it was observed that his consciousness was beginning to become compromised."

"Sometimes he closes his eyes and sometimes he opens them" and "when he hears voices, he sometimes reacts," Navaro-Valls said. "He sometimes appears to be sleeping, to be resting with his eyes closed," he said. Navarro-Valls said the eighty-four-year-old pontiff had made repeated efforts to say one phrase in particular. He said observers had managed with difficulty to piece the words together, and that they seemed to be "I have looked for you. Now you have come to me and I thank you." The spokesman said the phrase appeared to refer to the young faithful in particular who had gathered below his window in St. Peter's Square, to pray for his well-being. Meanwhile the square swelled with pilgrims awaiting what now seemed the inevitable news of John Paul's death.

Saturday evening, a special rosary was prayed in the square for the Pope, led by Sandri, who had been his public voice throughout this crisis. Just as that rosary ended, the news for which everyone had been waiting began to break.

The End

Finally, death came for Karol Wojtyla, who, as John Paul II, had stood astride his times as few global leaders ever had. At 9:55 p.m. Rome time, Vatican reporters' cell phones flashed an SMS message indicating that an urgent declaration from Navarro-Valls was in their e-mail box. That notice read:

> *The Holy Father died this evening at 9:37 pm in his private apartment. All the procedures envisioned in the apostolic constitution* Universi Dominici gregis *promulgated by John Paul II on February 22, 1996, have been set in motion.*

Most reporters never got past the first four words, immediately swinging into motion with long-prepared plans for coverage of John Paul's passing and its aftermath.

Later, members of the Pope's most intimate circle said that John Paul II had died just as a Mass led by his private secretary, Archbishop Stanislaw Dziwisz, had ended. Saturday was the vigil Mass for the Feast of Divine Mercy, a devotion associated with the Polish St. Faustina Kowalska, whom John Paul canonized on April 30, 2000, making her the first saint of the new millennium. The devotion to Christ's divine mercy is rooted in a series of revelations Faustina believed she received from Jesus, Mary, and saints such as Teresa from 1931 to 1938, and the heart of her message is that human beings cannot be merciful to one another unless they first acknowledge their dependence on God's mercy. John Paul always believed it was no accident that this message of mercy was revealed to a Polish nun between the two world wars, in a moment of supreme mercilessness. Once again, therefore, the Pope's timing even in death was flawless, as he put a spotlight one final time on a devotion so near to his heart.

There were also reports that the Pope's last word, at the end of the Mass that began around 8:00 p.m. Rome time, was "Amen." Some observers expressed skepticism that he would be capable of speaking, given the respiratory difficulties that plagued him in his final days. Nevertheless, it seems fair to assume that "Amen" was in his heart if not on his lips as that Mass drew to a close. In Aramaic, the dialect of Hebrew that Jesus spoke, "Amen" means "yes," and if ever there was a man who said a resounding "yes" to both life and death, it was Pope John Paul II.

At the Pope's bedside for that final Mass were his closest friends and collaborators. Dziwisz was there, his private secretary for almost forty years, and the closest thing to a son this loving father ever had. Also in the room was Cardinal Marian Jaworski, the archbishop of L'viv in Ukraine, who served as a young priest together with Wojtyla in Poland. Back in those days, Jaworski had lost one of his hands in a train accident on his way to a pastoral assignment that Wojtyla had asked him to cover, and ever since Jaworski has worn a metal device under a black glove where his hand once was. A sign of the intimacy between the two men was that in earlier years, when Jaworski would come to Rome and stay in the papal apartment, Wojtyla would cut his meat for his old friend. Also present at the Pope's deathbed was Archbishop Stanislaw Rylko, president of the Pontifical Council for the Laity, another old Polish associate; Monsignor Mieczyslaw Mokrzycki, Dzwisiz's deputy; and Fr. Tadeusz Styczen. Three Polish sisters who took care of the papal household were also by the Pope's side, including Sr. Tobiana, their superior, an ever-present shadow during John Paul's life. Whenever the Pope traveled, Tobiana was with him, always carrying the black bag that contained his medicines. At the moment the Pope died, this group broke out into the hymn *Te Deum Laudamus*, often sung to thank God for some special blessing. In this case, the blessing was the life and happy death of Pope John Paul II.

The Pope's body was taken to his private chapel for a final farewell from his household and most intimate collaborators, images of which for the first time were recorded and later released for broadcast by the Vatican Television Center. Then the body was moved to the Sala Clementina, where the first ripples of what would become a tidal wave of humanity, come to pay their respects, began to build.

TAKING STOCK

Oddly enough, having prepared for the death of John Paul II night and day for more than five years, having run through endless scenarios on both logistical and journalistic fronts, the one thing that I never anticipated is that I would have a personal, emotional response when the moment finally came. After all, not just any man had died—John Paul loomed large in my life, to say nothing of the billions of lives he touched around the world. I met him eight times, traveled with him to twenty-one nations, and probably wrote, all told, millions of words about him. While I realize there are reasonable criticisms to be made of various aspects of his papacy, what seems beyond question is that he was a man of deep faith and integrity, a good person striving by his lights to serve God, the Church, and humanity. His final days taught me—taught all of us—how to face impending death with both grit and grace, and it's a lesson I will never forget.

All that came to a crescendo during the funeral Mass, as I was sitting next to Christiane Amanpour and my colleague Delia Gallagher on the CNN set overlooking St. Peter's Square, watching the Papal Gentlemen pick up the Pope's casket and turn it around for one final farewell to the crowd. At that moment I had to choke back tears, realizing in an instant that I would never write another sentence about John Paul II in the present tense. I flashed on memories of burying my own grandfather not long ago, and once again I felt I had suffered a loss that was in some sense irreplaceable.

This is not the place for an evaluation of John Paul II's life and legacy. In the immediate aftermath of his death, lengthy obituaries were published around the world, including my own of more than nine thousand words, which can still be found on the Web site of the *National Catholic Reporter*. Historians, Vatican writers, and others will be sorting through his record for decades to come, and it will take time for his enormous impact on the Catholic Church and the wider world to emerge with clarity. John Paul was a complex man who ruled in turbulent times, and there is a legitimate discussion to come about particular choices he made or policies he pursued. A great man does not always accomplish great things, and certainly his reign had its ups and downs. New biographies and new studies will soon line the shelves alongside what was already a massive collection of literature devoted to his life, thought, and almost twenty-seven-year-long pontificate, the third longest in the almost two-thousand-year history of Roman Catholicism.

Suffice it here to close with a few fleeting words, some final impressions about a man whose passing leaves a psychological and emotional hole that will be difficult to fill.

What, then, to say of Pope John Paul II toward the end? That image of him sitting slumped over in his rolling throne (the Vatican would never call it a "wheelchair"), his eyes either closed or almost, his face contorted. Was it pain, anxiety, a crushing sense of so much still to do? In the final analysis, Karol Wojtyla, deeper than his politics and beyond his early-twentieth-century Polish Catholic cultural formation, was a mensch. He was a strong, intelligent, committed human being, someone whose integrity and dedication represent a standard by which other leaders can be measured.

John Paul was a selfless figure in a me-first world. Cardinal Roberto Tucci, who planned John Paul's voyages before retiring in 2001, once said he had briefed John Paul hundreds of times on the details for his various trips. Not once, Tucci said, did the Pope ever ask where he was going to sleep, what he would eat or wear, or what his creature comforts would be. The same indifference to himself could be seen every time the Pope stepped, or, in the end, was rolled upon the public stage.

This is the key that unlocks why John Paul drew enormous crowds, even where his specific political or doctrinal stands may be unpopular. It's a rare ideologue for whom condoms or the Latin Mass represent ultimate concerns. Deeper than politics, either secular or ecclesiastical, lies the realm of personal integrity—goodness and holiness, the qualities we prize most in colleagues, family, and friends. A person may be liberal or conservative, avant-grade or traditional, but let him or her be decent, and most of the time that's enough. This realm of *menschlichkeit*, authentic humanity, is where John Paul's appeal came from. For a Pope of a hundred trips and a million words, perhaps the most important lesson he offered was the coherence of his own life. When he urged Christians to *Duc in Altum*, to set off into the deep, it resonated even with those who sought very different shores.

When I was asked on CNN at the end of his long funeral Mass to sum up my feelings on the passing of John Paul II, what came to mind were Hamlet's words reflecting on the death of his own father: "He was a man. Take him for all in all, I shall not look upon his like again."

I don't expect to ever see another pope, or another man, quite like John Paul II.

Part Two

"HABEMUS PAPUM"

Chapter Two:

THE FUNERAL EFFECT

John Paul II was a magnet for humanity. According to most estimates, he was seen in the flesh by more people than any other human being who ever lived. He regularly drew millions when he traveled, including the 4.5 to 5 million people in Manila in 1995 for World Youth Day, and the 10 million who turned out in Mexico City in 1979. The only events that compare are the Hindu Kumbh Mela festival of January 2001, when 10 million people bathed in the Ganges River over twenty-four hours, and the funeral of Ayatollah Khomeni in June 1989, which drew 3 to 10 million. Yet these are one-off affairs; John Paul drew such crowds on a regular basis, so much so that anything less than a million for a papal Mass was styled by the press as a disappointment. Even the great Christian crusader Billy Graham doesn't have this kind of drawing power.

For that reason, it was no particular surprise that lots of people would turn out to pay respects to John Paul as his body lay in state in St. Peter's Basilica, or to attend the funeral Mass in St. Peter's Square on Friday, April 8. It was equally no surprise that these events drew massive television audiences worldwide, which was why networks from every language and continent flew in their most important anchors to host the coverage, and why they had paid top-dollar for Roman rooftop locations for the last several years. The surprise was rather in how many came—

by some estimates, as many as 5 million during the week from the Pope's death through his funeral—and how raw and deep their emotions were. The outpouring of grief and love for John Paul literally flooded the streets of Rome for the better part of a week, jolting even the world-weary Romans, who pride themselves on having seen it all before.

The surprise was that the events surrounding his death and funeral would be not just a major civic event and television extravaganza, but that they would become a critically important factor in the politics leading up to the selection of John Paul II's successor. In some cases for the first time, the cardinals became aware during that week that they were not just electing a leader of the Roman Catholic Church, they were electing a man who would be humanity's most important voice of conscience, a major player in global affairs. They became more conscious than ever before that they had to find a man of stature, who could command the respect and attention of the entire world. For that reason, a "Luciani solution," referring to the first conclave of 1978 and the election of Cardinal Albino Luciani of Venice as John Paul I, a simple, smiling man whom no one would mistake for a visionary, seemed out of the question. The massive international reaction to John Paul's death drove home to the cardinals the revolution he had worked in terms of the global standing of the office, and thereby reshaped the politics of the election of his successor. They had to find a pope of substance, someone who could withstand the withering comparison to John Paul II.

It's that political impact that observers have come to call the "funeral effect."

BACKGROUND: GRUMBLING ABOUT A POPE *AD EXTRA*

Prior to John Paul's death and funeral, it was by no means certain that a towering personality is what some cardinals were looking for in his successor.

When the College of Cardinals gathers to elect a new pope, part of the exercise is to take stock of the pontificate that's just ended, trying to assess both its strengths and its weaknesses. The choice of a successor is, to some extent, conditioned by the desire to find a man who can remedy those weaknesses and address the previous pope's unfinished business. For that reason, in an attempt to garner clues about what kind of man they'd be looking for in a successor, journalists had spent the last several years asking cardinals how they weighed the pluses and minuses of the pontificate of John Paul II.

Unsurprisingly, the list of positives most cardinals adduced was extensive. He was a magnificent evangelist and apostle, most cardinals said, making 104 trips outside Italy to 129 nations, revitalizing the role of the pope as the successor not just of Peter but also, in a sense, of Paul, the peripatetic apostle who brought the Gospel to the world. John Paul, they said, was a superb pastor, inspiring faith and devotion everywhere he went, especially among the young. There is an entire generation of "John Paul II" priests in the Catholic Church today, many of whom had their first stirrings about a vocation when taking part in one of the World Youth Days, those massive gatherings of Catholic youth instituted by John Paul and sometimes dubbed a "Catholic Woodstock." This was also a pope of historic outreach, revolutionizing the Church's relationship with the Jews, with Muslims, and with other Christian denominations. He was a teacher, a mystic, and a man of deep and constant prayer, whose example of self-giving love will live in the memories of a whole generation of Catholics.

And yet . . . and yet, many cardinals said, all these gifts came at a price. There was a certain inattention to the nuts and bolts of ecclesiastical governance on John Paul's watch, a sense that this pope's passion was so directed *ad extra*, meaning outside the Church, that sometimes routine business *ad intra*, or inside the Church, suffered. Evidence included the occasional dysfunction of Vatican offices, with one curial agency saying one thing and another contradicting it, with no visible consequences from the Pope. This polyphonic disarray was evident in matters large and small, from what exactly the Vatican thought about the Iraq war, where every day it seemed another Vatican official offered an opinion, with the routine disclaimer that he was speaking "only for himself," to the tawdry spectacle of what the Pope did or did not say about the Mel Gibson movie *The Passion of the Christ*. This neglect of internal administration, some cardinals said, was also reflected in the occasionally low quality of episcopal appointments over the last twenty-six years, as well as the slow and ambiguous response from Rome to the sexual abuse crisis in the United States. In that sense, some cardinals said quietly, management had suffered under John Paul. Moreover, some of the same cardinals objected to what they saw as the "personalization" of the papacy under John Paul, the rock star qualities of the man, the mega-events in St. Peter's Square, and the highly choreographed travels, which seemed sometimes to put the focus on the messenger rather than the message. The risk was that John Paul's teaching came to be seen as an extension of his personality, something that depended on him, rather than the long and constant tradition of the Church.

This was not just the opinion of conservative cranks who never adapted to their loss of control over the papacy. Even cardinals sometimes perceived as more liberal shared the concern. On the eve of John Paul's funeral, for example, Cardinal Godfried Danneels of Belgium told me in an interview granted on the condition that it be published after the conclave, "The Pope's charism was an openness *ad extra*. He was never preoccupied by what was going on in Rome. It was just never his cup of tea."

In the ruminations of some cardinals prior to the death of John Paul II, some had thought that perhaps a less charismatic figure, one who would travel less, engage in fewer spectacles, and stay behind his desk and govern more, would be appropriate as his successor. For that reason, a somewhat less dramatic, less theatrical, less ubiquitous pope, someone less given to public relations and imaginative gestures, might be what the Church needed after such a whirlwind of a pontificate. From this point of view, it was not important to elect another giant; a competent administrator and good-hearted man would be enough. By no means did every cardinal feel this way, but some came to Rome thinking that it might be healthy for the Church to avoid aggressive leadership for at least a brief period, in order to take stock and sort through John Paul's legacy.

Then John Paul II died, and the cardinals watched what happened next.

LYING IN STATE

When word of John Paul's death broke, there was already a large crowd in St. Peter's Square that had just finished praying a rosary on behalf of the Pope. "We all feel like orphans this evening," Archbishop Leonardo Sandri, the *sostituto*, or "substitute," told the tens of thousands of people who were on hand as soon as official word came of John Paul's death.

The body of Pope John Paul II was dressed in his vestments and moved to the Sala Clementina, on the third level of the Apostolic Palace, on Sunday, April 3. The Sala Clementina is a large reception room often used for semi-public and private audiences with various groups. It was in this room, for example, on June 4, 2004, that President George W. Bush presented John Paul II with the Medal of Freedom, the highest civilian honor bestowed by the American government.

The Pope's body was laid on a sloped olive-sheeted bed and propped on a stack of three gold pillows. Near the bed were a wooden crucifix and a paschal candle symbolic of Jesus Christ as the light of the world in the face of darkness and death. His body was watched over by the Swiss Guard. During a period of private visitation during the day of April 3 and the morning of April 4, Vatican officials, a contingent of officials from the Italian government, journalists, and other select groups viewed the body.

On April 4, the body was moved onto a red velvet bier, with his head propped on three red pillows. The Papal Gentlemen, regaled in black morning coats and white gloves, were consecrated as pallbearers and stood alongside the Pope. Martínez Somalo, dressed in red and gold vestments, officiated at the sprinkling rite. He blessed the Pope with the holy waters of baptism three times: to the right of the Pope, at his head, and then to his left. An acolyte then brought to the Camerlengo a censer and boat. Martínez Somalo incensed the Pope three times. A long procession was begun in order to transfer the body of Pope John Paul II from the Sala Clementina, through the colonnades of the Apostolic Palace, and into St. Peter's Square. A procession of monks, priests, and bishops paced slowly along a route toward St. Peter's Basilica. The College of Cardinals, trailed by Ratzinger and Martínez Somalo, followed them. As the ritual proceeded, Gregorian chants were sung by several religious orders with the people responding to each verse with the ancient Greek prayer "Lord, have mercy," or *Kyrie eleison*. The Litany of the Saints was sung. After each name of a martyr or saint was chanted, invoking his or her intercession between God and the people, participants in the procession sang the Latin words *Ora pro eo*, meaning "Pray for him." That was a departure from the traditional "Pray for us," or *Ora pro nobis*.

An estimated total of four million people, in addition to more than 3 million residents of Rome, made the pilgrimage to Rome to see the Pope during this period. The number of mourners multiplied rapidly as the city's population converged on the square, filling its oval contours with a sea of downcast faces and flickering candlelight. In the first twelve hours after the death of the Pope, Rome city officials estimated that some 500,000 people converged on the square, rivaling the largest crowds ever assembled there. Movement around the area of the Vatican became almost impossible, given the throngs of people who crowded every inch of space. Over the next several days, the crowd would be further swelled by pilgrims from every corner of the Catholic world, but above all from Poland, saying a final farewell to the country's undeclared king. An estimated 1.5 million Poles converged on Rome for the funeral Mass alone.

John Paul's departure had opened a void, and his followers were struggling to fill it, with a display of raw emotion that often startled even the mourners themselves. Prelates led the square in song and prayer with wavering voices, and the massive audience responded with tears, thousand-mile stares, and upward glances at the trio of illuminated windows, looming high above the scene, that marked the newly vacated papal apartment.

"Rome without the Pope isn't Rome," explained Barbara De Angelis, twenty-four, an anthropology major at Rome's La Sapienza University.

Like many in the city, she had spent the day in the square, sifting through clusters of tourists and well-wishers, aiming to get the inside scoop on John Paul's deterioration. Now she had her answer. "Breathe it in. It's all over," she said, surveying the scene.

Applause erupted from different ends of the square, a traditional gesture of Italian mourning. In an address from the Quirinale Palace, a former papal residence that now hosts the Italian president, Carlo Azeglio Ciampi reflected on how the late pontiff had "shaped our conscience."

"Italy weeps for a father," Ciampi said, expressing the sentiments of millions of Italians who had embraced this Polish pope.

Public mourning also found expression in a burst of late-night traffic that plugged the narrow byways around the Vatican. "Romans don't follow the Pope, they live him," observed Luis Gonzales, a native of Guatemala City, Guatemala, who moved to Rome forty years ago. Gonzales offered John Paul high marks for his performance as the bishop of Rome—a role that for many was affirmed minutes after his election when the polyglot pope addressed St. Peter's Square in Italian, instructing the people of Rome to "correct me if I err." Gonzales also praised the pontiff's subsequent acquisition of Romanesco, the local dialect.

Amid the crowds of arriving Romans, clumps of foreign tourists staked out their positions and dug in. Josh Rogers, twenty-one, of South Hadley, Massachusetts, sat in the square with his luggage, dumbstruck by the timing of John Paul's death. "It's my first trip to Rome, and the Pope is dead," he said. "Now what happens?"

Throughout the night into the early morning, mourners lingered in the square lighting candles. And when day broke, patches of spilt candle wax caked the cobblestones. Sunday soccer and variety television, Italy's other national pastimes, had both been canceled. At newsstands, Italy's factional print media expressed a rare moment of unity. The communist newspaper *Il Manifesto*, a vocal critic of the Church, blew an unprecedented kiss to the pontiff with a banner headline that read "You don't make another!"—a revision of the popular Roman saying that if "one pope dies, you make another."

As the hour of John Paul's requiem Mass approached, the weather warmed and shops selling religious objects bustled. The multitudes had returned, bearing flags, banners, and solemn expressions. Seasoned papal mourners noted the robust turnout and the crush of media coverage. "Everyone is watching us," said Emma Costantini, seventy-seven. "But I'm used to it." John Paul was her fifth pope. Graziano de Marinis, sixty-eight, was also mourning his fifth pope—the one he "knew best." In his wallet he carried a photo taken in 1981 of John Paul kissing his then six-year-old son Marco during a visit to his local church. Marinis tucked a copy of Rome's *La Repubblica* newspaper under his arm. The banner simply read "Addio Wojtyla."

On Monday morning, April 4, I had the opportunity to be part of a group of journalists permanently accredited to the Vatican who were taken into the Sala Clementina to pay a final farewell. It was in many ways an anticlimactic experience, given that the Pope already looked artificial and waxen, not the man bursting with life and energy we all had known. For me, the only human touch was seeing John Paul wearing the same scuffed red shoes I had grown accustomed to seeing in the Vatican and on the road; it was a reminder of how much ground all of us had traveled with him, both metaphorically and physically.

When John Paul's body was moved to St. Peter's Basilica for public viewing on the afternoon of April 5, the real tidal wave of humanity began to gather force. Lines had begun forming at 8:45 a.m. Monday, even though the public viewing was not slated to begin until later that evening. Volunteer crowd controllers clad in neon ponchos locked arms at street intersections, slowing the flow of bodies to guard against trampling. Vatican officials announced that the basilica would remain open almost around the clock, closing only from 2:00 a.m. to 5:00 a.m. to allow clean-up and maintenance. The press of humanity was, at times, overwhelming.

"I can't breathe," Ellena Medori, a thirty-four-year-old accountant, yelled when the masses forced her up against a railing on Monday night.

The tension increased around 1:30 a.m., with the deadline looming for the basilica to close for three hours. Shouts went up from the crowd to keep it open so they could see the Pope, and officials eventually reduced the break to one hour, between 3:00 and 4:00 a.m. That news, however, did little to calm the emotional press on the street.

"They're pushing again from behind," Medori shouted.

Straining from behind was Mirco Sanzovini, twenty-two, a biology student at La Sapienza, who had come prepared for his estimated five-hour wait. He was two hours in and swigging espresso from a stainless-steel thermos. He had been cut off from his mother thirty minutes earlier when the crowd controllers locked him in. Others in line came with tambourines, guitars, and signs bearing the names of their parishes. The city of Rome, meanwhile, had positioned over a hundred ambulances brought in from all over Italy in case of emergencies, and a first-aid tent was erected just off St. Peter's Square. Throughout this period, Rome's civil authorities would get high marks for the efficiency and imagination with which they responded to the extraordinary events.

By the time the doors of St. Peter's were closed for the last time Friday morning, some pilgrims had waited as much as sixteen hours just to spend a few fleeting seconds before John Paul's body. Seen from above, the long lines of mourners looked like mighty streams, a sort of Tigris and Euphrates of humanity, washing into the square from the Via della Conciliazione, the broad avenue leading to St. Peter's built by Mussolini, and from the side streets to the left and right. The crowd was a fascinating demographic mix of the elderly, some of them among the most faithful Roman Catholics of all, whose hearts were breaking at the loss of a pope who had been their moral compass for more than a quarter-century; young couples, drawn by a sense that this man, even in death, could somehow make a difference in their lives and the lives of their children, nudging them toward the good in a world where wrong choices lurk around every corner; and the young themselves, tens of thousands of them, driven by a deep awareness that this was *their* pope, a man who loved youth, who believed in youth, and who sacrificed for young people as few adult figures of any era ever have. Together, they formed an impromptu city within a city, braving the cold of below-average temperatures in sleeping bags, managing to maintain an air of reverence as Vatican loudspeakers repeatedly played hymns and litanies to the saints.

On CNN Tuesday night, one American pilgrim said he had come to join the line directly from Fiumicino Airport. He was still holding his luggage, and said he planned to sleep on the street, putting in as much time as it took for his opportunity to say good-bye. Mourners who fell ill were cared for by forty-two Red Cross doctors from the central Italian region of Emilia Romagna. They treated 180 persons in just the first twelve hours at a field hospital in the nearby Piazza Risorgimento, many of them young people who "arrived at the Vatican absolutely un-prepared for waiting in line for this long," said Dr. Enrico Sverzellati. Most were treated for dehydration, heatstroke, or chills caught at night, while many others fainted. Doctors reported that it was not just the physical ardor that caused some mourners to collapse, but also the fevered emotions that John Paul's passing had generated.

Hundreds of priests in Rome made their way to St. Peter's Square and environs in order to deliver pastoral care to the multitudes, hearing confessions, for example, around the clock. Many later described the ex-perience as unforgettable, relating anecdotes of people who opened their hearts to a priest for the first time in decades, sometimes for the first time ever. Some priests said there were conversions to Catholicism in the crowd, as pilgrims from other Christian churches, from other faith tra-ditions, and from no religious stance at all found themselves swept up in the mystery of the moment. Whether this fervor would endure is an-other question, but as a final tribute to the evangelizing capacity of John Paul's papacy, it struck most observers as impressive.

None of this was lost on the cardinals who, in short order, would elect the new pope.

Each morning, the cardinals met in the new hall of the Synod of

Bishops (as of Wednesday, April 6, 116 cardinals, including some of the over-eighty cardinals, took part in that morning's session, meaning the vast majority of electors were already present, twelve days before the conclave would begin). In order to get to the Vatican, they had to drive or walk past these unending streams of people who had accepted great physical hardship and endless delays in order to make contact with John Paul II one last time. The cardinals had occasion to converse with the mourners, to hear them talk about the powerful affect John Paul's teaching and example had on them. Cynics pointed out that many of these same people probably would not give up an hour later in the week to go to Sunday Mass. One Roman friend argued that if people really wanted to give up sixteen hours to do a good deed, they should visit a relative or help the poor. It was true so far as it goes, but to many cardinals such carping missed the point. They could not help but be impressed with the love and devotion the late Pope had inspired, however it translated into religious practice or more exacting standards of personal morality; even for those who had often followed the Pope in life, these scenes had a profound impact. Other cardinals, who had not been to a papal Mass or watched many of the large-scale events in St. Peter's Square, were experiencing the John Paul II magic for the first time. Still others, whose memories of such phenomena had dimmed as the Pope became steadily less active in his final months, were reminded once more of the awesome charisma John Paul had possessed.

Another powerful factor shaping the cardinals' consciousness was the around-the-clock media coverage these long lines were generating. Media outlets came to cover a funeral, and had planned to fill most of the time between the Pope's death and the funeral Mass with canned packages exploring his life and legacy. To a great extent, however, the people themselves became the story. For an entire week, the mass media forgot about the sex abuse scandals, the latest legislation on gay marriage in Spain, and the vocations crisis in Roman Catholicism, and focused on a story line that Ratzinger would later crystallize into a catchphrase at his inaugural Mass: "The Church is alive!" Even for cardinals long accustomed to seeing their boss draw crowds, this spontaneous, utterly unorganized outpouring was a jolt. Almost to a man, they were stirred by what they saw in the streets of Rome, and then on television, over those days. They realized one last time that John Paul II had raised the public profile of the papacy to historic heights, and many concluded that there could be no going back on the precious resource such visibility afforded the Roman Catholic Church.

Cardinal Justin Rigali of Philadelphia, who spent years working at the Vatican and was in St. Peter's Square for three other papal funerals, called the outpouring for John Paul the most dramatic he had ever witnessed.

"This is the fourth funeral for a pope that I personally participated in. I think this exceeds everything," he said. "This is the most extraordinary thing that ever happened."

During this period, I happened to bump into Cardinal Julian Herranz, one of the world's two Opus Dei (a sometimes controversial, theologically conservative organization of laypeople and clergy within the Church) cardinals and someone I have interviewed extensively for my forthcoming book on Opus Dei. Herranz and his secretary were walking down the Via Paolo VI, near the Vatican, as I was on my way back from an appointment in the Jesuit headquarters just down the street. I asked Herranz, a man who has worked in the Roman Curia for forty-four years and who currently heads the Pontifical Council for the Interpretation of Legislative Texts, what he made of the vast crowds to see the Pope.

"It's deeply moving," he said. "It's a sort of popular rebuttal to Hans Küng's criticism of the Pope." Herranz was referring to a lengthy article published in the Italian daily Corriere della Sera just before John Paul's death, offering a detailed criticism of John Paul's reign. Echoing the very phrase that Ratzinger would later invoke, Herranz said, "The Church is alive. Look at these young people, and you can see it on their faces . . . the Church lives."

Such were the thoughts circulating in the minds of cardinals as they ruminated on the choices awaiting them when the conclave opened.

THE FUNERAL

Those thoughts gathered additional strength from the April 8 funeral Mass, attended by almost a million mourners in and around the Vatican and millions more at satellite locations in Rome and worldwide, making it one of the largest religious gatherings of modern times. World dignitaries, religious leaders, and throngs of the faithful gathered in St. Peter's Square. Moreover, the ceremony was watched by hundreds of millions around the globe. Archbishop John Foley, an American who heads the Pontifical Council for Social Communications, held a briefing for broadcast journalists the day before, and referred to the event with a straight face as "possibly the most important broadcast in history." In any other context, the comment might have seemed laughably hyperbolic; in this setting, however, no one seemed prepared to challenge Foley's claim. By general consensus, it was the most-watched event in the history of television, taking into consideration its global audience of some 2 billion people.

Formally known as a Mass of Requiem, the event began with the doors of St. Peter's Basilica locked and dignitaries asked to stand outside the Church. Only the College of Cardinals and the patriarchs of the Eastern Rite were allowed inside for a private ceremony, in which Pope John Paul II was placed in a cypress coffin, the first of three. Before the Pope was laid in the coffins, Dziwisz had the honor of placing a white silk veil over the face of the Pope. Along with the body was a sealed document, a eulogy detailing the life and works of Pope John Paul II. Three bags, each containing one gold, silver, or copper coin for each year in Pope John Paul II's reign, were placed beside the body—the only monetary compensation he received for his service as pope.

After the private ceremony, the doors were opened while the dignitaries were seated. Ratzinger and his 164 concelebrant cardinals prepared for a procession from inside the basilica to a marble apron in the middle of the square, where the Mass was to be held. The procession began with the introductory hymn, "Eternal Rest Grant Him, O Lord," followed by Psalm 64, "To You We Owe Our Hymn of Praise, O God of Zion." Borne on the shoulders of the Papal Gentlemen, the coffin, with Pope John Paul II's coat of arms burned into the lid, was carried into St. Peter's Square. An acolyte holding a red leather-bound Book of the Gospel preceded the coffin, while the Papal Gentlemen laid the coffin on a red carpet directly in front of the altar.

During the singing of the processional hymns, Ratzinger and his concelebrants removed their miters and bowed to kiss the altar. The concelebrants then placed their miters back on their heads and took their positions at two lines of gold chairs, similar to thrones. The altar was then blessed and incensed. When the songs ended, Ratzinger recited a prayer for Pope John Paul II. The congregants offered a prayer of confession and then sang *Kyrie eleison*, which had also been sung during the transferal of the Pope's body from the Apostolic Palace to St. Peter's Basilica.

The Liturgy of the Word followed. A first reading taken from the Acts of the Apostles, chapter 10, was read in Spanish. Psalm 22 was sung. The second reading was read in English, taken from the Letters of Saint Paul to the Philippians. Later, the Book of the Gospels was carried by an English deacon, Paul Moss, to the ambo (pulpit). The reading came from the Gospel of John, stating, "For this is the will of my father that everyone who sees the son and believes in him may have eternal life." Moss then chanted John's account of a dialogue between Jesus and Saint Peter. Jesus asked three times, "Do you love me?" He then told his disciple, "Follow me."

At the conclusion of the Mass, Ratzinger led the Rite of Final Commendation and Farewell. He asked the College of Cardinals and patriarchs of the Eastern Rite to converge on the casket of Pope John Paul II. The congregants were called to prayer.

"Dear brothers and sisters, let us entrust to the most gentle mercy of God, the soul of our Pope John Paul II," he read out. "May the Blessed Virgin Mary . . . intercede with God so that he might show the face of his blessed Son to our Pope, and console the Church with the light of the resurrection."

The choir sang the Litany of the Saints. In a final break with tradition in John Paul's papacy, names of the saints canonized by Pope John Paul II, such as St. Maria Faustina and St. Josemaría Escrivá, were included. After the Litany of the Saints, the patriarchs, archbishops, and metropolitans of the Eastern Rite approached the coffin of Pope John Paul II for their own rituals of commendation and farewell. They incensed the casket and led each other into prayer. Together with the College of Cardinals and patriarchs of the Eastern Rite, they all witnessed the sprinkling of the casket with the waters used in the sacrament of baptism. Incense was used once again. The liturgy of the Eastern Rite was conducted in Greek.

The Mass of Requiem was officially ended with congregants standing, singing the words, "May the angels accompany you into heaven, may the martyrs welcome you when you arrive, and lead you to Holy Jerusalem." The Papal Gentlemen then carried the coffin of Pope John Paul II for interment, with the rite led by Martínez Somalo. As is customary, John Paul II was entombed in three nested coffins. The cypress coffin was sealed and tied with three red silk ribbons. It was then lowered into a larger solid zinc casket, which was soldered shut. This was adorned with three bronze plaques: a simple cross at the head of the coffin, a plaque with the Pope's name and dates of birth and death at the center, and Pope John Paul II's personal coat of arms at the foot. The zinc casket was finally lowered into a larger walnut casket, bearing three identical plaques, which was shut with nails of pure gold. Pallbearers took the unified coffin through the "Door of Death" on the left side of the altar of St. Peter's Basilica. At that point a single bell tolled. The pallbearers took the coffin down the stairs near the statue of St. Longinus at the base of the canopy of Gian Lorenzo Bernini. The coffin was lowered into the ground, as the Pope requested, and covered with a plain stone slab featuring his name and birth and death dates. Martínez Somalo ended the Rite of Interment with the words, "Lord, grant him eternal rest, and may perpetual light shine upon him." Those present sang *Salve Regina*, "Hail, Holy Queen."

The funeral itself was a masterpiece of symbolism. Following in the tradition of Paul VI, an opened book of the Gospels was placed on the coffin lid—its pages turned by the breeze as the funeral progressed. By the end, the book actually laid closed on the casket, seeming to symbolize the closing of John Paul's earthly life. Behind the casket, the College of Cardinals sat clad in crimson robes, which according to Roman Catholic tradition symbolizes the blood of Jesus Christ. Other church leaders sat to the right of John Paul II in white vestments.

Opposite them sat an audience of equal proportion that included kings, queens, presidents, and prime ministers from the secular world, most of whom dressed in black. Kofi Anan, secretary-general of the United Nations, was among the first to arrive.

Prominent personalities arrived a few at a time, including German chancellor Gerhard Schroeder, Ukrainian president Victor Yushenko, Afghan president Hamid Karzai, then French president Jacques Chirac, King Abdullah of Jordan, and the Spanish royals along with Prime Minister Jose Luis Rodriguez Zapatero. After them arrived Brazilian president Lula and his wife. Tony Blair and Prince Charles, who postponed his wedding with Camilla Parker Bowles for Saturday in order to attend the Pope's funeral, also filed in. (As a British footnote, the event marked the first time that the Archbishop of Canterbury, the future monarch, and the prime minister all attended the funeral of a pope together.) Among the last to arrive because of protocol and security reasons were U.S. president George W. Bush, his father and former president George Bush Sr., former president Bill Clinton, and Secretary of State Condoleezza Rice. The congregation, which included Syrian president Bashar Assad and Israeli president Moshe Katzav, sometimes made strange bedfellows. Reports later circulated that Assad and Katzav shook hands during the Rite of Peace in the Mass, which Archbishop Wilton Gregory of Atlanta, speaking on CNN, later dubbed "John Paul's first miracle." The dignitaries also included 142 leaders of non-Christian religions, testimony to John Paul's persistent and genuine outreach to the other religions of the human family.

Over 10,000 police and soldiers monitored security for the Mass, with 1,430 officers assigned specifically to the heads of state and other dignitaries. A flight ban was in effect to prevent security threats from the air—private light aircraft were not allowed within a thirty-five-mile radius of the center of Rome until Saturday afternoon. Italian air force jets were on standby to intercept intruders, and helicopters were put on "slow mover interceptor" mode in order to head off attacks by small aircraft. Security measures were also adopted to cope with a range of other threats, including attacks from biological, chemical, and nuclear weapons. Antiaircraft missile batteries were put in place in several locations in and around the Italian capital. All these precautions testified to the extraordinary nature of the event; never before had so many heads of state and other VIPs, representing such diverse backgrounds and political outlooks, gathered to mourn one man's passing. It was dramatic visual testimony to the moral, and also political, capital accumulated by John Paul II during his almost twenty-seven-year reign.

As the funeral came to a close, applause erupted throughout the square and resounded through the throng that filled Via della Conciliazione, the main avenue leading to St. Peter's Square. It continued for seven minutes. The crowd also repeatedly erupted into the rhythmic chants of *Giovanni Paolo! Giovanni Paolo!*, so often associated with events in St. Peter's Square and elsewhere. Faithful who could not attend the Mass filled the fields of Tor Vergata, the site where John Paul II held one of the largest rallies of his papacy on World Youth Day in 2000. The funeral was simultaneously followed around the world in places as diverse as the northern Iraqi city of Kirkuk and Tokyo, Japan. Rome itself groaned under the weight of visitors. Side streets were clogged in a permanent pedestrian rush hour, mostly by kids with backpacks. Tent camps sprang up at the Circus Maximus and elsewhere around the city to take the spillover from hotels. Hawkers jacked up prices of everything from bottled water to papal trinkets.

On the eve of the funeral, the Vatican released John Paul's last will and testament, penned in Polish over twenty-two years beginning five months after his election in October 1978. In it, he said he wanted to be buried "in the bare Earth" and have prayers and Masses celebrated after his death. The Pope had revised his thinking about his burial spot over the years, initially asking the College of Cardinals to accede to requests from Poland for burial there, then eventually leaving the matter entirely in their hands. John Paul's body was thus eventually laid to rest in the grotto beneath the main floor of St. Peter's Basilica, in the spot vacated by Pope John XXIII after his beatification in 2000. John Paul's remains are marked by a simple white tombstone with the dates of his pontificate. As soon as the Vatican reopened St. Peter's Basilica after the funeral Mass, it, too, became a magnet for pilgrims. Even during the two-day conclave, the long lines of people waiting to visit the Pope's resting place never abated.

THE HOMILY

Against this backdrop, Ratzinger's homily rapidly evolved from a mere funeral speech into a turning point in the history of the Church. It began with Ratzinger standing before the congregants, his reading glasses perched on his nose, speaking in flawless Italian, greeting the political figures and religious leaders who had gathered.

In somber tones, he then drew parallels between St. Peter's willingness to follow Jesus Christ and John Paul II's journey from the grip of tyrannical dictatorships in Poland to the seat of Roman Catholicism's highest office. He recalled well-known moments from the pontiff's youth, from his days working in a chemical plant under Nazi occupation and from his years as a clandestine seminarian in communist Poland.

"Rise, let us be on our way!" the homily continued, citing the title of John Paul II's 2004 autobiography. "With these words [John Paul II] roused us from a lethargic faith, from the sleep of the disciples of both yesterday and today."

Ratzinger told of John Paul's life as a bishop, cardinal, and pope:

> *The Holy Father was a priest to the last, for he offered his*
> *life to God for his flock and for the entire human family, in a daily*
> *self-oblation for the service of the Church, especially amid the*

sufferings of his final months. And in this way he became one with Christ, the Good Shepherd who loves his sheep. The Pope who tried to meet everyone, who had an ability to forgive and to open his heart to all, tells us once again today, with these words of the Lord, that by abiding in the love of Christ we learn, at the school of Christ, the art of true love.

Our Pope—and we all know this—never wanted to make his own life secure, to keep it for himself. He wanted to give of himself unreservedly, to the very last moment, for Christ and thus also for us. And thus he came to experience how everything which he had given over into the Lord's hands came back to him in a new way. His love of words, of poetry, of literature, became an essential part of his pastoral mission and gave new vitality, new urgency, new attractiveness to the preaching of the Gospel, even when it is a sign of contradiction.

Finally, he told of the Pope's devotion to Mary and the Divine Mercy of Christ. The cardinal's last words invoked the memory of Pope John Paul's attempt to greet the crowd in St. Peter's Square on Easter, words that he never got out:

None of us can ever forget how in that last Easter Sunday of his life, the Holy Father, marked by suffering, came once more to the window of the Apostolic Palace and one last time gave his blessing urbi et orbi. *We can be sure that our beloved pope is standing today at the window of the Father's house, that he sees us and blesses us. Yes, bless us, Holy Father. We entrust your dear soul to the Mother of God, your Mother, who guided you each day and who will guide you now to the eternal glory of her Son, our Lord Jesus Christ. Amen.*

Many construed the ending of the homily to mean that the Pope had already entered into heaven, and had become a saint; given Ratzinger's unimpeachable doctrinal credentials, no one was prepared to challenge him.

Ratzinger became emotional at certain parts of his homily, especially in that final reflection of the inability of Pope John Paul II to speak in the last days of his life. Altogether, the homily was interrupted approximately thirteen times with outbursts of applause by the congregants, and Ratzinger seemed visibly moved by the response. At one point, his eyes, partially shielded by his reading glasses, appeared to well up with tears.

Perhaps the most indelible memory for anyone who experienced the homily was the way the crowd, quite literally, became Ratzinger's conversation partner. At first Ratzinger seemed startled by the applause, but quickly he learned to wait for it, not to proceed until the mourners had been heard. Banners reading *Santo Subito*, "sainthood now," could be seen across St. Peter's Square, and repeatedly the crowd broke out into strong and deep chants of *santo, santo*, "saint, saint." It seemed a classic illustration of the way cases for sainthood are supposed to work in the Catholic Church. It's supposed to begin with a popular devotion, what the medievals called *fama santitatis*, or the "fame of sanctity," which the Church then examines and ultimately ratifies in an after-the-fact fashion. Evidence that the cardinals were influenced is not hard to come by; in the wake of the funeral Mass, a petition was circulated within the daily General Congregation meetings calling on the next pope to move rapidly toward the beatification and canonization of John Paul II. Discussion of the topic arose within the General Congregation, and Ratzinger called on Cardinal Jose Saraiva Martins, head of the Congregation for the Causes of Saints, who explained that there is an ancient custom of sainthood by "popular acclamation," and that the next pope could waive the mandatory five-year waiting period, as was done by Pope John Paul in the case of Mother Teresa. She was beatified in 2003, just six years after her death.

Public reaction to Ratzinger's performance was striking. NBC's Brian Williams captured the sense of many viewers when he called the homily a "warm, warm remembrance." It was precisely the emotion of Ratzinger's homily that struck many cardinals. This is not a man known for wearing his heart on his sleeve, but there he was, with tears in his eyes, talking about the late Pope's love and self-sacrifice. For cardinals who had concerns about Ratzinger's capacity to project emotion to a vast audience, the homily gave them a new sense of the man.

Of course, most of these cardinals knew Ratzinger well in private, and viewed him as a badly misunderstood figure. They knew his gentleness, his impish sense of humor, and his genuine lack of what the Italians call being *gonfiato*, inflated with a sense of one's own importance. Yet many wondered about his capacity to allow those qualities to shine through in public settings. The funeral Mass thus did much to allay those concerns. To hear the Vatican's doctrinal enforcer talking about "the art of true love" seemed to mark the emergence of a "new Ratzinger," or, to put the matter differently, it marked a new stage in his capacity to bring the man many cardinals already knew in private into better alignment with his public image.

There is a sense, therefore, in which the funeral Mass marked the formal beginning of Ratzinger's candidacy for the papacy. (CNN's Jim Bitterman interpreted Ratzinger's repeated invocation of Jesus' exhortation from the day's gospel—"Follow me!"—as a kind of campaign slogan. While that may have been overreaching slightly, Bitterman's sense that Ratzinger was gathering steam proved prophetic.) The Italian papers began to be full of "scoops" and "revelations" about the strength of the pro-Ratzinger vote, suggesting that his base of support was energized by his performance, seized with a new sense that this was not merely the expression of a longing, but a realistic political possibility.

THE IMPACT

No one who watched these scenes play out could be unmoved, and this was especially true of members of the College of Cardinals, who were stunned by this vast popular eruption of love and admiration at the very moment when they were struggling to take stock of the pontificate that had just ended. There is no doubt that the events of the week, the infinite lines to see John Paul's body lying in state and the massive crowds who roared "*santo, santo*" at his funeral, had tremendous psychological impact on the cardinals as they prepared to enter the conclave. If any had arrived in Rome entertaining questions about whether the pontificate of John Paul was fundamentally a success, the experiences of this week eviscerated those doubts. No one could watch the respect paid to the Pope by the VIPs of the world, coupled with his massive popular following, and not draw the conclusion that John Paul II had done something right.

Speaking as these events drew to a close, a number of cardinals made clear that they were deeply stirred by the events of the previous week—and that the emotions had left an impression on their judgments about the kind of pope they needed in order to build on this legacy, which now seemed deeper and more powerful than most of them had imagined.

"It reflects the great impact that John Paul II had on the world," Cardinal Roger Mahony of Los Angeles told the *National Catholic Reporter*. "He was the people's pope. He loved people, and they understood that."

Asked if John Paul would have enjoyed the vast crowds who turned out to bid him farewell, Mahony had no doubt.

"He would have loved it," Mahony said. "He wanted to connect with people. He was a good pastor, and now the flock is coming to see its pastor."

Cardinals also noted that the events of the week, especially the lying in state and the funeral, had generated a stretch of positive media coverage for the Catholic Church that was unprecedented in modern times. Many could not stop thanking the press for the round-the-clock positive treatment of John Paul II's death and its aftermath.

"I want to thank all of you very much for the way you have reported on the death and dying of the Pope," Cardinal Cormac Murphy-O'Connor of Westminster, England, said to a group of journalists shortly before a press blackout was imposed in the week leading up to the conclave. "It has been honest, edifying, and generally very fair."

Asked how to explain the vast response to John Paul's death from both elites and the grass roots, Murphy-O'Connor cited two factors. First, he said, thanks to John Paul's constant travels and outreach, Catholicism was better understood by the world at large. Related to that, he said, John Paul II left a legacy of demonstrating that the Petrine ministry, meaning the office of the pope, is in service not just to the Catholic Church but to the world at large.

"No doubt all his frequent flier miles made a huge difference," the cardinal said, smiling.

"He brought it into a new dimension," Murphy-O'Connor said. "He gave it a new role, and new influence, as a moral voice. Because of the global village in which we live, and the means of communication that exist today, he was able to speak to the entire world. The significance of all this is being seen now for the first time. The world has listened."

To the extent that cardinals had been thinking about electing a pope whose interests would be much more *ad intra*, the events of this week caused them to think anew. They now realized they needed a pope who would not simply take care of the Church's internal business, but someone who could reach out, who could inspire and challenge, someone who could leave a mark on his times in a way analogous to John Paul II. The events of this week, in other words, had the cumulative effect of raising the bar for John Paul II's successor.

A RATZINGER BOOST

What conclusions did the cardinals draw from these experiences?

First, that the global communications industry could be a friend of the Church as well as a critic—if the pope knows how to project a positive message in a media-savvy fashion.

Second, that John Paul's outreach to the young must continue, since the legions of young Catholics who roared with such enthusiasm in the lines waiting to see the Pope's body and at the funeral Mass represented the nucleus of a dynamic, living Catholicism in the future.

Third, that the overall thrust of John Paul's pontificate, whatever its failures and disappointments, was a success. The events of the week between his death and the funeral, in the minds of many cardinal-electors, fortified the case for continuity with the pontificate that had just drawn to a close.

Fourth, that the new pope had to be someone of international stature, someone who could hold his own on the world stage and make the Church's voice heard in moral and cultural debates, someone who could make the Church relevant. John Paul II more than held his own alongside the Thatchers and Kohls, the Reagans and Clintons and Blairs of his era; in some sense, he towered over them all, and his moral and intellectual leadership was universally recognized, even among those (and there were many) who did not agree with much of what the Pope stood for at the level of content. That fact was confirmed by the staggering turnout of heads of state and political leaders who arrived for the funeral. Watching the extraordinary global response to his death, the 115 cardinals who would elect John Paul's successor were conscious that the next pope would also have to be someone with this kind of stature, someone of whom the Roman Catholic Church could be proud, not just for his goodness and decency, but also for his intellectual depth and geopolitical vision. The list of such men in this College of Cardinals, as in any small group of potential leaders, was not exceptionally long.

Intuitively, it did not seem that some of these conclusions would automatically translate into support for Ratzinger's candidacy. The shy, bookish Ratzinger was not known as a charismatic crowd-pleaser, especially with the young, and his media profile was mixed at best. Yet of the four conclusions listed above, probably the one that loomed largest for most cardinals was the argument for continuity with John Paul II, and on this score, in retrospect, Ratzinger was the obvious choice. He was the intellectual architect of the main lines of the late Pope's reign, and no one in the College of Cardinals knew John Paul's mind and heart better. If the cardinals were looking for someone to uphold and build upon the thrust of what John Paul set out to achieve, many felt they could do no better than to look to the figure who had been his right-hand man since 1981, just three years after the Pope himself took office. The fact that John Paul had extended Ratzinger in office three times beyond the normal five-year term of a curial prefect, that the Pope so obviously felt he could not do without Ratzinger's advice and guidance, all by itself marked Ratzinger out as the best possible protector of John Paul's legacy. Moreover, because of Ratzinger's keen understanding of the Roman Curia and the broader dynamics of ecclesiastical governance, he could ensure that John Paul II's legacy did not simply vanish, but was translated into structural and institutional reality.

As for the media, the cardinals themselves opted for a rather striking encore to their praise of the media's coverage of the death and funeral of the Pope: They decided not to talk to the press in the period between the funeral on April 8 and the opening of the conclave on April 18. As word of the press blackout began to circulate, many journalists, especially from the Italian papers, leapt to the conclusion that it must have been Ratzinger, as dean of the College of Cardinals, who imposed the restriction, in keeping with his image as "Cardinal No." In fact, however, this was not the case. Inside the daily General Congregation meetings of cardinals, pressure had been building for days for an explicit ban on conversations with the press, largely from some curial cardinals as well as some of the Latin Americans who felt it was unfair the way cardinals from Europe and America commanded a disproportionate share of media attention, allowing them to set the public agenda for the conclave through the press. During the period immediately after the blackout went into effect, three cardinals told me on background that it was not Ratzinger who imposed the policy. Indeed, they said, he resisted calls for a formal ban.

In our preconclave interview, Danneels made this explicit, relating that Ratzinger had said in the General Congregation meetings that it was a "human right" of cardinals to speak to whomever they chose. Other cardinals confirmed this account. Instead of an explicit ban, therefore, the cardinals struck a sort of gentleman's agreement among themselves to be discreet. Through Navarro-Valls, they also issued invitation to the press to leave them alone; as Navarro-Valls described it, "This is not a prohibition, it's an invitation."

In other words, to the outside, the maneuvering over the press among the cardinals perhaps seemed a typical authoritarian exercise from Ratzinger. Among the cardinals themselves, however, it was precisely the opposite. Ratzinger respected their individual liberty, had shown sensitivity to the press, and once again seemed victim of an unfair type of character assassination in the broader public discussion. These internal perceptions did much to soften Ratzinger's image among cardinals who did not know him well, and cause them to think anew about what kind of pope he might make.

On the question of international stature, Ratzinger was clearly among the standouts. He is a widely respected intellectual who has published lucid works of theology and cultural criticism on a staggering variety of subjects. Even in ultra-secular France, where respect for institutional religion is not exactly at an all-time high, Ratzinger has been twice honored for his intellectual accomplishments. On November 6, 1992, he was inducted into the Academy of Moral and Political Sciences of the Institute of France, and in 1998 he was installed as a commander in the French Legion of Honor. This, in other words, would be a pope with whom the world would have to reckon.

Finally, as for the question of youth and the "common touch," no one pretends that Ratzinger can muster quite the same charisma as John Paul II. Yet his powerful performance during the funeral Mass, and the immediate rapport he seemed to establish with the cheering crowd, caused at least some cardinals to look past the old stereotype of Ratzinger as an aloof authoritarian incapable of relating to ordinary people.

In his own mind, Ratzinger's standout performances probably had nothing to do with improving his chances at election, and everything to do with paying off one final debt to the man he served and loved for a quarter-century, John Paul II. Yet whatever his intent, the reality is that these two weeks transformed Ratzinger from one possibility in a crowded field into a juggernaut whose candidacy proved unstoppable.

"His leadership at the Pope's funeral was such that we have to give Ratzinger some consideration," an African cardinal told me on background on Sunday, April 10, eight days before the voting began.

This cardinal acknowledged candidly that he wasn't yet sold. "How would I explain that the best we could do was a seventy-eight-year-old man already beyond the retirement age for bishops?" he mused, thinking about how he would present the outcome back home. As a man of the global south, this cardinal also confessed that he wanted a pope whose local church would be solidly behind him, a man who could put a face on the energy and dynamism of Catholicism in places like Africa and Latin America. It wasn't clear to him at that stage that an elderly German cardinal fit that bill.

Then came a telling comment.

"Still, what I saw at that funeral . . . it seemed to me that Ratzinger was taking on something of the style of John Paul II, rather than his own style," he said. "It certainly made me think."

Obviously, it made some others think, too.

Chapter Three.

THE INTERREGNUM

Though some may wish to dispute the point, it seems abundantly clear that Cardinal Joseph Ratzinger, having turned seventy-eight just two days before the conclave began, did not run for the job of pope. Just before his election, he told staff members at the Congregation for the Doctrine of the Faith that he hoped the new pope would allow him a few more months on the job, and then he would step down, as he had long dreamt of doing. Three times over the course of the last fifteen years—in 1991, 1996, and 2001—Ratzinger had asked Pope John Paul II for permission to retire so that he could return to Germany, to Regensburg in his native Bavaria, to live with his brother Georg and resume writing full-time on theology, liturgy, spirituality, and ecclesiology. Each time, the Pope refused, and Ratzinger accepted his wishes, but his eagerness to set aside the burdens of office was clear to those who knew him.

Moreover, the new pope confirmed his lack of hunger for the job on Monday, April 25, just after his election, in an audience with German pilgrims.

"As slowly the balloting showed me that, so to speak, the guillotine would fall on me, I got quite dizzy," he said. "I had thought I had done my life's work and could now hope for a peaceful end of my days. . . . So with deep conviction, I told the Lord: 'Don't do this to me! You have younger and better men who can do this work with different verve and strength.'"

Among other things, this was undoubtedly the first time in church history that a new pope has compared his election to a death sentence.

Then, Benedict XVI conceded that his prayer had been in vain: "This time, He didn't listen to me."

Cynics might see this as the normal pro forma show of humility from a victor, but there's every reason to believe that Ratzinger was deadly serious. The truth is that most cardinals do not want to be pope. On a spiritual level, cardinals take seriously the Catholic belief that the pope is Christ's vicar on earth, and knowing themselves as they do, fully cognizant of their frailties and weaknesses, most have a hard time taking themselves seriously as a candidate for that role. On a human level, the papacy is a burden one carries from the moment of election to the moment of death. There is no six-year term to serve, followed by writing one's memoirs and then afternoons on the golf course. It is a bone-crushing job that one is never allowed to set down, and for a man who had envisioned spending his golden years in his study, reading and writing, playing the piano, and taking quiet strolls on Bavarian afternoons, it must weigh especially heavily. For all those reasons, we are obligated to take Benedict XVI at his word: He did not want to be pope.

Yet if Joseph Ratzinger *had* been running for pope, it would be difficult to imagine a more skillful campaign than his performance as dean of the College of Cardinals in the period from the death of John Paul II on April 2 through the opening of the conclave on Monday, April 18. Though it is too much to say that those two weeks got him the job, without them, it's much more difficult to imagine that Joseph Ratzinger would be sitting on the Throne of Peter today.

Ratzinger was elected dean of the College of Cardinals in December 2001, after Cardinal Bernard Gantin of Benin, having reached the age of eighty, asked to be relieved of the post. (Although cardinals lose their voting privileges at the age of eighty, it is not automatic that the dean renounces his position. In 1978, the year of two conclaves, the dean who presided over both interregnums was eighty-five-year-old Cardinal Carlo Confalonieri of Italy.) The election to replace Gantin was carried out by the ten cardinals who then constituted the order of cardinal-bishops within the College of Cardinals and was confirmed by Pope John Paul II.

Though the transition was little-noted at the time, it was perhaps the single most decisive moment in the chain of events that resulted in the election of Pope Benedict XVI. One could argue that the eighty-three-year-old Gantin, without even being present in the conclave, was among its most influential players. In a certain sense, he was the inadvertent architect of Ratzinger's election. By making way for Ratzinger to become the dean of the College, he allowed Ratzinger to tower over the interregnum, and the momentum Ratzinger built over those two weeks proved to be unstoppable.

As the cardinals assembled in Rome, however, it was by no means a foregone conclusion that Joseph Ratzinger would emerge as the next pope. Most cardinals later said that they arrived in Rome with several names running through their heads; one American cardinal told me that he entered the interregnum period with a personal list of twenty candidates he regarded as serious contenders. In that environment, cardinals had to form impressions of the various candidates quickly, and no one had a better opportunity than Ratzinger to present himself. As dean, he presided at the funeral Mass for John Paul II on April 8 and at the Mass *pro eligendo papa*, "for electing the pope," which took place on April 18, the morning of the conclave. More important, he presided at the daily meetings of the General Congregation, the assembly of cardinals that proved critically influential in shaping the preconclave discussions. Because of these roles, he was also the most sought-after figure in informal conversation, giving him an unrivaled opportunity to speak with his brother cardinals one-on-one or in small groups, making him the central point of reference during the entire process. These forums gave him the chance to leave a personal impression that no other cardinal could match.

Had Joseph Ratzinger not already been an impressive candidate, his leadership during that period would likely have meant very little. (Had Gantin still been dean, for example, it's unlikely that the exposure of those two weeks would have transformed him into a serious contender to be pope.) Yet for those cardinals who entered the deliberations with reservations about Ratzinger, and there were many, the interregnum offered an opportunity to test those reservations against the reality of the man they saw before them. The outcome suggests that Ratzinger passed the test with flying colors.

THE PRESS BLACKOUT

As noted earlier, Ratzinger was not responsible for the gag order on the College of Cardinals, preventing them from speaking to the press. In fact, the way he was blamed for the restriction in the press actually seemed to help him among some cardinals, who saw it as another instance of Ratzinger unfairly shouldering the blame for policy decisions that were not his own.

That aside, however, Ratzinger was inarguably the candidate who benefited most from the effect of the blackout, since he became by default virtually the only cardinal whose voice appeared in print or on television during the ten days between the funeral and the conclave, at least in any form other than prepackaged interviews from long ago. Not only did Ratzinger dominate the internal discussions among the cardinals, he also dominated the media discussion, mostly because there was little else to digest by way of public comment. Thus his homily at the funeral became the most-discussed bit of oratory in the preconclave period, contributing to the sense of "Big Mo," or momentum, around his name heading into the balloting.

Why did the cardinals decide to go silent?

First, the cardinals and their press advisers understood that once the papal funeral was over, the press would shift from asking "life and legacy of John Paul II" questions to more aggressive questions about the state of the Catholic Church, and about the next pope. In general, cardinals found the second sort of question far more awkward and difficult to answer, especially given the way it invited speculation.

Second, the cardinals were concerned about protecting the liberty of the conclave. This is the reason they are cut off from the outside world once the conclave begins, so that foreign governments, activist groups, and other interested parties cannot exert influence over their deliberations. It's the same concept as the secret ballot in democratic societies—cardinals must be free to vote for the person who, in their consciences, they feel would be the best man for the job. The concern was that in the preconclave period, the media rather than the cardinals might end up setting the agenda for their discussions.

Third, the cardinals were also concerned about honoring the vow of confidentiality they made about the daily meetings of the General Congregation, as well as the conclave itself. With the best of intentions, sometimes in conversations with journalists things slip out, and can end up having unforeseeable negative consequences. Simply saying "no" in theory insulated them from this possibility. (In reality, however, at least this motive for the policy was honored more in the breach than the observance. Each day the Italian papers were full of detailed, and remarkably accurate, reports of what had been said by various cardinals the day before.)

Fourth, there was the simple logistical fact that if cardinals were constantly shuttling from one TV location to another, they would have proportionately less time to accomplish what was the primary purpose of that week—reflecting privately with one another on the issues facing the Church, the profile of a leader needed to face those challenges, and ultimately who that leader ought to be. If they didn't have the time to talk with one another, some argued, the quality of their deliberations might be impaired.

Fifth, some cardinals, especially those from Europe and North America, were more accustomed to dealing with a massive, at-times hostile press corps than cardinals from other places. The advantage of a blanket policy of caution was that those cardinals uncomfortable with media relations would have an automatic reason to say "no."

Sixth and finally, this was supposed to be a period not just of political caucusing, but also of prayer. The cardinals felt they shouldn't be so pressed that they couldn't find the time for spiritual reading, prayer, and reflection.

These were the reasons most commonly given for the pull-back from engagement with the press. Whether they are ultimately convincing is a matter of perspective, but in any event it adds up to something more than the simple desire to pull a curtain down on the preconclave activity. More to the point, the policy, as well as the public reaction to it, gave another unforeseeable boost to the candidacy of Joseph Ratzinger.

COMPLEXITY THAT PRODUCED SIMPLICITY

Heading into the conclave of 2005, many observers regarded it as one of the most difficult conclaves to handicap in recent memory. This judgment was based on three factors:

- Following the election of Karol Wojtyla in 1978, the Italian monopoly on the papacy had been shattered forever. While the next pope could be an Italian, and indeed there seemed to be some strong Italian candidates, he did not *have* to be Italian. The field was wide open, so that in a sense all 115 cardinals, and not just the 21 Italians, had to be regarded as potential popes. Moreover, this was the first conclave in which the Italians were not clearly "in charge," meaning that the real candidates were not identified ahead of time by an inner group of Italian kingmakers. This time, it was the entire college that tried to grope its way toward identifying candidates, which made the preconclave dynamics much trickier.
- Many of the cardinals did not know one another well. An inner core of the 115 electors, those who worked in Rome or who traveled to the Vatican regularly on business, had a good sense of one another, but other cardinals, who lived in far-flung dioceses and

who did not come out of the Vatican diplomatic corps or other standard ecclesiastical career paths, knew only what they read in the newspapers or saw on television. They came into the preconclave period without a strong personal awareness of the strengths and weaknesses of the various candidates. Moreover, because of their lack of connections in Rome, it was not immediately clear to them how to plug into the informal, subterranean conversations they knew were happening. While an inner circle of cardinals began meeting almost immediately to talk things over, this other group, represented especially by residential cardinals from the global south, was much more disengaged. The unpredictability of how they might react represented a potential "wild card" heading into the deliberations. Moreover, given that most cardinals did not begin openly discussing the succession until after the funeral of John Paul II, this meant they only had ten days to come to a decision.

• There was no one dominant issue looming over the conclave of 2005, as had sometimes been the case in the past. In 1878, for example, the burning issue was the so-called Roman question, of whether the papacy could resign itself to the loss of temporal power and the reality of the new Italian republic. The election of Cardinal Gioacchino Pecci of Perugia (Pope Leo XIII), in this context, was a vote for a more conciliatory approach than that of his immediate predecessor, Pius IX. In 1963, the towering issue was the fate of the Second Vatican Council (1962–65), and the election of Cardinal Giovanni Battista Montini as Pope Paul VI was a clear signal that the cardinals wanted the council to continue. This time around, however, the cardinals listed a slew of issues that were on their minds: secularism in Western Europe, the rise of global Islam, the growing gap between rich and poor in the north and the south, and the proper balance in church governance between the center and the periphery. Before the fact, it was unclear what kind of candidate these reflections would produce.

Given the complexity the above factors suggest, many observers were expecting a protracted conclave with a surprise result. In the event, however, things shook out in exactly the opposite fashion. Rather than complicating the election of the next pope, the obvious complexity of the preconclave dynamics produced a desire for simplicity. Given the pressures of time and unfamiliarity, many cardinals concluded that rather than risking the unknown, it made more sense to opt for a "safe" choice—that is, a man whose qualities, experience, and aptitudes were known to all. (By "safe," one should not understand an interim, caretaker figure. The point is rather that in an environment in which there was pressure to settle quickly on a candidate among a large set of unknowns, many cardinals felt the most prudent course was to opt for someone whose worldview and personal approach were well-established.) One cardinal said before the fact, "This is a choice we dare not get wrong," and in the end it seems that most agreed this was not the time for a roll of the dice. The option they chose to cut through the complexity was a known quantity, even if it meant electing someone whose age, nationality, and controversial track record was perhaps not what some of them went into the conclave seeking.

ISSUES

Before the press blackout descended on April 8, many cardinals had given extensive interviews to the press, and a consensus view of the issues they believed would face the next pope began to emerge from these conversations. It's worth taking a moment to examine what the cardinals saw as the agenda of the next pontificate as they entered the conclave.

Secularity
Given that the majority of cardinal electors were European (fifty-eight Europeans, as opposed to fifty-seven from everywhere else), and given that even the non-Europeans generally have spent long stretches of time

in European cities, especially Rome, European realities tend to loom large in the collective imagination of the College of Cardinals. These days in Europe, those realities are often problematic for the Catholic Church.

It's not just that the Vatican recently lost a bitter fight to have the preamble of the new European constitution make a reference to God, or that Italian politician Rocco Buttiglione was blackballed as the European commissioner of justice because of his traditional Catholic views on abortion and homosexuality, or even that the new Spanish government has waged what is tantamount to a cultural crusade against Roman Catholicism on issues such as homosexual marriage. Deeper than these specific battles, several trends converged to suggest to many observers a kind of "ecclesiastical winter" in today's Europe:

- A residual anticlericalism in many quarters that still sees the Church as an enemy of cultural progress, and that regards the Church's primary interest as the defense of its own power and privilege;
- Declining vocations to the priesthood and religious life, with some religious orders literally dying out;
- Low Mass attendance rates, in some cases in the single digits in northern European countries;
- Declining fertility rates, with the lowest recorded in traditional Catholic strongholds, such as Spain and Italy;
- Declining cultural influence, with, for example, twelve nations that have regularized same-sex unions, and three that have granted full marriage rights to same-sex couples.

There is little question that these are tough times for institutional Christianity in Europe, so much so that some cardinals wondered if European candidates ought to be excluded from consideration as the next pope by the mere fact of being European.

"If we elect a pope from Honduras or Nigeria, there would be a very dynamic and excited local church behind him, as there was with John Paul II and Poland," one cardinal from the developing world said

April 10. "If we elect someone from Belgium or Holland, can you imagine the Belgians or the Dutch getting excited? He simply wouldn't have the same base of support, the same energy behind him."

It's easy enough to identify secularity as a challenge. The hard part is knowing what to do about it, and here ideas among the cardinals tended to cluster into three main options.

First was the reform option. This current holds that in order for the Church to be a credible dialogue partner for contemporary Europe, it must better reflect the values that animate European culture—transparency, democracy, human rights. A less authoritarian church, one that is more open and accountable, will stand a better chance of finding a hearing in contemporary European conversation. "Europe" here functions as a metaphor for secularized Western culture, which is increasingly becoming the culture of the world. Danneels of Belgium is one prominent exponent of this position. He has repeatedly argued that the contemporary Western mind is allergic to arguments from authority, so that the Church needs to learn instead to speak in the language of beauty.

Another option was "aggressive engagement." This view held that the crisis in European Catholicism is not one of structures but of nerve. The Church's problem is that it has become too timid, too cowed by the challenges of secularism, and the danger is being assimilated to the dominant ethos of relativism and immanentism. Instead, this view held, the Church should proclaim its traditional truths loudly and boldly, with no compromise and no apology. In the end, this view held, a robustly evangelical approach will win over Europe, because it expresses the truth about the meaning and purpose of human existence. Cardinals Camillo Ruini and Angelo Scola of Italy represented this view.

Finally, a third camp believed that in the present moment, Europe (at least the post-Christian, postreligious culture of western Europe) is to some extent beyond the reach of evangelization. It's pointless to hope that Christianity will be a mass presence in this historical period. Instead, as Ratzinger himself has said many times, the aim ought to be to make Christianity "a creative minority." The goal should be to defend Christian identity rather than to make it acceptable to a culture hostile on principle to what it stands for, concentrating on forming a new generation excited about the faith, however small in number they may be, who can emerge at a future point when the false promises of hedonism and secularism have run their course.

These options were more like ideal types than real groupings, and most cardinals found themselves to some extent in all three, or in none, depending upon the precise question under examination. Nevertheless, the groups illustrate the complexity of the choices that faced the conclave on this question.

Governance

As already mentioned, there had been grumbling for some time among some cardinals, as well as within the Vatican, that John Paul II's style was so directed to the outside world—through his travels, his documents, and his ecumenical and interreligious dialogue. For Americans, perhaps the most obvious manifestation of this inattention to internal business would be the sexual abuse crisis. Many American Catholics wanted John Paul II to intervene earlier and more aggressively to insist that bishops be held accountable if they failed to adequately supervise their priests, thereby placing children at risk of abuse. Instead, the Pope treated the crisis as largely a matter for the local church to resolve, restricting himself to general statements of repugnance at sexual abuse and confidence in the American bishops.

Others were frustrated with the extent to which the Roman Curia has appropriated to itself powers that previously had been reserved to local churches. Nowhere has this tendency been clearer than in the liturgy, where control of the process of liturgical translation has been recentralized in Rome. Some complained that even minor decisions are being made by Roman officials that should be left to the judgment of local authorities.

When some cardinals talked about the need for a pope more concerned with governance, they meant someone who will supervise bishops more closely, take greater personal responsibility for the appointment of bishops, and insist on a more coordinated common line in the

Vatican. Others meant a pope who will "tame" the Roman Curia, insisting on a program of decentralization, known in Catholic parlance as "collegiality." This tends to be a special concern both of progressives in the developed world, who tend to resent Roman rigidity, as well as bishops in the developing world who may be conservative on matters of doctrine but want to see some room for greater "inculturation" of that doctrine, meaning allowing it to be expressed in ways appropriate to the local culture.

The commonality among these various ways of expressing the governance issue was a widely held sense among the cardinals that the internal administration of the Church had been neglected for too long, and that the next pope needed to be a man with a proven aptitude for administration.

Islam

In the post-9/11 world, there's a kind of general recognition that the relationship between the Islamic world and the West, and thus between Christianity and Islam, will be among the most decisive factors shaping world events. For better or worse, the Islamic world perceives the pope as the most important leader in the Christian world, and for that reason the policy of the next pope vis-à-vis Islam will be a critically important force in shaping this relationship.

Moreover, there's a growing concern among some Christian observers that Christian energies may be flagging, especially in Europe, just as Islam is gathering momentum. Already there are more practicing Muslims who go to mosque on Fridays in the United Kingdom than Anglicans who attend services on Sunday, and estimates are that Muslims could make up one-quarter of the French population, the "eldest daughter of the Church," within a generation. The fear in some quarters is that Europe, which has traditionally been the cradle of Christian civilization, could end up as little more than an outpost of the Islamic world.

Once again, it's easier to name the concern than to forge policy in response to it. One group of cardinals, who could be labeled "doves" on the question of Islam, emphasized the need for ever greater levels of dialogue with different Islamic movements and institutions. They argued that because the Christian West is richer and more powerful on the global stage, it's incumbent upon Christians to take the first step, to avoid saying or doing anything inflammatory, and to accept what at times may seem a certain irrationality and suspiciousness as part of the historical "baggage" of this relationship. It's also important, this camp believed, to reach out to moderate centers of Islamic opinion, and to work to resolve the social justice issues that are sometimes at the root of terrorism that appeals to Islamic principles.

This view, for example, was expressed in a session with the press by Cardinal Cormac Murphy-O'Connor of Westminster, England.

"I would hope that the way of dialogue would increase," Murphy-O'Connor said, "and make inroads among the other parts of Islam. This needs to be done with urgency for the sake of peace in our world." Murphy-O'Connor argued that Islamic immigrants in Europe, including those in the United Kingdom, could become a "bridge" between the West and Muslim populations in the Arab world.

Other cardinals, however, believed that while there are plenty of moderate Muslims, "moderate Islam" is a bit of myth, at least in the sense of an organized and politically meaningful movement. The short-term future, they believed, is more likely to be characterized by conflict rather than by dialogue, especially in those zones of the world where Christians and Muslims rub shoulders: sub-Saharan Africa, Asia, and the Middle East. Catholicism should be prepared for this conflict, they suggested, through a policy more akin to "tough love." One focus for this attitude is the issue of "reciprocity." If Muslim immigrants to the West insist upon religious freedom and the protection of law, they argue, the same treatment should be extended to Christians in the Islamic world. If the Saudi Arabian government can spend $65 million to finance the construction of a sprawling mosque in Rome, for example, then perhaps Christians ought to be able to legally build churches in Saudi Arabia, something that is presently barred by law. Similarly, this camp was strongly convinced of the need to revitalize the Christian roots of Europe, that Europe is in a sense too important to fail. Accelerating Islamic immigration into

Europe, while not a threat in itself, they suggested, nevertheless puts additional pressure on the Church to remind Europeans of their historical and cultural identity. One cardinal associated with this view is the emeritus bishop of Bologna, Cardinal Giacomo Biffi.

Rich and Poor

During the General Congregation meetings, in the latter stages when each cardinal was able to speak about the situation facing his local church, many of the cardinals from the south spoke in emotional terms about poverty, chronic underdevelopment, corruption, war, and disease. They urged their brother cardinals to engage the Church in a struggle for a more just world order, one that would reflect Christian convictions about the dignity of all persons and the universal destination of the goods of the earth. This plea was not so much a proposal for new theological reflection, since the tradition of Catholic social teaching since the late nineteenth century had already put the Church squarely on the side of the poor, but a cry from the heart for a new level of engagement and passion from the Church on the subject.

The next pope, according to these cardinals, should bring the same passion to bridging the north/south divide that John Paul II did to the rupture between East and West. Like John Paul, the pope had to be a voice of conscience for the marginalized and forgotten peoples of the world, they urged. This demand did not break down along liberal/conservative lines, as even cardinals from the south who would conventionally be seen as quite conservative doctrinally echoed the point. Whatever else the next pope does, these men seemed to be saying, he would have to confront the social reality of structural sin with energy and imagination.

How did this set of issues result in the election of Joseph Ratzinger?

Unlike a secular political election, one cannot always connect the dots in clear fashion between the issues the cardinals discuss and the man they elect. First of all, they were looking for the best man, not necessarily the best platform. Cardinals often do not "vote issues" in the way journalists are accustomed to tracking them. Second, many cardinals were genuinely convinced that they had set the agenda for the next pope collectively through the General Congregation meetings, so that to some extent, in terms of these issues, it almost didn't matter whom they elected. Having listened to the discussion, they felt, the pope would feel bound to act on it.

Yet Ratzinger's background and set of strengths did, nevertheless, correspond well in the mind of many electors with the issues they had identified. Given his consummate mastery of the Western intellectual and cultural tradition, he seemed to many exactly the right man to engineer a response to secularism. As a proven Vatican administrator, yet a man free of the normal ties of loyalty in the Roman Curia, he could get a handle on church governance. On Islam, he was known to respect the strong doctrinal traditions of Islam and for positive dealings with Islamic leaders one-on-one, but he was also someone who would not be afraid to be tough when the situation called for it. His comments last year about Turkey's admission to the European Union, for example, struck some external observers as provocative, but to many in the College of Cardinals, they were evidence of a man not afraid to buck a "politically correct" environment when issues of Christian identity beckon. On the north/south question, Ratzinger had shown surprising sensitivity during the General Congregation meetings, at one point insisting that the European and American cardinals limit their remarks so that cardinals from Africa and Asia could be heard.

The more the cardinals thought about what the next papacy would be like, in other words, the more they could see Joseph Ratzinger, despite his age and his reputation, doing the job.

PUBLIC PERFORMANCES

Well before John Paul II died, Joseph Ratzinger had the determined support of a number of cardinals as his successor. In the last five years, I have interviewed roughly 65 of the 115 cardinals who elected Pope Benedict XVI. Most did not discuss the names of potential candidates, preferring to talk about the issues facing the Church and the profile of the kind of man who would be necessary to face those challenges. Four cardinals, however, told me point-blank that they intended to vote for Ratzinger at least on the first ballot of the conclave, to see where his candidacy might go. They included cardinals from Latin America, the Pacific Rim, and Europe, so I knew that Ratzinger had a formidable basis of support.

At the same time, however, one North American cardinal said something I suspect was also in the backs of the minds of some electors: "Ratzinger may be the best man for the job," he said, roughly a year ago. "But my concern is how I would sell this back home."

During the interregnum, Ratzinger went a long way to addressing precisely those reservations, showing a more conciliatory, open, listening side of himself; proving to have surprising resources as a man on the public stage.

He exhibited these qualities first of all during the two capstone public appearances of this period, the funeral Mass and the Mass for the election of the pope that opened the conclave. We have already noted how the well-crafted homily Ratzinger delivered at the funeral Mass, combined with his surprising rapport with the crowd, suggested to some cardinals that he might have surprising reserves of strength as a public figure.

Having established his capacity to project a kinder, gentler image on the public stage, Ratzinger then turned in another kind of performance during the Mass *pro eligendo papa* on April 18, the opening day of the conclave. Delivering a powerful critique of trends in contemporary Western culture, he reminded the cardinals of why he was considered a front-runner in the first place—because, whatever one makes of the content of his positions, he possesses a powerful intellect and the courage of his convictions. This is not a man afraid to speak what he sees as the truth, however inconvenient or jarring that truth may seem.

It's worth quoting the heart of that homily at length:

> *How many winds of doctrine have we know in these recent decades, how many ideological currents, how many modes of*

*thought. . . . The small ship of thought of many Christians has
often been agitated by these waves—tossed from one extreme to the
other; from Marxism to liberalism, from collectivism to radical
individualism; from atheism to a vague religious mysticism; from
agnosticism to syncretism and so on. Every day new sects are born,
and what St. Paul said about the deception of humanity is
demonstrated, about the craftiness that tends to lead to error. To
have a clear faith, according to the Creed of the Church, is often
styled as fundamentalism. Meanwhile relativism, meaning allowing
oneself to be carried away "here and there by any wind of
doctrine," appears as the only attitude suited to modern times.
What's being constructed is a dictatorship of relativism, which
recognizes nothing as definitive, and that regards one's self and
one's own desires as the final measure.*

*We, however, have another measure: the Son of God, the
true man. He is the measure of true humanism. A faith is not
"adult" that follows the waves of fashion and the latest novelty; an
adult and mature faith is profoundly rooted in friendship with
Christ. It's this friendship that opens us to everything that is good,
and that gives us the criterion for discerning between the true and
the false, between deception and truth. We must mature in this
adult faith, and it's toward this adult faith that we must lead the
flock of Christ. It's this faith—only this faith—that creates unity
and realizes itself in charity. St. Paul offers us in this regard, in
contrast with the constant vicissitudes of those who, like children,
are tossed about by the waves, a beautiful word: to live the truth in
charity, as a fundamental formula of Christian existence. In
Christ, truth and charity coincide. To the extent that we come
closer to Christ, also in our own lives, truth and charity will find a
solid base. Charity without truth would be blind; the truth
without charity would be like "a clashing cymbal."*

This was strong medicine, and in the immediate aftermath of the
homily, some (myself included) suggested that it might actually work

against Ratzinger's candidacy. By so openly striking a negative, critical note about the surrounding culture, some felt, Ratzinger had sent exactly the wrong signal to the cardinal-electors, reminding them of the dour "enforcer" image that he had carried for the previous twenty-four years. While few cardinals would disagree with the content of what Ratzinger had said, some observers felt that cardinals might be troubled by its tone, since so many had said that above all they were seeking a pope who could offer hope to the world. Such a dark view of contemporary culture, at least in the developed West, did not seem especially optimistic, and optimism is usually the fuel of electoral politics. A few (again myself included) even greeted the homily as proof positive that Ratzinger was not running for office, in that it was the opposite of conventional political oratory.

To some extent, however, this was a case of selective attention on the part of the press and other observers. We accented the toughest parts of the homily, without paying adequate attention to the rest of the text. Here's how Ratzinger ended his reflections:

> *Everyone wants to leave something that lasts. But what lasts? Not money. Buildings don't last; neither do books. After a certain period of time, more or less lengthy, all these things disappear. The only thing that lasts into eternity is the human soul, the human person created by God for eternity. The fruit that lasts is therefore what we have planted in peoples' souls—love, understanding; the gesture capable of touching hearts; the word that opens the soul to the joy of the Lord. Therefore, let's pray to the Lord so that he helps us to bear fruit, a fruit that lasts. Only this way can the earth be transformed from a valley of tears into the garden of God.*

These were decidedly un-Ratzingerian notes, at least measured against his public image. Here was one of the principle theologians of the Catholic Church acknowledging that his own intellectual legacy, the books he produced over a lifetime, ultimately count for nothing if they don't lead people to an experience of God's love. Here was Ratzinger the dry academic undergoing a metamorphosis into Ratzinger the poet, talking about a "valley of tears" and "the garden of God," about gestures capable of stirring hearts. What many cardinals took away from this homily, they said later, was a sense of admiration for a man who could both lucidly present a set of challenges, and yet not end up sounding pessimistic or defeatist.

The homily was not a campaign speech, with no soundbites, no catchphrases, no "shining city on a hill"–style rhetoric. Yet if the cardinals were looking for someone who seemed to have a read on the challenge of secularism in the West, who was not blind to its perils but seemed to have a viable Christian alternative to propose, who was a realist about what could be accomplished but not someone prepared to concede defeat, Ratzinger clearly began to loom as the obvious choice.

PRIVATE PERFORMANCES

If his public performances were important, by a universal consensus among the cardinals who lived these two weeks from the inside, it was his conduct behind closed doors that truly made the difference. Again, it's not that his leadership in the General Congregation meetings or in informal talks with other cardinals won him the election, but rather that they were instrumental in lowering the anxieties of cardinal-electors who approached his candidacy with reservations. Reducing those anxieties was, therefore, the critical factor in transforming Ratzinger from a strong candidate but one whose capacity to reach 77 votes out of 115 remained in doubt, to something approaching a consensus choice.

What were some of those reservations?

- That as a top official of the Roman Curia for twenty-four years, someone who had only a brief (two and half years) and mixed record as a diocesan bishop, Ratzinger might be insensitive to pastoral realities;
- In a similar vein, that Ratzinger's background in the Curia might

leave him ill-equipped to practice collegiality—that is, collaborative governance with other cardinals and bishops, for which many bishops have long clamored;

- That Ratzinger's age and health might render him too delicate to shoulder the crushing responsibilities of the papacy, a special consideration in light of the long and very public decline during John Paul II's final years;

- That a northern European intellectual might not bring the special sensitivity to social justice issues about which many cardinals from the global south felt passionately;

- That Ratzinger's ambivalent public image might hamstring his pontificate from the beginning, deepening the polarization in a church already badly fractured in some parts of the world;

- That Ratzinger's professorial disposition, more at home in a study than on stage, might leave him incapable of transmitting the energy and dynamism that the Church needs, especially if it is to find new life in Europe.

In the period between the death of John Paul II on April 2 and the opening of the conclave on April 18, the General Congregation, the daily assembly of cardinals that met in the new synod hall inside the Vatican grounds, met thirteen times. Ratzinger presided over each session, and in the end his leadership left a deep impression, though it took a while for this impact to sink in. During the early sessions, the cardinals were constrained to go line by line through the text of *Universi Dominici Gregis*, John Paul's fourteen-thousand-word document issued in February 1996 setting out the rules, in minute detail, for the election of his successor. Several cardinals privately questioned why the whole body had to study the text in such detail; since they'd all known since 1996 it would come to this one day, they asked, wouldn't it be more productive to presume they had all read it and simply ask if there were any questions? Yet Ratzinger was doggedly determined to make sure that everyone was clear about how things would work, and perhaps just as important, to make sure that everyone had a chance to voice questions

or concerns, even on relatively minor issues such as the date of the funeral and the date of the opening of the conclave. In other words, he
seemed to want these to be genuinely *collegial* decisions, an important
signal of things to come.

The atmosphere changed after the funeral, when the cardinals
shifted from an examination of the rules of procedure to a much more
wide-open discussion of the issues facing the Church, which gave all of
them a chance to air the situation as it looked from their own local perspective. Some cardinals came out of these meetings grumbling that the
atmosphere was too much like a Synod of Bishops, with long-winded
speeches and little opportunity for real interaction. Several mentioned
that it was especially difficult to keep the over-eighty cardinals, of whom
there were between fifty and sixty in the room, to stick to the seven-
minute time limit. Everyone, however, seemed impressed with the way
Ratzinger guided the discussions.

First of all, whenever a cardinal raised his hand to speak, Ratzinger
immediately called upon him by name. In a College of Cardinals in
which some people felt they didn't know one another especially well,
here was at least one man who knew everyone. That reaction was the
fruit of more than twenty-four years of meeting with cardinals during
their *ad limina* visits to Rome, hearing their concerns when they came
to the Vatican on other bits of business, taking part in the plenary assem-
blies of other offices of the Roman Curia alongside them, and rubbing
shoulders with them at various congresses, symposia, and other ecclesiastical events. In Ratzinger, in other words, the cardinals saw someone
who really knew the members of the college, not as abstractions but as
individual persons.

Moreover, Ratzinger seemed to be making a genuine effort to listen, and to ensure that everyone's voice was heard. At more than one
stage in the proceedings, cardinals said, he intervened to ask those who
had not yet spoken to do so. When he had to summarize a discussion,
he always seemed fair to the various points of view that had been expressed. Speaking on deepest background, two cardinals said they felt
Ratzinger heard them in a way that John Paul II did not always manage;

one, for example, said that while John Paul II always recognized him, he sometimes had to be prompted to recall his name, something that never happened with Ratzinger. Perhaps as pope, some of them found themselves ruminating, Ratzinger would be less tempted to personalize his reign, less given to imposing his own devotional, liturgical, and stylistic tastes, and more willing to surround himself with strong collaborators who would be able to provide him with a stronger, albeit informal, system of "checks and balances."

One cardinal said his own decision to support Ratzinger's candidacy came during these General Congregation discussions, at a point when two cardinals with backgrounds in canon law found themselves arguing over the legal dimension of a particular problem that had arisen. Ratzinger intervened, as this cardinal remembered it, saying: "That may be what the law says, but what should our pastoral response be?" The comment, the cardinal said, convinced him that Ratzinger was not necessarily the authoritarian curial figure his public image sometimes suggested.

Critical, too, was the picture of Ratzinger's place in the Roman Curia that emerged from these conversations. As one cardinal expressed the point, "Ratzinger is *in* the Curia but not *of* the Curia. He came in as a cardinal, and doesn't have the same sense of loyalties and careerist logic that some others do." In other words, cardinals who did not already know Ratzinger well developed the sense that he would approach problems objectively, on the basis of genuine conversation with the principals, and not primarily through the prism of curial politics or bureaucratic logic.

"I really think he'll listen to us," one European cardinal said after the election was over. "Based on what I saw in this period, I think he will be a surprisingly collegial pope."

Impressive, too, during this period was Ratzinger's stamina and energy. As dean, it fell to him to guide all the meetings of the cardinals and oversee much routine administration, yet he also found time to craft powerful homilies and prepare himself for the ceremonial duties associated with the position. His keen attention during the meetings, and his capacity to follow lengthy discussions with what seemed complete comprehension, convinced a few cardinals who had doubts about his physical capacity to do the job.

Finally, Ratzinger's linguistic skills proved an enormous electoral asset. Cardinals, like second-tier executives in any hierarchy, are concerned among other things about their access to the boss. In an international organization, language plays a key role; if the boss can't understand you and you can't understand him, or if at best you can only manage broken conversations that fail to convey nuance and subtext, it creates obvious communications barriers and therefore concern about whether the person in charge can truly grasp your concerns. During the informal discussions leading up to the conclave, Ratzinger always addressed cardinals in their own language (unless it happened to be a non-European language, in which case he used the major European language most familiar to that cardinal). Generally, he did so flawlessly, without any of the gaps in comprehension that often accompany someone speaking in a third or fourth language. Thus the cardinals who interacted with Ratzinger came away with a sense that this is a man with whom they could speak and be understood, without mediation or translation.

NEGATIVE CAMPAIGNING

Despite the gentlemanly tone of discussions among the cardinals, and their genuine desire to regard the election of the pope as a process of discernment rather than a bare-knuckled political exercise, sometimes even papal politics turn nasty. Such was the case again in 2005, as various attempts to sabotage candidates wafted through the Roman air during the interregnum.

Examples include:

- Italian media reported rumors that Cardinal Angelo Scola of Venice had been treated for depression, suggesting a sort of psychological instability that might disqualify him for the Church's highest office;

- Other reports pointed out that Cardinal Ivan Dias of Mumbai has diabetes, a telltale sign of ill health that might undercut what had been a growing swell of positive talk about him, at least in the local press; in addition, an e-mail campaign allegedly initiated by members of his own flock in India made the rounds, including complaints of an "unapproachable, stubborn and arrogant style."

- A book in Argentina, given wide attention in the Spanish-language media, alleged that Cardinal Jorge Mario Bergoglio had been unacceptably close to the military junta that dominated that country in the 1970s, even that he was complicit in the persecution of two liberal Argentinian Jesuits, something his defenders stoutly denied; another e-mail campaign, this one claiming to originate with fellow Jesuits who knew Bergoglio back when he was the provincial of the order in Argentina, claimed that "he never smiled."

- Reports surfaced alleging that both Cardinal Joseph Ratzinger and Cardinal Angelo Sodano, considered by some to be leading candidates, were in poor health, raising questions about their physical capacity to be pope.

No one really had the time to trace down all these rumors, and in a sense that was the point. The hope was that the mere fact that negative things were being said, whether or not they turn out to be true, would be enough to derail a particular candidacy. (In Ratzinger's case, at least, it didn't work, largely because the cardinals had two weeks in which to form their own assessments about his physical capacities.)

A safe rule of thumb about such reports is to assume they're false until proof to the contrary emerges. The point is reminiscent of John Paul II's standard line when reporters would ask about his health. "I don't know," he would quip. "I haven't read the newspapers yet." Moreover, sometimes these attempts at sabotage aren't even especially imaginative. A friend in the Vatican diplomatic service, for example, called me during the interregnum period to ask why no one seemed to be talking about Sodano's well-documented role in efforts to free former Chilean dictator Augusto Pinochet when he was detained in Great

Britain in 1999, facing potential extradition to Spain. Though there are a variety of ways to interpret Sodano's interventions, not all of them unflattering, at least a critique along these lines would have had the virtue of being rooted in reality. (In the end the point turned out to be moot, since no one took Sodano seriously as a candidate.)

This sort of murmuring is part of the inevitable backdrop to a papal campaign season, one that's more analogous to British rather than American politics—the race lasts only a couple of weeks, instead of almost three years. In the American cycle, there's usually time to sort out whether alleged documents about George Bush's National Guard service, for example, are authentic or not; in the frenzy of an abbreviated papal campaign, however, there's just no time to do that kind of legwork.

Cardinals insisted that they were not influenced by any of this, and to some extent that's no doubt true; many of them knew one another, and are able to form personal judgments on the matters in question. On the other hand, given the quick judgments they have to make, sometimes just the hint of skeletons in the closet can be enough to cause them to think twice. Indeed, people launch these rumors for the same reason that political advisers in the United States craft attack ads—because, like it or not, sometimes negative campaigning works. It should be emphasized that these smear campaigns originate outside the College of Cardinals, not inside, and that there is generally a very genteel, respectful tone to the discussions among the cardinals themselves. At the same time, they still had to face tough choices about what issues matter for the future of the Church, and which man is best suited to meet those challenges. Whether they liked it or not, that involves them in building coalitions and advancing candidates—in other words, in politics.

BEHIND CLOSED DOORS

Cardinals were not relying exclusively on impressions formed during the General Congregation meetings, or in the press, to shape their attitudes toward the election. As is always the case leading up to a conclave, informal meetings were taking place around the edges, among cardinals who had been friends over long stretches of time, among cardinals who shared a similar sense of where the Church ought to go, and especially among cardinals who spoke the same language.

Unlike previous conclaves, these sessions took place almost entirely in discreet Roman locations, in the private apartments of curial members, in the national colleges where many cardinals were staying prior to their sequestration in the Casa Santa Marta, and in various ecclesiastical facilities around town. In part because of the press blackout and the consequent desire to shun publicity, cardinals for the most part stayed away from their favorite Roman trattorie as during these two weeks—for some of them, this was perhaps the biggest sacrifice of the interregnum. (Not everyone followed suit, however. On the day after John Paul's funeral, I bumped into Cardinal Tarcisio Bertone of Genoa, Ratzinger's former secretary at the Congregation for the Doctrine of the Faith, at Armando's, my favorite Roman eatery just off the Borgo Pio. When I asked Bertone what he made of his former boss's chances, he beamed.)

In the initial stages, the most important gatherings tended to take place by language group. One such get-together, for example, took place at the end of the first week at the Venerable English College on Via Monserrato, just off the Piazza Farnese, home to seminarians from Great Britain who are studying in Rome, as well as a handful of other clergy connected in one way or another to the United Kingdom. This particular get-together was hosted by Cardinal Cormac Murphy-O'Connor of Westminster, who emerged as a point of reference for the English-speaking cardinals in the run-up to the conclave. In such sessions, away from prying eyes and ears, cardinals were able to chat freely about various candidates, and to get a sense of what other cardinals were thinking. The English-speaking group emerged as a surprisingly important factor in the conclave, given that English is the first or second language of roughly twenty-five cardinals—four more than the entire Italian block, for example, of twenty-one.

As one cardinal put it, "Some were rather uncomfortable with the free-flowing nature of these conversations, but that's what you have to do if you're going to get anywhere."

Based on after-the-fact recollections from cardinals about these informal meetings, some cardinals proved more indefatigable campaigners than others. By all accounts, one of the most articulate and forceful organizers of the pro-Ratzinger campaign was Cardinal Christoph Schönborn of Vienna, perhaps the closest thing to a kingmaker in the conclave of 2005.

"When you talked to other cardinals about Ratzinger, most of them would say, yes, he's a good candidate, but there's also this man or that man," one cardinal recalled after the conclave had ended. "Not Schönborn. For him, it was God's will that Ratzinger be pope, and that was it."

Such passion is hardly surprising, given the close ties between Schönborn and Ratzinger, which some have said is almost like a father/son dynamic. As a young Dominican theologian, Schönborn joined one of Ratzinger's seminars while completing postdoctoral work at Regensburg, and later became a regular at annual gatherings of Ratzinger's students, More than fifteen years ago, under Ratzinger's patronage, Schönborn and two other priests started a residence in Rome for young men discerning a vocation to the priesthood. The name is the Casa Balthasar. The young men there are steeped in the theological works of Hans Urs von Balthasar, Henri de Lubac, and Adrienne von Speyr, a visionary and lifelong collaborator with Balthasar. Over the years Ratzinger sometimes spends an evening there, and was in the habit of attending a board meeting in February. In 1987, Ratzinger named Schönborn the general editor of the new universal *Catechism of the Catholic Church*.

Yet no one suggests that Schönborn played the role in 2005 that his predecessor as the cardinal of Vienna, Franz König, played in 1978, thrusting a relatively unknown cardinal of Krakow into the limelight as a papal contender. Joseph Ratzinger was anything but unknown, especially within this electoral college, and he entered with a determined base of support that did not need Schönborn's encouragement. What

Schönborn was able to provide was a passionate testimony about Ratzinger's character and heart that apparently had impact among a few fence-sitting electors.

In the week prior to the conclave, most cardinals said, the election of Joseph Ratzinger did not yet appear to them a shoo-in. Several cardinals in these informal talks expressed serious reservations, chief among them the "baggage" Ratzinger carried from his years at the Congregation for the Doctrine of the Faith. By general consensus, these concerns came especially from some of the American and German cardinals, where Ratzinger is an especially polarizing figure. This reality was the origin of a story in the Italian papers about an American/German "block" determined to veto Ratzinger's candidacy. The reality was much more diffuse and disorganized than the story made it seem, but the hesitation among some cardinals from those two countries was real.

It's not difficult, for example, to identify Cardinal Walter Kasper, the head of the Pontifical Council for Promoting Christian Unity, as one cardinal who seemed to be striking notes that did not add up to a vote for his fellow German, Ratzinger. In a candid sermon before hundreds at Santa Maria in Trastevere on April 17, Kasper aimed to debunk perceptions that John Paul's legacy should be seen as a litmus test for future popes.

"Just as it is forbidden to clone others, it is not possible to clone Pope John Paul II," Kasper said. "Every pope ministers in his own way, according to the demands of his era. No one was ever simply a copy of his predecessor."

As the head of the Vatican's ecumenical affairs office, Kasper has openly sparred with Ratzinger over the years. He was a vocal critic of Ratzinger's *Dominus Iesus*, a 2000 document that reasserted the superiority of Catholicism over other faiths and Christian denominations. He has also called for curial reform and decentralization of Vatican power, positions that contrast sharply with Ratzinger's emphasis on the priority of the universal church. Rivalry between the two men can be traced back to their native country when Kasper, as a bishop in Rottenburg-Stuttgart, backed a pastoral letter encouraging divorced and civilly remarried Catholics to take sacraments. Ratzinger, already John Paul's theological watchdog, rejected the letter.

Kasper opened his April 17 sermon with candid comments about what was on his mind.

"It's easy to guess what I'm thinking about. We are about to elect a new pope in next week's conclave," he said. While Kasper was cautious to avoid going into a description on the next pope, he concentrated a large portion of his homily on the importance of finding a candidate with strong pastoral skills—a quality some say Ratzinger lacks.

"Like the Gospel says, the pastor needs familiarity, mutual caring, and reciprocal trust between him and his flock," Kasper said. "Let's not search for someone who is too scared of doubt and secularity in the modern world."

As already noted, Ratzinger's performance during the interregnum went a long way toward assuaging such reservations. Yet his candidacy also needed the help of a few other kingmakers, senior cardinals in the various language groups and geographical blocks who were able to address some of the concerns voiced by their brother cardinals. I interviewed one such kingmaker after the fact, asking him how he responded when concerns about Ratzinger's "baggage" arose in these informal talks.

"I reminded them that we all know what the Congregation for the Doctrine of the Faith is about," he said. "The top man there is somebody whose job it is to look after the faith. It's hard to come out of that gleaming white as a kind of liberal."

Precisely that reputation, however, this cardinal argued, might prove to be an asset.

"It's a bit like the way de Gaulle was the only man who could have solved the problem in Algeria, because no one could question his credentials as a French nationalist," he recalled saying to his brother cardinals. "Ratzinger may be able to do some surprising things on ecumenism, with other religions, and on collegiality, because certainly nobody will be able to accuse him of heresy."

Further, this cardinal said, in the last analysis, he staked his argument on "the quality of the man."

"In electing him, I felt he would be fair in listening to the real concerns of people, including the bishops," he said. "This is the man who appeared to us over these ten days, and I think that simply overrode the other considerations."

THE OPPOSITION

None of that should suggest, however, that the election of Joseph Ratzinger as Pope Benedict XVI was an entirely placid affair. In fact, there was a strong current of opposition to his candidacy within the College of Cardinals, but it ultimately proved too disorganized and ineffective to halt his momentum.

One rumor that made the rounds in the preconclave period is that the extensive discussion of Ratzinger in the Italian papers was a deliberate invention of Italian cardinals, intended to cause a panicked stampede to any available alternative. According to this theory, the most plausible such alternative would be Cardinal Dionigi Tettamanzi of Milan. This typically Italian conspiracy theory saw the Ratzinger boomlet as a deliberate concoction intended to provide a boost to the man many saw as the leading Italian candidate. As we will see in the next chapter, if this was indeed the intent, it failed rather spectacularly, since Tettamanzi's candidacy never caught fire. Instead, it seems the stories were based on solid reporting, meaning that Ratzinger did indeed have strong support.

One other Italian candidate who seemed slightly more plausible to some cardinals was Tettamanzi's predecessor in Milan, Cardinal Carlo Maria Martini, long considered the leading liberal candidate to be pope. Like Ratzinger, Martini is a man of unquestioned intellectual stature and cultural refinement, a talented linguist, and a proven pastoral leader. Some of the more reform-minded cardinals in the college hatched plans to make a push for Martini on the grounds that they had to fight fire with fire—if the "funeral effect" meant that a gray, transitional figure was now out of the question, that the next pope had to be a man of substance capable of winning the respect and attention of the world, Martini fit the bill.

The fatal flaw in this strategy, however, was that Martini has a form of Parkinson's disease, and the prospect of another pope ready to begin the long, slow decline characteristic of John Paul's final years was simply too much for many cardinals to accept. Many cardinals agreed after the fact that had it not been for this factor, Martini might well have been a serious challenger to Ratzinger, despite his age, his resignation from active duty, and his obvious disinterest in the job. The failure of the reform-minded forces to settle on an alternative candidate testifies both to their disarray, and, to some extent, to their lack of imagination.

Finally, some Latin American cardinals went into the conclave interested in the idea of electing a pope from Latin America, home to almost half of the Catholics on the planet. Many had a sense that it would be deeply meaningful for Latin American Catholicism to produce a pope, not to mention a real shot in the arm with respect to the "sects," aggressively missionary neo-Protestant evangelical and Pentecostal movements that have been eating into traditional Catholic strongholds up and down Latin America. These cardinals by and large had settled on Cardinal Jorge Mario Bergoglio of Buenos Aires, Argentina, as their candidate. A Jesuit, Bergoglio has a reputation as a man of great humility, deep spirituality, and unwavering commitment to rather traditional doctrinal views. In that sense, some of the Latin Americans felt, he could attract some of the Ratzinger votes but at the same time appeal to moderates attracted to the very idea of a non-European pope.

Such was the state of things as the curtain opened on the conclave on the afternoon of Monday, April 18.

Chapter Four:

THE CONCLAVE

The magic of elections is that they happen when they happen, not before. No matter what the "polling" suggests, however formal or informal it may be, no one knows with certainty what the outcome will be until the votes are counted. Every election is in some sense a drama whose ending is unscripted, and this was also the case in the conclave of 2005. After the fact, it's tempting to regard the election of Joseph Ratzinger as so obvious that the event itself seems a mere formality, but that was not what it felt like at the time. While Ratzinger entered the conclave with obvious momentum, the result could have gone in other directions, and it took the intersection of intangible factors and determined support to make him pope.

By their own choice, the 115 cardinals who would elect the next pope began their lock-down early, moving into the Casa Santa Marta, the $20 million hotel on Vatican grounds where they would stay during the conclave on Sunday night, ahead of the Mass *pro eligendo papa* the following morning. Several cardinals said they felt the need for a "jump start," since the behind-the-scenes conversations up to that point had been scattered, and not everyone had been involved.

It wasn't just the broader public that was curious about how things would shake out. Of the 115 cardinal-electors, only two, Ratzinger and

Cardinal William Baum from the United States, had ever been through this process before. (The other under-eighty cardinal who took part in the two conclaves of 1978, Cardinal Jaime Sin of the Philippines, was too ill to attend.) Even those who went in with a strong idea of what they would like to happen, therefore, also carried a sense of the unknown, wondering if things would unfold as they hoped.

Cardinals with a background in religious life compared the conclave to a chapter meeting for the election of superiors in a religious order, in the sense that you just don't know what's going to happen until things get under way.

"People might have various ideas about who the candidates should be," Cardinal Wilfrid Fox Napier of Durban, South Africa, a Franciscan, said. "But until you get in the room and see whose name starts to attract a consensus, you really don't know how it's going to turn out."

It was with this atmosphere of adventure that the cardinals filed into the Sistine Chapel on the afternoon of April 18.

THE PROCESSION

In exact fulfillment of the *Ordo Rituum Conclavis*, the liturgical book prepared by the Papal Master of Ceremonies, Archbishop Piero Marini, in accord with the specifications of John Paul's *Universi Dominici Gregis*, the 115 cardinals began their procession from the Hall of Blessings through the Sala Regia and into the Sistine Chapel at 4:30 p.m. on Monday, April 18, the date they had set for the start of the conclave twelve days earlier. (The ritual actually calls for them to begin in the Pauline Chapel, at the opposite end of the Sala Regia, but that chapel is undergoing restoration and was unavailable.)

The cardinals were led by a cross-bearer and a cleric carrying aloft a book of the Gospels, along with members of the Sistine Chapel Choir who intoned the Litany of Saints. They were also joined by the man who would give them their final meditation before getting down to business, Cardinal Tomáš Špidlík of Czechoslovakia, an over-eighty cardinal known as a passionate advocate of unity between Eastern and Western Christianity. Marini was present, along with a handful of aides. The cardinals themselves walked in reverse order of seniority, with the cardinal-deacons first, then the cardinal-priests, and finally the cardinal-bishops, with Ratzinger as the dean of the College in the final position. As the cardinals arrived in the Sistine Chapel, they took their assigned seats, again determined on the basis of seniority, and awaited Ratzinger's arrival to sing the *Veni, Creator Spiritus*, or "Come, Creator Spirit," invoking the guidance of the Holy Spirit in the deliberations before them.

Two days before, a group of journalists had been invited up to the Sistine Chapel to get a sense of the arrangements in the space where the cardinals were now gathered. Vatican spokesperson Joaquin Navarro-Valls had described the blocking devices in place in the chapel to impede attempts to communicate or eavesdrop, and jokingly challenged journalists to try their cell phones. Apparently the devices had not yet been switched on, because I was able to call my wife's number from a few feet away from the spot where Cardinal Ennio Antonelli of Florence was now sitting.

Following the hymn, the cardinals took a collective oath. It reads:

> *We, the cardinal electors, collectively and individually, present*
> *in this election of the Supreme Pontiff, promise, pledge and swear*
> *to observe faithfully and scrupulously all the prescriptions contained*
> *in the Apostolic Constitution of the Supreme Pontiff John Paul II,*
> Universi Dominici Gregis, *published on February 22, 1996.*
>
> *We likewise promise, pledge and swear that whichever of us*
> *by divine disposition is elected Roman Pontiff will commit himself*
> *faithfully to carrying out the munus Petrinum as Pastor of the*
> *Universal Church and will not fail to affirm and defend*
> *strenuously the spiritual and temporal rights and liberty of the*
> *Holy See.*
>
> *Above all, we promise and swear to observe with greatest*
> *fidelity and with all persons, clerical or lay, secrecy regarding*
> *everything that in any way relates to the election of the Roman*

Pontiff and regarding what occurs in the place of election, directly
or indirectly relating to the results of the voting; we promise not to
break this secret in any way, either during or after the election of
the new Pontiff, unless explicit authorization is granted by the
same Pontiff; and never to lend support or favor to any
interference, opposition or other form of intervention, whereby
secular authorities of whatever order and degree or any group of
people or individuals might wish to intervene in the election of the
Roman Pontiff.

In a remarkable departure from previous practice, Vatican Television carried both the procession and the oath-swearing live, so it was broadcast live around the world, offering the public for the first time a glimpse into this centuries-old ritual. Following this collective oath, each cardinal then proceeded to the Book of Gospels, which had been placed in the center of the chapel, and added his individual guarantee:

And I N, Cardinal N, do so promise, pledge and swear, so
help me God and these Holy Gospels which I now touch with my
hand.

When the last cardinal has finished, Marini uttered the famous words *Extra Omnes*, or "everyone out," which meant that everyone except he, Špidlík, and the cardinal-electors had to exit. (Marini's dramatic flair left something to be desired, and I ended up inadvertently talking over his pronouncement on CNN.)

After Špidlík finished his meditation, he and Marini were also obligated to leave, and the door of the Sistine Chapel was locked. (As a bit of trivia, the door is locked from the outside and the key is held by the colonel of the Swiss Guard, so that when the cardinals wished to exit they had to knock.) At that stage, the rules of procedure called for Ratzinger to ask if anyone had any remaining questions about the requirements of *Universi Dominic Gregis*, and if they had, a discussion would have followed. In the event, there were no matters of importance raised, and so the cardinals proceeded directly to a first ballot.

The election of the 265th pope in the 2,005-year history of the Roman Catholic Church had begun.

INSIDE THE SISTINE CHAPEL

Sometimes people picture in their mind's eye a highly charged political atmosphere inside the Sistine Chapel, with caucuses of cardinals hurriedly whispering in corners, desperately attempting to mobilize support for or against certain candidates. Indeed, I had this image myself before interviewing Cardinal Franz König in Vienna in 2002, two years before his death. König had been part of the conclaves of 1963 and the two of 1978, and I asked him about the "electricity" that I imagined must be palpable inside the Sistine Chapel during the election of a pope.

"Actually, if you could watch what happens inside, you'd be bored to tears," König laughed.

The reality is that all the politics of a conclave happen around the margins, over dinners and coffees and in other informal settings. The goings-on inside the Sistine Chapel are, by way of contrast, entirely ceremonial. In each round of balloting, every one of the cardinals has to process to the altar beneath Michelangelo's fresco of the Last Judgment and place his ballot on a paten, then deposit it in an urn (not a chalice as in previous conclaves; these urns were specially designed by Marini for the occasion). They vow that they have voted for the candidate whom before God they believe should be elected, and then return to their seat. The counting is an elaborate process involving three cardinals, and their work has to be checked by another three cardinals to ensure that it's accurate. All told, one round of balloting can take an hour or more to complete, so that two ballots are, in effect, a morning's or afternoon's work.

During an interview on CNN following the election of Benedict

XVI, Cardinal William Keeler of Baltimore explained what some cardinals do to fill the time. "One cardinal told me, while he was listening to the votes being counted, he said three rosaries," Keeler said. "And another said, well, I said two, and so, a third said, 'Well, I prayed mine with greater piety, and it was just one.'"

That's how the conclave works on the inside—there are long stretches of time spent in silence and in prayer, with no floor speeches, no dramatic moments when a kingmaker pops up and swings his support to another candidate, no concessions and no victory laps. The drama of a conclave resides in the political preparation that goes on around the edges. The counting of votes inside determines if that preparation pays off, or if the unexpected takes over from the prefabricated.

A POPE IN FOUR BALLOTS

Interviewing cardinals after a conclave is a bit like interviewing witnesses to an auto accident. While you can usually get agreement on the big picture, everyone remembers the details slightly differently. In part, this is due to the vagaries of human memory; in part, it's due to the oaths of secrecy cardinals take. In light of that oath, each cardinal negotiates slightly differently what he feels at liberty to say, and many respond to questions with hints, or ambivalent circumlocutions that have to be interpreted to be understood. As a result, one has to be careful about purported "reconstructions" of the conclave, especially claims about the number of votes received by various candidates. I do not provide precise round-by-round totals in this section, and I am skeptical of all such accounts. My rule of thumb has been that I will treat as verified only those points confirmed for me by at least three cardinal-electors, so that the version of events provided here is as reliable as humanly possible.

The general picture of how things went inside the conclave of 2005 seems, by this stage, reasonably clear.

Cardinal Joseph Ratzinger was elected Pope Benedict XVI on the fourth ballot, putting the conclave of 2005 in a tie for second place among the fastest conclaves of the last 102 years. Only the conclave of 1939, which elected Pius XII on the third ballot, was more rapid, and that election unfolded against the backdrop of the Second World War, when it seemed obvious to most cardinals that they should elect someone who could keep a steady hand on the Vatican's diplomatic rudder. To some extent, therefore, the election of Cardinal Eugenio Pacelli, the secretary of state under Pius XI and the former papal ambassador to Germany, was a foregone conclusion. (Some were surprised that it actually took three ballots, expecting an election by acclamation on the opening afternoon.) The first conclave of 1978 also produced a pope on the fourth ballot, Cardinal Albino Luciani, the patriarch of Venice. The swiftness of that result was due largely to the skillful preconclave organizing by Cardinal Giovanni Benelli, who swung his support to Luciani in order to block the candidacy of Cardinal Giuseppe Siri of Bologna, a strong conservative who might have backtracked on some of the reforms of the Second Vatican Council.

On Monday, April 18, at roughly 8:00 p.m. Rome time, the first evening of the conclave, smoke began to pour from the chimney atop the Sistine Chapel. That chimney had been installed earlier in the week in preparation for the conclave; it does not regularly sit atop the chapel, as there is no routine need for a furnace. To facilitate the burning of the ballots, two devices had actually been placed inside the Sistine Chapel. One was a small cast-iron furnace in which the papers are burned, which has been in use since the conclave of 1939 (the dates are etched in a semi-circle around the top of the stove). The other device produced bursts of compressed air in order to send the smoke up the lengthy chimney and outside into the Roman air.

For a brief instant Monday night, as had been the case in virtually every conclave of recent memory, the smoke was an ambiguous gray, and some in the crowd began cheering, thinking the cardinals had shattered all precedent and elected a pope on the first ballot. Shortly, however, it became clear that the smoke was black, meaning that the result was negative. In a press briefing earlier in the week, the Vatican had announced that bells would go off when a pope was elected, so that the world would not have to rely exclusively on the smoke. In a minor glitch, however, the bells of St. Peter's that ring at the top of every hour to mark the time went off at 8:00 p.m. just as the smoke was emerging, so some in the crowd mistakenly took this as meaning that the Church already had its pope. As it became clear that the smoke was black, however, the crowd dispersed and people began heading to one of the many fine trattorias in the neighborhood of the Vatican.

The black smoke reflected the fact that on the first ballot votes were scattered among a variety of candidates, though by all accounts the strongest showing belonged to Ratzinger. Several cardinals said that Ratzinger received something on the order of 40 votes of the 115 cast at this stage, placing him more than halfway toward the 77 he would need to become pope. Several cardinals said afterward that this first showing was important, because while there had been scattered expressions of support for Ratzinger from various quarters during the interregnum, and a few cardinals for years had been talking about Ratzinger as the pope, this was the first indication that Ratzinger's candidacy was a serious push with a realistic prospect of success.

There were also votes for Martini, though apparently not as many as originally reported in some media outlets. Like Ratzinger, there's no evidence to suggest that Martini wanted the job, and much to indicate that he did not. After retiring as archbishop of Milan in July 2002, Martini has spent most of his time in Jerusalem, returning to the biblical studies that were his passion earlier in his career. He had repeatedly indicated that this is how he wishes to spend whatever time he has left. That desire, coupled with his questionable health, led many cardinals to disregard him as a contender.

"I don't think we ever took Martini seriously, largely because of his health," one European cardinal said after the voting ended.

In the immediate aftermath of the conclave, rumors swirled around Rome that Martini had run "neck and neck" with Ratzinger on the opening ballot, but then formally "withdrew" as a candidate, sending the reform forces into disarray. The implicit suggestion, at least in some reporting, was that Martini might have staged a serious challenge to

Ratzinger had he stayed in the race. None of the cardinals with whom I spoke after the conclave ended, however, could confirm that Martini had ever taken himself out of the running, formally or informally. These cardinals said there was no declaration from Martini on the subject during the conclave.

"There's no time for such statements," one cardinal said. "I can tell you for sure that no one got up, even informally, and said, 'I've got something to say.' It just didn't work like that."

While it's possible, therefore, that Martini may have mentioned something over dinner or over breakfast to a small group, none of the eight cardinals with whom I spoke afterward heard any such report. All eight said that even if such a statement had been made, it would not have affected their votes, which probably means that they weren't planning to vote for Martini in any case. For the most part, the theory that Martini formally "withdrew" from the race appears to have been an ex post facto exercise among stunned progressives seeking some explanation for how the election of Ratzinger could have happened so quickly.

An American cardinal was blunt: "Martini wasn't elected because he didn't have the votes," he said. "Simple as that."

After that first ballot of Monday evening, the cardinals retired to the Casa Santa Marta, just back from the Paul VI audience hall, across from the entrance to the excavations underneath St. Peter's Basilica. It features 108 guest suites, each with a living room and a bedroom, and 23 single rooms, all with private baths. The cardinals had a simple dinner, then retired. They regrouped at 7:30 a.m. for Mass in the chapel of the Casa Santa Marta, a modern wood-and-glass design with enough room for slightly over 100 people, just enough space for the 115 electors and their aides. By 9:00 a.m., having walked the few hundred yards or taken a small minivan made available to them, the cardinals were back inside the Sistine Chapel, ready for the second and, if necessary, third round of voting.

On the second ballot, Ratzinger's support increased, reaching if not slightly surpassing fifty votes. For many cardinals this was a critical sign, because it meant that the support for Ratzinger on the first ballot was not just a tribute, but a statement of the desires of a solid chunk of the College. His support was not declining. The rest of the votes were scattered across a variety of other names, but no one seemed to be emerging as a clear alternative to Ratzinger. Among the Latin Americans, the top vote-getter was Cardinal Jorge Mario Bergoglio, the Argentinian. Despite that support, some cardinals candidly doubted that Bergoglio really had the steel and "fire in the belly" needed to lead the universal church. Moreover, for most of the non–Latin Americans, Bergoglio was something of an unknown quantity. A handful remembered his leadership in the 2001 Synod of Bishops, when Bergoglio replaced Cardinal Edward Egan of New York as the *relator*, or chairman, of the meeting after Egan went home to help New Yorkers cope with the 9/11 terrorist attacks. In that setting, Bergoglio left a basically positive but indistinct impression.

While some analysts later described Bergoglio as the "progressive" candidate after Martini, he is hardly a darling of reform-minded liberals in Latin America, who remembered his battles as the Jesuit provincial in Argentina during the 1970s, when he insisted on a more traditional reading of Ignatian spirituality in opposition to Jesuits beginning to embrace liberation theology and the move toward social engagement. It was precisely this reputation that led some to regard Bergoglio as a potential compromise candidate between doctrinal conservatives and some moderates who felt the election of a Latin American would be positive symbolism for the Church. While Bergoglio was in effect the conclave's second-place finisher, and one African cardinal described the voting as "something of a horse race" between Ratzinger and Bergoglio, other cardinals said they never really took seriously the idea that Bergoglio would be elected.

"Many were the names of Latin American cardinals mentioned in the press as *papabili*, but in the voting, they were nowhere to be seen," Cardinal Francisco Errazuriz Ossa, archbishop of Santiago, Chile, later told the Associated Press. Indeed, Errazuriz, president of the Latin American bishops' conference, CELAM, had been touted himself as a papal contender in some quarters.

By the third ballot, Ratzinger's support crossed the magic fifty-eight-vote threshold, meaning that he now had sufficient support to command an absolute majority in the conclave. Though no one said so out loud, all the cardinals realized that under the 1996 rules promulgated by John Paul II in *Universi Dominic Gregis*, the conclave could decide after seven days of voting, or roughly thirty-four ballots, to switch to election by a simple majority, which meant that a candidate with that level of support, assuming it was stable, could simply ride out a few more ballots, even if he fell short of two-thirds of the vote, and then be elected. Given that Ratzinger's support was not only holding but growing, after the third ballot most of the cardinals felt the handwriting was on the wall.

After the fact, several cardinals commented on how surprised they were that some of the names of potential *papabile* they had been hearing about for years, such as Cardinal Dionigi Tettamanzi of Milan, had made no showing whatsoever; one report said that Tettamanzi collected no more than two votes. While that number is unconfirmed, it's clear that his candidacy never gathered any steam. Long-touted front-runners such as Sodano, Francis Arinze of Nigeria, Claudio Hummes of Brazil, Ruini, Kasper, and Dias were likewise nowhere to be seen in the results. As the cardinals broke for lunch, it seemed crystal clear that no serious challenger was going to emerge to Ratzinger, and the afternoon vote would be merely a formality.

Shortly before noon Rome time on April 19, smoke again began to billow out of the Sistine Chapel chimney, and after another period of initial confusion, it was clearly black. The world now knew that the cardinals had gone through three ballots without electing a pope; what they didn't know was that inside, the deal was all but done. Already some commentators began talking about the possibility of a prolonged conclave, although others pointed out that in 1978, John Paul I was elected on the fourth ballot.

Observers were confused when, after the noontime smoke seemed to have tapered off, a new burst began to appear. In fact, the Sistine Chapel stove into which the ballots and notes taken by the cardinals had to be placed for burning has a limited capacity, and 230 ballots from two rounds of voting, plus dozens of sheets of other paper, simply didn't all fit at once. There were thus two separate burnings, meaning two bursts of smoke. This would be the only time the world would see a double burst, however, because in the afternoon session it would require only one round of voting to produce a new pope.

As the cardinals returned from *pranzo*, the midday meal, and a brief rest, an atmosphere of expectation hung in the air. Most cardinals said afterward that they returned to the Sistine Chapel expecting to produce a pope on the first ballot of the afternoon session, and it was abundantly clear who that would be. Ratzinger clearly understood what was about to happen. When, just two hours later, he was asked by Cardinal Angelo Sodano by what name he would be known as pope, he was ready with his answer—Benedict XVI—as well as a fairly lengthy explanation of its significance.

Once the counting of the ballots began, the repeated intonation of "Ratzinger" left no doubt as to the outcome. Most cardinals were following the counting on their own tally sheets, so that when Ratzinger reached the magic number of 77, a brief gasp was heard in the chapel, followed by a strong round of applause. Cardinal Joachim Meisner of Cologne later remarked that the new pope looked "a little forlorn" at the instant of his election; certainly no one understands better the enormity of the job than Ratzinger, who stood at John Paul's right hand for twenty-four years. By the time the final tally was over, Ratzinger had collected almost 100 of the 115 votes, which is the standard dynamic on the last ballot in a conclave—when it becomes clear who is destined to win, most cardinals join the majority in order to give the new pope the broadest possible mandate and base of support.

Had the new pope been anyone but Ratzinger, it would have been Ratzinger's duty as dean of the College of Cardinals to approach the man who had been elected and ask if he accepted election. In this case, however, the honor fell to the vice-dean, Sodano, the Vatican's secretary of state. After the ballots were all counted and the result confirmed, Sodano approached Ratzinger and asked: "Do you accept your canonical election as Supreme Pontiff?" Ratzinger pronounced the fateful words "I accept," and from that moment he was pope. Sodano then asked by what name he wished to be known, and Ratzinger was ready with his response: "Benedict XVI."

At that moment, cardinals began lining up to the new pope to pay their respects. Benedict was then led off to the "room of tears," where the famous Gamarelli family of tailors had three sets of papal vestments ready, one for a large pope, one for a small, one for a medium. Pope Benedict stepped comfortably into the vestments and prepared himself for what would come next.

Shortly before 5:50 p.m. Rome time, smoke once again began to billow from the Sistine Chapel chimney. Though the smoke again seemed a shade of gray, the timing clearly indicated that a pope had been elected; had the cardinals gone through two rounds of balloting, the smoke would not have appeared until sometime around 7:00 p.m. local time. Smoke at this hour could therefore only mean that they had reached a conclusion. Still, the promised bells did not begin to go off, and despite the repeated swells of cheering that came from the crowd in St. Peter's Square, commentators held off making the call until official confirmation arrived. At 6:00 p.m., the hourly bells of St. Peter's chimed once again, sending onlookers into new paroxysms of confusion, wondering if that meant the result was negative as it had been the night before.

Finally, at roughly 6:10 p.m., the massive bells of St. Peter's began to toll again, this time to signal the election of a new pope, followed by the bells of most of Rome's three hundred churches. For the next several minutes the city resounded with what American poet Edgar Allan Poe once called the "tintinnabulation that so musically wells / from the bells, bells, bells, bells." It was a spectacularly aesthetic moment, but more important, it meant someone had been elected. Given the speed of the result, many people leapt to the conclusion that Joseph Ratzinger was the winner.

Shortly thereafter, that instinct was confirmed.

However foregone the result may seem now, it's worth observing one final time that things could have turned out differently. Had Martini not been ill, for example, it's possible that he could have mounted a se-rious run for the papacy. A bit like Ratzinger, many cardinals believe that Martini's public image as an extremist (in his case, on the left) is unde-served, and in any event, no one doubts his intellectual or cultural prepa-ration. This is a man, after all, who has published an exchange of correspondence with Italian novelist Umberto Eco, and many readers felt the cardinal's literary style was the more impressive of the two. Or had there been a Latin American candidate of Ratzinger or Martini's stature, he might have stolen the show. The fact that Bergoglio made a strong showing, despite the reservations that some cardinals harbored, reflects the hunger in some quarters to break the European grip on the leadership of the Church. Every election to some extent turns on cir-cumstance, and in this case the potential impediments to a Ratzinger vic-tory simply never fell into place.

"HABEMUS PAPAM"

At 6:43 p.m. Rome time, the senior cardinal deacon, Cardinal Jorge Medina Estevez of Chile, stepped onto the central balcony of St. Peter's Basilica. In a personal flourish that is not part of the official protocol, he greeted the "dear brothers and sisters" gathered in the square in several languages. Then he got down to business, intoning the fateful Latin for-mula *Habemus Papam*, meaning "We have a pope."

Observers watching the scene closely noticed that Medina had a slight smile on his face from the moment he stepped out onto the bal-cony. Then, as he told the crowd the name of the new pope, he said, "Joseph, Cardinal of the Holy Roman Church . . . Ratzinger." He dragged out pronouncing the last name slightly longer than ritual re-quired, obviously relishing the suspense.

It's no conjecture to suggest that Medina was delighted with the outcome. Like so many members of the College of Cardinals, his roots with Ratzinger run deep. In the early 1970s, he and Ratzinger served to-gether on the International Theological Commission, an advisory body to the Congregation for the Doctrine of the Faith created under Pope Paul VI. At the time, Ratzinger and Medina shared concern that the reforms spawned by the Second Vatican Council were getting out of hand; in 1972, both men were among eight members of the commission who addressed a letter to the Pope urging him to be cautious about liturgical changes. When Medina became the Vatican's top liturgical officer more than two decades later, from 1996 to 2002, he would aggressively pursue a "reform of the reform" along these lines. The friendship between the two theologians blossomed over the years, as their reservations about post–Vatican II trends brought them together. In his 1997 memoir *Milestones*, Ratzinger identifies himself with other former *periti*, or theological experts, at Vatican II who became disillusioned, including Henri de Lubac, Philippe Delhaye, M. J. le Guillou, and Medina Estevez. These bonds of brotherhood no doubt were on Medina's mind as he presented his old friend, Joseph Ratzinger, to the world as Pope Benedict XVI.

Shortly after Medina's announcement, the new pope stepped out onto the same balcony to receive the cheers from the crowd below. Before delivering the pro forma *urbi et orbi* blessing, Ratzinger followed the example of his immediate predecessor, Pope John Paul II, and made a few remarks to the crowd. It was the first sign, tiny though indicative, that he intended to follow the example of outreach and spontaneity of John Paul, rather than returning to a more iron-clad deference to Vatican protocol.

"Dear brothers and sisters," the new pope said. "After the great Pope John Paul II, the Cardinals have elected me, a simple and humble worker in the vineyard of the lord." The tens of thousands of faithful in St. Peter's Square roared their approval. In another small but revealing move, the new pope did not elect to return to the royal plural of past pontificates, but very naturally referred to himself in the first person singular. Then Ratzinger, not known as a man of impromptu gestures or great bursts of public emotion, clasped his hands and raised them over his head in a gesture of victory.

"The fact that the Lord can work and act even with insufficient means consoles me, and above all I entrust myself to your prayers," he said.

Some in the crowd began to chant "*Benedetto! Benedetto!*," using exactly the same intonation and rhythm they only recently used for "*Giovanni Paolo!*," and applause echoed through the square. Longtime Romans and Vatican-watchers expressed surprise at the sight of the man who stepped out in the papal robes on this chilly Roman night, beaming and waving. This was not, many remarked, the image of Joseph Ratzinger acquired over the years in a thousand and one articles about the "Panzer-Kardinal" and "God's rottweiler."

Benedict XVI spent his first night as the 265th pontiff dining with his fellow cardinals at the Casa Santa Marta. With this act, the new pontificate was under way.

WHY RATZINGER WON

In attempting to explain Joseph Ratzinger's election as Pope Benedict XVI, one is tempted toward one of two equally banal answers: that the Holy Spirit dictated the outcome, or that he got the most votes. The first is inarguable from a faith perspective, and the second flirts with being tautologous. Neither, however, is terribly informative about what went on behind the closed doors of the Sistine Chapel.

In summary form, what were the factors that swung this election to Joseph Ratzinger? Based on conversations with cardinal-electors after the conclave, the following points seem to have been most decisive.

The Best Man

First, he was an outstanding man in a College of Cardinals not long on truly outstanding men. Ratzinger is the sort of figure who, in any group of 115 distinguished international leaders, whether businesspeople or politicians or academics, would stand out. He has a remarkable range of intellectual interests, is fluent in a number of languages, has a ferocious work ethic, and is a superb listener and learner. While there are a number of other cardinals who are fine men with good academic backgrounds, solid track records as pastors and administrators, and who genuinely love their people and are loved by them, few have quite the same gravitas as Ratzinger. Carlo Maria Martini, Godfried Danneels, Francis George of Chicago, Walter Kasper, or Christoph Schönborn perhaps belong in the same category, but each for various reasons was considered unelectable, and never emerged as a serious candidate. From that point of view, the cardinals were deadly serious when they said they wanted to elect the best man for the job. One cardinal said after the conclave that if Ratzinger's election had no other effect than convincing the world to read his theology, that alone would be worth it.

"Man for man, he was superior to the lot of us," as one cardinal put it succinctly in a postconclave interview.

After the fact, most cardinals insisted that the "best man" factor was the primary, if not exclusive, factor that had driven their votes. Other considerations, they said, such as age, nationality, doctrinal positions, and career path gave way under a prayerful consideration of who would be the best individual to lead the Church. There's no reason to doubt this, and given the foreseeable negative reaction to Benedict XVI in some quarters, powerful reason to believe that for at least some cardinals, electing him was an act of courage.

At the same time, it would be dishonest, and inaccurate, to leave the impression that more routine political considerations did not play a role in the outcome. One cardinal, for example, told me that he had considered voting for Cardinal Angelo Scola of Venice, based on his impressive theological background as a member of the *Communio* school inspired by Hans Urs von Balthasar and his track record at the Lateran University, but in the end did not do so because of his age, sixty-three. This cardinal felt that another long pontificate following John Paul's almost twenty-seven-year reign would be unhealthy for the Church. An African cardinal made clear that all things being equal, he would have preferred a candidate from the global south, representing a local church where there would have been "bells, fireworks and dancing in the streets" in reaction to the pope's election. Bergoglio's strong showing suggests, at least in part, that a number of cardinals thought in these terms. Some no doubt voted for Ratzinger in the end to avoid a protracted division within the College of Cardinals, and that, too, is a political calculation.

In the end, most elections are not decided by a single factor, but by an intersection of circumstances and reflections that are generally unrepeatable. For example, the election of Karol Wojtyla in 1978 was the result of a deadlock among two front-runners, Benelli of Florence and Siri of Bologna, which led the cardinals to seek a "compromise" outsider. Many Vatican analysts assumed the pattern would repeat in 2005, so the hunt was on for "compromise" candidates who did not clearly belong to either the "conservative" or "liberal" camp. Just as generals are usually fighting the last war, Vaticanisti often handicap the last race. The lesson for future conclaves, then, is not to exclude the traditional criteria by which candidates are usually evaluated, but also not to forget that the cardinals will not necessarily feel bound by them, and that candidates of genuine substance should not be overlooked because conventional wisdom says they don't fit the typical profile.

The Best Campaign

Second, despite not wanting the job, Ratzinger ran the best campaign. As described in chapter three, his performance during the interregnum was perfectly calibrated to remind his conservative base of support of what they admired about him, but to reassure cardinals of other temperaments that he was not the man of his public image, not a brooding and dictatorial figure. He appeared as a man of substance, generous and open, willing to work cooperatively, and capable of standing in front of massive worldwide audiences and doing the Church proud. No one could watch Joseph Ratzinger over those two weeks and not regard him as a potential pope.

The Best Campaign Staff

Third, and again despite not campaigning for the job, Ratzinger had the best campaign staff. For years, a core group of cardinals, composed of

Pope John Paul II greets Cardinal Joseph Ratzinger, then Prefect of the Catholic Church's Congregation for the Doctrine of the Faith, in December 2003.

Pope John Paul II waves to the faithful from a window of Rome's Agostino Gemelli hospital where he appeared on Sunday, February 6, 2005.

The seven American Catholic Cardinals pose with the Archbishop of Miami and the president of the Catholic University of America in January 2005. *Standing, from left:* Bishop William Lori, president of the CUA board of trustees; Cardinal Theodore McCarrick, Archbishop of Washington; Father David O'Connell, president of CUA; Archbishop John Favalora of Miami; and Cardinal Justin Rigali of Philadelphia. *Seated, from left:* Cardinal Edward Egan of New York; Cardinal Adam Maida of Detroit; Cardinal Francis George of Chicago; Cardinal William Keeler of Baltimore; and Cardinal Roger Mahony of Los Angeles.

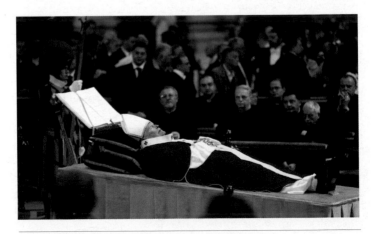

Pope John Paul II lies in state in Saint Peter's Basilica in the Vatican. The worldwide outpouring of emotion triggered by the Pope's death unexpectedly became a factor in the pre-conclave politics.

Cardinal Joseph Ratzinger blesses the coffin containing the body of Pope John Paul II, during the funeral mass in St. Peter's Square at the Vatican, Friday April 8, 2005.

Austrian Cardinal Christoph Schoenborn prays during a Mass in St. Peter's Basilica at the Vatican, Monday, April 18, 2005, in his last public appearance before the conclave began later that day. Schoenborn was one of the most ardent advocates of the election of Cardinal Joseph Ratzinger to the papacy.

Italian Cardinal Carlo Maria Martini, *center*, walks in procession to enter the grottos containing the tomb of Pope John Paul II following a Mass in St. Peter's. For some, Martini was considered the main "liberal" alternative to the candidacy of Cardinal Joseph Ratzinger.

Argentine Cardinal Jorge Bergoglio, who would become the main Latin American candidate in the 2005 conclave, celebrates a Mass in honor of Pope John Paul II at the Buenos Aires Cathedral in Buenos Aires, Argentina, Monday, April 4, 2005.

Cardinals enter the Sistine Chapel at the Vatican, on Monday, April 18, 2005, at the beginning of the conclave.

Cardinal Jorge Arturo Medina Estevez of Chile announces the "Habemus Papam," the Latin expression for "We have a Pope," from a balcony of St. Peter's Basilica at the Vatican, on Tuesday, April 19, 2005, following the election of Pope Benedict XVI.

The newly elected Pope Benedict XVI waves to the crowd from the central balcony of St. Peter's Basilica at the Vatican.

Pope Benedict XVI greets and blesses the crowd from the central balcony of St. Peter's Basilica at the Vatican, on Tuesday, April 19, 2005.

Pope Benedict XVI, flanked by Cardinal Angelo Sodano of Italy, left, and Eduardo Martinez Somalo of Spain, right, makes his first visit to his new residence at the Vatican on April 20, 2005.

Pope Benedict XVI celebrates his installment Mass in St. Peter's Square at the Vatican, on Sunday, April 24, 2005.

Pope Benedict XVI greets Metropolitan Chrisostomos, a top envoy for Ecumenical Patriarch Bartholomew I, the spiritual leader of the world's Christian Orthodox Churches, during a meeting in the Sala Clementina at the Vatican, Monday, April 25, 2005.

Pope Benedict XVI tours St. Peter's Square during the first general audience of his new pontificate Wednesday, April 27, 2005, pledging to work for reconciliation and peace.

Pope Benedict XVI greets the faithful during the first appearance of his papacy from the window of his apartment overlooking St. Peter's Square at the Vatican, on Sunday, May 1, 2005.

curial figures and admirers from other parts of the world, had been determined to see him elected. The new pope has talked about the future of Christianity in the West as a creative minority that has an outsized impact on the broader culture, and in miniature, that seems to have been the story of the 2005 conclave.

In June of 2004, for example, I interviewed one Latin American cardinal on background about the election of the next pope, and his blunt comment was: "I would like very much Ratzinger." In the spring of 2003, I sat at a cafe in the Piazza of Santa Maria in Trastevere in Rome with a cardinal from another part of the world who was visiting the Vatican on business, and had a similar conversation. This cardinal's unambiguous view was "Ratzinger is the man the church needs as pope." Neither man works in the Roman Curia. Going into the conclave of 2005, therefore, there was no mystery that Ratzinger would have votes. During the interregnum, these cardinals were by far the most determined and organized force in the preconclave politics. One cardinal who played a key role in this regard was Schönborn, who insisted repeatedly that it was "God's will" that Ratzinger become pope. No other candidate had anything like this committed base of support.

Inside the conclave, Ratzinger's base managed to get out to a quick lead and built on it, while the possible alternatives foundered. All of which just goes to show that forming a consensus isn't always a matter of crafty horse-trading, but of having the fastest horse!

The Funeral Effect

Fourth, Ratzinger benefited from the "funeral effect." While it might have been thinkable before John Paul's death to elect a quiet, pastoral Italian to allow the Church to catch its breath, the reminder the funeral issued of the international stature gained for the Church under John Paul, and the momentum of his pontificate, meant that the cardinals knew they had to elect another serious, world-class leader. Based on everything they knew of Ratzinger, as well as his performance over the interregnum, he was ideally suited for the part. He is a man to whom the world will listen.

A Known Quantity

Fifth, Ratzinger was a known quantity among cardinals who did not know one another well. Many cardinals, especially those from the global south and those created as cardinals in John Paul's final consistories of 2001 and 2003, came to Rome worrying aloud that they had not had the opportunity to develop personal impressions of their brother cardinals. As things turned out, because of the informal taboo on discussing the succession until the funeral Mass was over, they really had only ten days to make these judgments. In the end, many of them seem to have decided that rather than risk the unknown, they would opt for a proven figure whose interaction with them had largely been positive.

"We've all had contact of some kind with Ratzinger over the years," one cardinal said afterward. "What most of us came away saying was, 'What a brilliant man, but also what a kind man.' When I've dealt with him, he's always been very careful and very collegial. He doesn't get credit for that. He's always done the research, he listens, and he often brings his people into the meetings so that everyone's on the same page. He's a man of cooperation and collaboration. He's honest and says what he believes."

Getting to the bottom line, this cardinal summed it up: "We like him."

Not an "Enforcer"

Sixth, and related to the point above, many cardinals believe that the man the world knew as the Vatican's "enforcer of the faith" is a caricature of the real Joseph Ratzinger, and that as Pope Benedict XVI, his true self will shine through—kind, humble, and deeply spiritual. Moreover, they insist, Ratzinger will be more collegial and collaborative than the Pope he served, John Paul II, because his pontificate will be driven less by personal charisma and more by collective reflection. Further, they say, Ratzinger has a history of naming qualified aides who are not simply yes-men. (Critics sometimes charge that both the staff and consultors of the Congregation for the Doctrine of the Faith represent a narrow band of theological opinion, but most would at least acknowledge that the current brain trust, led by the secretary, Archbishop Angelo Amato of Italy, and the undersecretary, Fr. Augustine Di Noia from the United States, know their stuff.) Ratzinger enjoys give-and-take, and though he will not yield on matters of faith, the cardinals say he can be surprisingly flexible on most other matters.

Along these lines, a majority of cardinals was also persuaded that despite his professorial streak and his shy side, Ratzinger can play to crowds and be a public figure, if not with the same charisma as John Paul II, at least with enough élan to provide the Catholic faithful with a positive image of their shepherd. Most notably, they were persuaded that he would continue the last pope's outreach to youth. Many conceded, however, that the showman's element of the papacy will be the steepest part of the learning curve for Benedict XVI.

"This is a very introverted man," one cardinal said. "Talk about purification . . . this will be very hard for him. But, people grow into it."

The Best Response to Secularism

Seventh, to the extent cardinals had identified secularism in Europe as one of the primary challenges facing the Church, Ratzinger seemed the man best positioned to articulate an answer. No one in the College of Cardinals understands the Western intellectual tradition better, no one has spent more time reflecting on the phenomenon of relativism, and no one seems to be more forceful in challenging the relativistic mind-set of the contemporary West on its own turf—that is, which worldview best protects human freedom and happiness. If secularism was the primary issue that drove this election, in other words, Ratzinger had the winning position.

While secularism was not the primary concern of most cardinals from the global south, many of them said afterward that they are convinced the next pope will also be a voice for the poor and for just development, if only because so many of them talked about it during the General Assembly meetings.

"The Pope sat through all of that," one African cardinal said. "He has to know our concerns."

The Impact of a Simple Majority

Eighth, Ratzinger was the first candidate to benefit from John Paul's rule allowing the cardinals to elect a pope on the basis of a simple majority after seven days of voting, or roughly thirty-four ballots. Most analysts had said before the fact that the cardinals would never allow the conclave to go on that long because they did not wish to appear divided, and that turned out to be true. Psychologically, however, everyone in the conclave knew that with a solid majority vote, Ratzinger's supporters could, if they wanted to, simply "run out the clock" until the thirty-fourth ballot was up, and then elect their man without two-thirds of the vote.

"Everybody had that in mind," one cardinal said later, adding that after Ratzinger crossed the fifty-eight-vote threshold, his election became "inevitable." In that sense, what John Paul II did, in effect, is to transform the election of the pope from a two-thirds vote into a simple majority.

This is not to suggest that Ratzinger would have been incapable of attracting two-thirds of the vote had the conclave gone on a few more ballots; obviously, in the end, he attracted far more than seventy-seven. The point, however, is that the game was over much more quickly once he crossed the fifty-eight-vote marker. Had that rule not been in place, the conclave might have gone on a few more rounds, creating at least the theoretical possibility for a serious challenger to emerge.

Ineffective Opposition

Ninth, it seems abundantly clear that the anti-Ratzinger vote in the College of Cardinals, such as it was, simply never was able to organize in a way sufficient to halt Ratzinger's momentum. In the critical preconclave period, when Ratzinger's candidacy was gathering steam, the more progressive cardinals never united behind a single candidate around whom a coalition might emerge, floating instead a seemingly endless series of possibilities: Martini, Hummes, Tettamanzi, even Ennio Antonelli of Florence. The fact that several of the "opposition" cardinals apparently voted for Martini in the early stages testifies to their paralysis, since it was clear from the beginning that no one with Parkinson's disease would be elected to succeed a pope who suffered from that illness so visibly for so long.

"Only Nixon Could Go to China"

Tenth, under the heading of "only Nixon could go to China," some cardinals felt the Church was long overdue for some needed reforms that only someone of Ratzinger's stature and unquestioned orthodoxy could engineer, beginning with a serious reform of the Roman Curia. The culture of the Curia, some cardinals believe (along with other bishops around the world), is too dominated by a self-justifying bureaucratic mentality that seeks power over the life of local churches for its own sake, that too often meddles in matters it really doesn't understand, and that flourished for twenty-six years under a pope whose passion for issues *ad extra* allowed the Curia largely to set its own course. If there is to be a shake-up in the Curia, many cardinals felt, only Ratzinger can pull it off. He knows the system, having worked inside it for twenty-four years, but is not *of* the system. He was already a cardinal before he arrived, so he has no debts to pay for advancement or access. He is his own man, and at least some cardinals expect serious changes in Rome in fairly short order.

REACTION

Perhaps the single greatest reservation many cardinals had about Ratzinger was the "baggage" he would carry into the papacy, meaning his reputation as a fierce enforcer who would divide and polarize the Church. In truth, this was not a great source of anxiety for cardinals from many parts of the world, such as Latin America, Africa, Asia, and eastern Europe, where Ratzinger's stands had not been a source of much public discussion over the years. For Europeans and North Americans, however, and above all cardinals from Germany and the United States, the potential for "baggage" was a live concern indeed.

I had indirect confirmation of the point when I bumped into

Cardinal Norberto Rivera Carrera of Mexico City in the Rome airport, awaiting a flight to Paris the day after the new pope's inaugural Mass. (Rivera Carrera was on his way home, while my wife and I were traveling to Paris for a writing retreat to produce this book.) I had met Rivera Carrera for the first time during John Paul II's trip to Mexico in 2002 for the canonization of Juan Diego, and so I went over to say hello. Speaking in flawless Italian, he asked me why I was headed to Paris, and I told him the purpose was to write a book about the conclave and the new pontificate.

"Your book will be balanced, I hope," he said.

"I hope so, too," I replied.

"That will be particularly important in the United States," he said. "There could be problems there."

Given such concerns, it is not surprising that immediately after the election, cardinals from the United States and Germany sprung into a public relations offensive designed to present Ratzinger to the world before the media and his critics had a chance to set the agenda.

Interviewed by CNN's Alessio Vinci shortly after the result was announced, for example, Cardinal Walter Kasper of Germany, the Vatican's top ecumenical official and a man often identified as a more progressive jousting partner of Ratzinger, urged patience.

"Well, I cannot tell about the conclave, but it was a very moving event," Kasper said. "And for me it's the first conclave I participated in, and a sense of high responsibility, not only for my own church but for all churches, for the whole of the world. And then, the first German cardinal after eight centuries, it's also something. Today was the feast day of the last German pope [Victor II]. He was a pope of reformers. And now, Cardinal Ratzinger, was before my colleague as professor, and now he's pope. It makes a moving atmosphere among us."

Kasper was generous in his praise of Ratzinger.

"Well, there are a lot of prejudices about him, and most of these prejudices are unfair. And I think you should leave these prejudices aside now and give him at least a chance. . . . I know him since the sixties when he was a professor at Münster. I was also a professor there, and we worked together. He can be a very charming person. He's a very bright person known everywhere, and I think he will be a pope of reconciliation and peace. It is the, I think, the inspiration he gave for his name: 'peace and reconciliation.' And the first meeting—short—I had with him, he told me, 'Well, now we will work together, walk together, on the paths to unity of the Churches.' And I think that's a good sign also for the ecumenical movement. He was formerly very engaged, especially in the dialogue with the Orthodox churches, and I think he will go on in this direction. I am happy to be able to work together with him."

Vinci reminded Kasper that he had said, just days before, that the conclave should not look for a "clone" of John Paul II.

"Clearly he's not a clone of John Paul II," Kasper replied. "These are very different personalities. They are very friendly to each other and work very well together. But they are different, very different. I think he's a pastoral man. He will be a pastoral pope, to be a pastor, since the office is job of a pope. And I think he will do his best with the gifts he has. And he has very rich gifts. . . . People wanted an outstanding person, and he is one without any doubt, and they wanted a man who is firm in faith and church doctrine but also a man who can explain faith. It's not only important to have the truth but to communicate truth. And he is very able to do this. And it can have a good impact in this direction in our very religiously indifferent modern world. . . . We work together until now. We will work together also in the future. Sometimes you have different aspects . . . when it comes to the real issue of faith, there was never a difference. But among professionals it is a normal thing to maintain different positions and different aspects. But now he's pope and it's a different relation now."

In terms of German reaction, the new pope also got a boost from an unexpected source: Swiss theologian Hans Küng, long seen as the champion of the liberal "loyal opposition" to John Paul II. He called Ratzinger's election "an enormous disappointment," but added: "The papacy is such a challenge that it can change anyone. . . . Let us therefore give him a chance."

The American cardinals likewise launched a media offensive, as six of them—Mahony, Maida, George, Egan, Keeler, and Rigali—appeared at a press conference at the North American College, the residence for American seminarians in Rome, to discuss the new pope on the morning after his election.

Cardinal Francis George of Chicago attributed popular impressions that Ratzinger was authoritarian to media "caricatures," which misrepresented Benedict's "humble genius." George described an encounter with a woman who worked at the Congregation for the Doctrine of the Faith, the Vatican office Ratzinger led for twenty-four years, who described the new pope as a "true Christian."

Cardinal Theodore McCarrick of Washington, D.C., said that Benedict XVI "wants to be collegial, wants the advice of cardinals, and wants the advice of the bishops. He'll ask for that advice in the synods, and on other occasions."

Cardinal Justin Rigali of Philadelphia described the way the new pope had invoked the memory of the last pontiff to hold the name Benedict, Benedict XV, as someone who "promoted peace in the world, and universal reconciliation." He predicted that the new Pope Benedict would pursue Christian unity, dialogue with other faiths, and a commitment to the social teachings of the Church, and would be "a great proclaimer of Jesus Christ in the world."

Cardinal Edward Egan of New York described Benedict as "extremely kind" and a "lovely gentleman." He challenged reporters to "start reading all his books, read what he has to say." Egan predicted that Pope Benedict "will come to be known for who he is, and much admired."

Cardinal Adam Maida of Detroit struck a similar note.

"I firmly believe that Cardinal Ratzinger with all of his gifts and talents, and even some of his shortcomings, will somehow be able to reach others," he said. "We prayed that God would send us a true shepherd, and those prayers have been answered." Maida pointedly said it was his expectation that all people would embrace the new pope with love and affection, and support him in his ministry.

Cardinal Roger Mahony of Los Angeles told reporters "to be very careful about caricaturing the Holy Father and putting labels on him." He added, "I've already seen some headlines doing that."

Finally, Cardinal William Keeler of Baltimore, whose longtime passion for Christian-Jewish dialogue gives him a special sensitivity to Jewish reaction, pointed out that a rabbi who had worked with Ratzinger was present at the NAC for the press conference, and said that he would testify how a recent document from the Pontifical Biblical Commission on the Hebrew Scriptures, with a preface written by Ratzinger, had been very help in Jewish/Christian relations. Keeler made the point in part because day-two discussion of Ratzinger's election, especially in the British press, featured prominent mention of the new pope's brief and unenthusiastic compulsory enrollment in the Hitler Youth.

In the end, the American cardinals may have had less to worry about in terms of public reaction than many had feared. A CNN/*USA Today*/Gallup poll of American Catholics conducted shortly after the white smoke came up from the Sistine Chapel found that 31 percent had a favorable reaction to the new pope, 9 percent unfavorable, and almost 60 percent said they didn't have enough information to reach a conclusion. In other words, more than 90 percent of American Catholics already like the Pope, or at least are willing to give him a chance. That's considerably less baggage than some early comments in the press had suggested, painting a picture of a Catholic community almost evenly divided between Ratzinger fans and critics.

Still, 9 percent of America's 65 million Catholics amounts to roughly 5.8 million people, which is a large pocket of opposition right out of the gate. Those numbers have been mirrored in polls across western Europe. Obviously, Pope Benedict is aware that some Catholics have trepidations about where his papacy will go, and at least part of the drama of the early stages of his pontificate will be determined by whether he is able to win at least some of these skeptics over. Like presidents and prime ministers, every pope gets a honeymoon. In the case of popes, the initial climate of goodwill is probably even stronger, because there is an overwhelming Catholic desire in most quarters to want to like, respect, and be proud of the pope. Benedict XVI thus has a window of opportunity to define himself and his pontificate before judgments begin to harden.

THE EXPECTATIONS GAME

When John Paul II was elected in 1978, he invited the cardinals to remain with him that night for dinner, and as champagne was served, he and a number of other cardinals broke out into traditional Polish folk songs. On the night of Pope Benedict's election, however, there were no Bavarian drinking anthems among the cardinals gathered in the Casa Santa Marta, merely a couple of hymns in Latin and a dinner featuring soup, cordon bleu, and spumanti. (One cardinal later described the fare as "good but not great.")

Yet the evening meal had barely been served when the political jockeying surrounding the new pontificate began, especially in the press.

In the Roman newspaper *La Repubblica*, for example, an article appeared the morning after Benedict's election claiming that the Congregation for the Doctrine of the Faith was preparing to issue four new documents that would now await Ratzinger's replacement. One would approve communion for the "innocent party" in a situation of divorce and civil remarriage; another would raise the retirement age for bishops from seventy-five to eighty; and third and a fourth would redefine church teaching on the divinity of Christ in an ecumenical key, and commit the papacy to the search for full Christian unity.

These reports, senior Vatican sources told the *National Catholic Reporter* on April 22, are "absolutely false." There are no such documents, nor any projects to produce documents along the lines suggested, within the Congregation for the Doctrine of the Faith, sources said. While it is possible that other Vatican offices might be thinking about such documents, a Vatican source said that nothing is close to publication.

On the question of Communion, Vatican sources said that the

Congregation for the Doctrine of the Faith is working on a study of the principles underlying reception of the Eucharist, responding in part to the debate raised in the United States over pro-choice Catholic politicians. It will not, however, produce a change of policy for divorced and civilly remarried Catholics. That issue was already addressed in a 1994 document of the congregation, "Reception of Communion: Divorced-and-Remarried Catholics." The heart of that document was the following affirmation: "If the divorced are remarried civilly, they find themselves in a situation that objectively contravenes God's law. Consequently, they cannot receive Holy Communion as long as this situation persists."

On the question of the retirement age, Vatican sources indicated that this question is not part of the competence of the Congregation for the Doctrine of the Faith, and in any event, no document on the subject exists in that office.

On the ecumenical question, the new pope has already expressed his commitment to the search for Christian unity, and his anticipated visit Monday to the Basilica of St. Paul Outside the Walls is a further symbolic indication of his desire to move in that direction. That congregation had conducted a symposium on the papacy following John Paul II's 1995 encyclical on ecumenism, *Ut Unum Sint*, the proceedings of which were published in 1998. At the moment, sources said, no further documents are planned.

If no documents exist, what's going on?

Longtime Vatican-watchers speculate that this is part of the traditional dance when a new pope is elected. Forces that would like to nudge his pontificate in one direction or another float trial balloons, in this case most prominently a relaxation of discipline regarding Communion for divorced and civilly remarried Catholics. Doing so will either compel the Pope to adjust his policies, or will exact a price in terms of public relations when expectations of a change are not met. It's all a standard part of the political game, observers say, and it would appear that even in its earliest hours, the pontificate of Pope Benedict XVI was not exempt.

FIRST MOVES

Whatever else may be said of him, Pope Benedict XVI is not a dumb man. He understands that his role as universal pastor is different from that of doctrinal guardian, and he also knows that some constituencies both inside and outside the Catholic Church initially received the news of his election with trepidation. His first few days as pope, in that light, seemed in part designed to reassure the anxieties of many interest groups and currents of opinion that might have had reason to fear a Ratzinger victory.

Mass in the Sistine Chapel, April 20

The morning after his election, Benedict XVI celebrated his first Mass as pope with the cardinals in the Sistine Chapel. For the occasion, he prepared a four-page speech in stylized Latin, laying out the basic principles that he said would guide his pontificate. He started off, as he did on the evening of his election, with a note of humility, saying he was strongly conscious of his own "inadequacy" for the task thrust upon him. Yet he said he felt John Paul's "strong hand holding my own," adding that he felt as if he could see his smiling eyes and hear his voice, saying one last time: "Be not afraid!"

The Pope then asked all the cardinals, and all the bishops of the world, to sustain him in his efforts, saying he wanted to truly be "the servant of the servants of God." It was an indirect way of saying that he wants to pursue a collegial mode of governance, crafting policy in collaboration with the bishops, striving to reassure those who would expect precisely the opposite from a Ratzinger pontificate. He quoted in this regard the document *Lumen Gentium* from the Second Vatican Council, signaling his desire to stand in continuity with the council's aim of strengthening the role of the College of Bishops. "Collegial communion," Benedict said, is essential to an effective proclamation of the living Christ to the world. The documents of Vatican II, Benedict said, have lost none of their relevance in the forty years that have passed since the formal close of the council. (This was read by many as an indirect way of saying that there is no immediate need to call another ecumenical council, an idea that has from time to time been floated by some reform groups in the Church.)

Benedict noted that his papacy is beginning in a year already dedicated by John Paul II to the Eucharist, and he affirmed that the synod scheduled for October on the theme of the Eucharist will go ahead. Some cardinals had suggested to the Pope in the immediate aftermath of his election that he might wish to postpone the synod, but Benedict vowed to press ahead, another way of suggesting that he wants to hear the contributions that the bishops will make.

Pope Benedict then turned to ecumenism, pledging to make a "primary commitment" of his reign "working tirelessly for the reconstruction of full and visible unity among all the followers of Christ." Moreover, Benedict said, he is fully aware that progress on this front requires more than "the manifestation of goodwill," but also "concrete gestures that enter into souls and stir consciences, inviting everyone to that interior conversion that is the presupposition of all progress on the path of ecumenism." In that regard, the Pope called for a deeper "purification of memory," an acknowledgment of past and present faults. The Pope took the opportunity to salute all Christians and to pledge to do everything possible to improve relations.

Benedict said the funeral of John Paul II made him ever more conscious that the pope must address himself not just to Christians but to followers of all religions and to all men and women of goodwill, and pledged to work for a "sincere and open" dialogue with the rest of the human family. In this context, he also confirmed the Catholic Church's commitment to work for "authentic social development," a way of saying that the Church's option for the poor will continue on his watch.

Benedict also pledged to continue John Paul II's outreach to the young.

"With you, dear young people, the future and the hope of the Church and of humanity, I will continue to dialogue, listening to your expectations with the intent of helping you to meet ever more deeply the living Christ, who is eternally young."

Inaugural Mass, April 24

Pope Benedict XVI received the symbols of his authority in a two-hour inaugural Mass, marked by a call for unity with other faiths and a pledge to govern the Church through cooperation rather than papal mandate. He accepted the fisherman's ring and seal—the symbol of his continuity with St. Peter—and a lamb's wool pallium, a sash that signifies the pope's role as the shepherd of the faithful.

In his homily, he recast these tokens of papal power as symbols of servitude, signaling a dramatic departure from his former role as the Church's chief doctrinal authority.

"My real program of governance is not to do my own will, not to pursue my own ideas, but to listen, together with the whole church," Benedict said. He extended his call to Christian churches "not yet in full communion" with the Catholic Church, and to the "Jewish people," whom he characterized as "brothers and sisters," heirs to an "irrevocable" bond with God, united with the Church through "a great shared spiritual heritage."

"Like a wave gathering force, my thoughts go out to all men and women of today, to believers and nonbelievers alike," Benedict said. The homily was interrupted almost thirty times by strong applause.

Benedict described the pallium as a "yoke" that "does not alienate us, it purifies us—even if this can be painful."

Cardinal Angelo Sodano, the Vatican's secretary of state, brought before the pontiff a golden bejeweled box with its lid ajar, exposing the glittering fisherman's ring, emblazoned with a relief of Peter casting his fishing net—the image traditionally used to seal apostolic letters. Benedict plucked it from the box and slid it onto his right ring finger. Twelve people representing Christ's disciples then lined up to kneel before Benedict and kiss his ring. Among the twelve chosen was a Benedictine sister, the first religious woman ever to participate in the ritual.

"I am not alone," Benedict declared, prompting loud cheers from the audience. "You see," he said, briefly lifting his eyes to the crowd in a brief departure from his text. "We see it. We hear it."

Sunday, Benedict cast his condemnation of Western ideological influence in a more subtle light.

"All ideologies of power justify themselves in exactly this way. They justify the destruction of whatever would stand in the way of progress and the liberation of humanity," he said. "God, who became a lamb, tells us that the world is saved by the crucified, not by those who crucify."

"Pray for me," he said, "that I may not flee for fear of the wolves."

Each time the crowd cheered their new pope, he appeared to receive the affirmation with gratitude. Although it was clear that the new pope did not have the same immediate gift for connecting with a crowd of his predecessor, it was also clear he was trying, and on this day that seemed quite enough for the supportive flock gathered in St. Peter's Square.

After the Mass concluded, Benedict mounted a white jeep and circled the square to the cheers of onlookers who held out their hands and flashed digital cameras. Beyond the square, an endless crowd packed the Via della Conciliazione, which was lined with mega-screens for the occasion. Similar screens were positioned outside Vatican City walls to accommodate late arrivals. City officials estimated that 100,000 pilgrims from the Pope's native Germany attended the event.

Dignitaries from more than 131 countries attended the Mass, including German chancellor Gerhard Schroeder, Prince Albert II of Monaco, and Florida governor Jeb Bush, head of the American delegation. In another sign of the new pope's ecumenical openness, the crowd included Archbishop of Canterbury Rowan Williams; Metropolitan Chrisostomos, a top envoy for Ecumenical Patriarch Bartholomew I, the spiritual leader of the world's Christian Orthodox; and a senior representative of the Russian Orthodox Church, Metropolitan Kirill. All met with the Pope later in the day.

Interreligious Audience, April 25

In the morning of April 25, Benedict XVI met with members of the Muslim community who had attended Sunday's installation ceremony.

He assured them the Church wanted to continue building "bridges of friendship" that he felt could foster peace in the world, and said he was particularly grateful that members of the Muslim community were present.

"I express my appreciation for the growth of dialogue between Muslims and Christians, both at the local and international level," he said. He noted that the world is marked by conflicts but longs for peace.

"Yet peace is also a duty to which all peoples must be committed, especially those who profess to belong to religious traditions," he said. "Our efforts to come together and foster dialogue are a valuable contribution to building peace on solid foundations. It is therefore imperative to engage in authentic and sincere dialogue, built on respect for the dignity of every human person, created, as we Christians firmly believe, in the image and likeness of God," he said.

Some Muslim leaders had reacted with apprehension to Benedict's election, based especially on comments he made in 2004 opposing the entry of Turkey into the European Union on the grounds that it might compromise the Christian identity of Europe.

St. Paul's Outside the Walls, April 25

The Basilica of St. Paul Outside the Walls, one of the four major patriarchal basilicas in Rome, was a particularly important port of call for the new pope for two reasons. First, it is administered by the Benedictines, the order named for St. Benedict, from whom the Pope had taken his name; second, it is associated with ecumenical outreach, so his appearance in this church took on special resonance for the leaders of other Christian denominations who had come to Rome for his inaugural Mass.

In his remarks, Benedict noted that St. Paul was the great apostle of the early church, a man who traveled throughout the ancient world to bring the message of Christ to the entire world. The Pope pledged that he, too, felt the urgency of the missionary mandate of announcing Christ, signaling that his would not be a sleepy pontificate in which the Church turned in on itself, but an attempt to build on the energy and dynamism of John Paul's reign. He also said that his approach to mission would not be through force or power, but through example. He cited the rule of St. Benedict, in which the fifth-century saint urged his monks "to put absolutely nothing before the love of Christ."

A BROADER MANDATE

Collaborators of the new pope say these words and gestures were not part of a calculated effort to mount a "spin" campaign, putting a false face on the "real" Ratzinger. They arise directly out of his long-standing passions, and mark the beginning of the transformation of Cardinal Ratzinger into Pope Benedict XVI, a man with a broader mandate, and a better opportunity to speak words of hope and brotherhood as well as doctrinal correction to the broader world.

If this *were* a spin campaign, however, it would be difficult to imagine a better one. The Pope struck the right notes, and everywhere he went he appeared smiling, waving to crowds, caressing infants, and even making impromptu jokes. When he showed up late for an audience with German pilgrims, for example, he quipped that he had been "Italianized" because of his long years in Rome, and pledged to work on his punctuality.

These early moves all played to generally positive reviews, though some cynics noted that paradoxically, Pope Benedict benefits from low expectations because of his rather fearsome reputation. In these early days, anything at all that comes across as optimistic, relaxed, and open is eagerly embraced, and perhaps overinterpreted, precisely because it was not what some people were expecting. Measured against such low standards, these critics say, almost anybody would get a "bounce" just by showing up.

Nevertheless, there was much that was genuinely intriguing in these telltale first steps of the new pope. It's early in the game, but all this suggests that the pontificate of Benedict XVI may turn out to be more complex, less predictable, than some early commentators had anticipated.

Part Three

A PAPACY
OF EPIC AMBITION

Chapter Five

WHO IS JOSEPH RATZINGER?

Though Cardinal Joseph Ratzinger had been a known quantity in the Catholic world since the Second Vatican Council, 1985 was the year that made him a star. In that year, his book-length interview with Italian journalist Vittorio Messori, titled in English *The Ratzinger Report*, became a publishing sensation around the world. Ratzinger's tart diagnoses of the problems facing the Church made him into a hero for Catholic conservatives, who had wondered if anyone in Rome saw the same crisis they did, and a lightning rod for the Church's liberal wing, a symbol of what they saw as a reactionary desire to "turn back the clock" on Church reform. Public discussion of the book was intense. During the 1985 Synod of Bishops, called to take stock of Vatican II twenty years after its close, Cardinal Godfried Danneels became so sick of answering questions about *The Ratzinger Report* during a press conference that he snapped, "This is not a synod on the book, it's a synod on the council!"

From that year on, Ratzinger occupied a place all by himself in the pantheon of Catholic celebrities.

As proof of the point, when Ratzinger turned seventy in 1997, two of the biggest secular publishing houses in Germany brought out new editions of his books, his picture appeared on the front cover of the largest mass-market newsmagazine in Italy, and virtually every newspaper and TV network in Europe prepared extensive profiles to mark the occasion. Just by virtue of having a birthday, Ratzinger was news.

By the standards of the normally shadowy world of the Roman Curia, Joseph Ratzinger, as the Vatican's top doctrinal official, was not just a star, but a mega-star. After being elected pope, the Italians quickly dubbed him "Papa-Razi," a play on the term paparazzi for those photographers who trail celebrities around, and the term has a curious fittingness for the preexisting celebrity status of Benedict XVI. He's perhaps the first pope of modern times who truly needs no introduction.

In that sense, offering a biographical sketch here of the new pope almost seems an exercise in redundancy. Still, as Walt Whitman once put it, "the child is father to the man," and so a brief overview of Ratzinger's life, especially his experiences in Nazi Germany and his later career as one of the most promising Catholic theologians of his generation, will be helpful in approaching the question of what kind of pontificate he is likely to lead.

In this regard, we are helped by the fact that Ratzinger himself has outlined the story of his life, at least prior to being made a bishop, in his 1997 memoir *Milestones*. This slim volume is required reading for anyone seeking to understand the mind of the new pope. Moreover, there is Pope Benedict's own prodigious literary output to draw upon, both as a theologian and a cultural critic. Prior to his election as pope, Cardinal Karol Wojtyla of Krakow, widely regarded as one of the more thoughtful members of the College of Cardinals in his day, had written three major books: *The Acting Person, Sign of Contradiction,* and *Love and Responsibility*. Pope Benedict, on the other hand, has written more than fifty books, along with a seemingly infinite series of journal articles, popular essays, and lectures, which range from the late 1950s up to just days before the conclave.

Given the abundance of this primary material, only the briefest of profiles is offered here, just enough to situate the Pope in time and place as a sort of backdrop to the coming drama of his pontificate. Doing so is perhaps especially important with respect to what is likely to be the characteristic struggle of his papacy—the battle against what he called a "dictatorship of relativism," and to recover the Christian roots of Europe.

CHILDHOOD

Joseph Aloysius Ratzinger was born on April 16, 1927, on Holy Saturday, in a small Bavarian town called Marktl-am-Inn, just across the border from Austria and the city that enchanted his youth, Salzburg. He was the youngest of three children in a lower-middle-class Bavarian household, and his parents were named Joseph and Mary. Joseph was a policeman, while Mary stayed at home during some periods of her life, and worked as a cook in bed-and-breakfast establishments in others.

Joseph's sister, Maria, was born in 1921, and his older brother, Georg, in 1924. Georg, like Joseph, became a priest (they were ordained the same day in 1951), and also like his brother has a passion for music. Georg went on to be a choir conductor. Maria spent most of her adult life as a caretaker for the brothers, especially Joseph; when Joseph was a professor, and later a senior churchman, she looked after his office and household. Maria died in November 1991, in the Roman apartment in the Piazza Leonina she shared with her brother, while Georg is retired in Regensburg.

In Bavaria, Ratzinger grew up in a homogeneous, deeply practicing Catholic environment. While his mother was the new pope's primary catechist, his father was deeply faithful as well, sometimes attending as many as three Masses on Sunday. In *Milestones*, Ratzinger recounts fond memories of his mother teaching him devotional practices, and of the deep impression that the Easter liturgies made on his religious imagination. It does not seem that the Pope ever seriously contemplated any other career than the priesthood (though he said at one point he considered working as a house painter); unlike his predecessor, Karol Wojtyla, he was never tempted by the theater or other walks of life. He also does not seem to have had any serious romantic relationships as a young man, though when asked at a press conference in Germany for the launch of *Milestones* why he didn't discuss any girlfriends in the book, he jokingly replied that "I had to keep the manuscript to one hundred pages."

As a young man, the Pope developed a lifelong love of music, especially Mozart, that native son of Salzburg whose melodies became the sound track of Pope Benedict's life. Of Mozart, he said in 1996: "His music is by no means just entertainment; it contains the whole tragedy of human existence." The Pope himself became an accomplished pianist, and in an interview published in the 1980s said he tried to get in at least fifteen minutes a day at the keyboard playing Mozart and Beethoven. Brahams, he sighed, is too difficult. His brother Georg was the conductor of the famed Regensburg choir, which had the honor of performing at the closing session of the Second Vatican Council. The new pope's musical tastes are not "catholic," however, in the sense of universal; he is not a fan of rock and roll, which he once called "a vehicle of anti-religion." One strains to imagine Pope Benedict, like John Paul II did in 1997, tapping his toes to a performance by Bob Dylan, or being dubbed by U2's Bono as "the first funky pontiff."

NATIONAL SOCIALISM

The main historical shadow that hung over Ratzinger's youth was the rise of National Socialism in Germany. He was six when Hitler came to power in 1933, and was eighteen when the Second World War ended in 1945. The Nazi period thus coincided with the formative period of his life, and his reflections on that experience continue to exert influence on his theological and political outlook today.

First, to clarify the relationship of the Ratzinger family, and the new pope specifically, with respect to National Socialism, it can be said with crystal clarity that the Ratzingers were not "pro-Nazi." The father on more than one occasion expressed criticism of the Brownshirts, and concern about the potential implications of those views for himself and his family triggered a series of relocations to progressively less significant

Bavarian assignments, until in 1937 he retired and the family moved to the Bavarian city of Traunstein. Ratzinger has written that his family belonged to a political tradition in Bavaria that looked to Austria and to France rather than to Prussia, and that therefore had little sympathy for Hitler's form of German nationalism.

In *The Ratzinger Report*, Ratzinger disassociated his cultural roots from Hitler and the Nazi movement: "The poisonous seeds of Nazism are not the fruit of Austrian and Southern German Catholicism, but rather of the decadent cosmopolitan atmosphere of Vienna at the end of the monarchy."

In 1941, when Joseph Ratzinger was fourteen, membership in the Hitler Youth became compulsory, and both he and Georg were enrolled. Yet Joseph did not attend activities, and as he recalls in *Milestones*, a sympathetic teacher in the high school in Traunstein allowed him to qualify for a reduction in tuition even though he did not have the mandatory Hitler Youth registration card.

In 1943, after Joseph had entered the seminary, he and his entire class were conscripted into the German army, spending most of his time as part of antiaircraft battalion guarding a BMW plant outside Munich. In a 1993 interview with *Time*, Ratzinger said he never fired a gun "in anger" during his military service, and eventually deserted. He ended up in an American prisoner-of-war camp, and was eventually released to continue his studies for the priesthood.

On the basis of this record, it seems clear that while Ratzinger did not take part in active resistance to the Nazi regime, he was by no means a supporter of the Nazis either. He and his family opposed Hitler.

(I pointed all this out on CNN after the Pope's election, in response to rumblings in the British press about Ratzinger's "Nazi past." My comments earned a kind of immortalization from Jon Stewart of the *Daily Show*, who said of the Hitler Youth controversy: "To be fair, membership in that group was compulsory, and as Ratzinger's biographer John Allen has noted, Ratzinger's tenure in the group was brief and unenthusiastic, as evidenced by his basement full of unsold Hitler Youth cookies.")

The brutality of the Nazi regime once touched the Ratzinger family personally. A cousin with Down's syndrome, who in 1941 was fourteen years old, just a few months younger than Ratzinger himself, was taken away in that year by the Nazi authorities for "therapy." Not long afterward, the family received word that he was dead, presumably one of the "undesirables" eliminated during that time. Ratzinger revealed the episode on November 28, 1996, at a Vatican conference organized by the Pontifical Council for Health Care. He cited it to illustrate the danger of ideological systems that define certain classes of human beings as unworthy of protection.

Perhaps more important than these biographical details is how Benedict XVI looks back on the Nazi period today, especially in the context of the lessons to be drawn for institutional Christianity. First of all, Pope Benedict is proud of the resistance offered to National Socialism by the Church. In *Milestones*, he writes:

> *Despite many human failings, the Church was the alternative to the destructive ideology of the brown rulers; in the inferno that had swallowed up the powerful, she had stood firm with a force coming to her from eternity. It had been demonstrated: The gates of hell will not overpower her. From our own experience we now knew what was meant by "the gates of hell," and we could also see with our own eyes that the house built on rock had stood firm.*

In *The Ratzinger Report*, he echoed the same point: "It is well known," he said, "that in the decisive elections in 1933 Hitler had no majorities in the Catholic states." The Nazi assault on the Catholic Church is inarguable; some twelve thousand priests and male religious were victims of persecution and harassment during the Hitler era, representing 36 percent of the diocesan clergy at the time.

As a historical matter, the extent of this resistance offered by the Church, and its impact on the course of events, is still a subject of debate. Ratzinger is obviously aware that some Catholics backed the regime, but he sees them as exceptions to an overall pattern of opposition. The point here is not to resolve those controversies, but to understand how the new pope remembers them.

Ratzinger has been critical of the way some Christian denominations in Germany, especially those he regarded as more "liberal," were corrupted by National Socialist ideology. In a 1986 lecture in Toronto, he said that "liberal accommodation . . . quickly turned from liberality into a willingness to serve totalitarianism." In *The Ratzinger Report*, he said that many Protestant churches were more easily co-opted by the Nazis because the idea of nationalism and a national church was more attractive to them, having decoupled themselves from the concept of a transnational institutional Christianity with a strong teaching office.

The Pope's conclusion, on the basis of these experiences, is that only a form of Christianity clear about its core beliefs, and equally clear about its system of authority, will have the inner strength to stand up against alien forces attempting to seduce or hijack it. While the threat posed by hostile cultural currents is not as clear today—because in Europe at least there are no Brownshirts burning churches or rounding people up in the middle of the night—the risk remains, especially in the form of rampant materialism and relativism in the West. The Church, he believes, must be equally vigilant to be sure it is not gradually assimilated to the prevailing cultural ethos. A system of theology decoupled from the institution or its authorities, Pope Benedict worries, leaves itself prey to other powers, which can manipulate that theology to sap the Church's strength from within.

RATZINGER THE THEOLOGIAN

After ordination in 1951, the young Joseph Ratzinger pursued a career as a theologian, teaching in a succession of German universities that were among the most vital and productive centers of theological energy of the time: Freising, Bonn, Münster, and, in 1966, Tübingen. These were the places where much of the intellectual scaffolding that would support the reforms of the Second Vatican Council was erected. So indebted was Vatican II to the German theological contribution, in fact, that one of the most famous early books about the council, by Fr. Ralph M. Wiltgen, was entitled *The Rhine Flows into the Tiber*.

Ratzinger was present for all four sessions of the Second Vatican Council as the *peritos*, or theological expert, for Cardinal Josef Frings of Cologne, Germany, whom Ratzinger had met and befriended while teaching at Bonn. Broadly speaking, Frings was part of the progressive majority at the council that spoke in favor of greater collegiality among the bishops, liturgical reform, greater ecumenical and interreligious openness, and a more transparent style of governance within the Church.

Ironically, Ratzinger was the principal ghostwriter of a speech Frings gave on the floor of the council on November 8, 1963, that denounced the "methods and behavior" of the Holy Office, today the Congregation for the Doctrine of the Faith, as "a cause of scandal to the world." Less than two decades later, Ratzinger was the prefect of that office himself, drawing some of the same kind of criticism he had once helped express. More than one critic accused Ratzinger of having come down with "scarlet fever"—that is, the ambition for high ecclesiastical office—though defenders point out that Ratzinger's career did not follow the traditional track of someone seeking a bishop's miter.

What changed between the Ratzinger of 1963 and the Ratzinger of 1981, the year he moved to Rome at John Paul's invitation to head the doctrinal office?

Ratzinger himself has long insisted, as he did in an interview with *Time* magazine in 1993, that his positions have not changed, but rather the context has. There's undoubtedly truth to that assertion. To speak in generalities, at least two currents were in play within the progressive majority at Vatican II: one, known as *ressourcement*, or a "return to the sources," looking to recover earlier stages of Christian tradition; another known as *aggiornamento*, or "renewal," looking to reconcile the Church with the modern world. One impulse, in other words, looked back, another looked forward. Ratzinger, under the influence of figures such as Augustine, Romano Guardini, and Hans Urs von Balthasar, was always more comfortable in the *ressourcement* camp. As the *aggiornamento* group gained dominance in the immediate post–Vatican II period, he worried that too much of the tradition was being squandered based on an uncritical reading of the goodness of "the world."

In *The Ratzinger Report*, he put the point this way: "I have always tried to remain true to Vatican II, to this *today* of the Church, without any longing for a *yesterday* irretrievably gone with the wind, and without any impatient thrust toward a *tomorrow* that is not ours."

At the same time, there's little question that on some issues, from the theological status of national bishops' conferences to liturgical reform, the later Ratzinger has struck more traditional and "conservative" notes. Though it is overly simplistic to express this in terms of a shift from "Ratzinger the liberal" to "Ratzinger the conservative," nevertheless something did change in his thought in the critical years since 1965, at the close of Vatican II, when Paul VI made him archbishop of Munich.

The pivotal point seems to have come in 1968, with the student revolutions that swept across Europe, including Tübingen, where Ratzinger was teaching. More troubling still, those uprisings often had the explicit support of sectors within the Catholic Church, which tended to identify Marxist socialism with Catholic social teaching. This was deeply troubling for Ratzinger, who felt he had already lived through one ruinous attempt at the ideological manipulation of the Christian faith in Nazi Germany, and therefore felt himself obliged to resist another. In the lengthy interview with German journalist Peter Seewald that became 1997's *Salt of the Earth*, Ratzinger said of this period: "Anyone who wanted to remain a progressive in this context had to give up his integrity."

The new pope himself has not shrunk from describing his attitude toward the postconciliar period in terms of the need for a "restoration," saying in *The Ratzinger Report*: "If by 'restoration' we understand the search for a new balance after all the exaggerations of an indiscriminate opening to the world, after the overly positive interpretations of an agnostic and atheistic world, then a restoration understood in this sense (a newly found balance of orientation and values within the Catholic total-ity) is altogether desirable and, for that matter, is already in operation in the Church."

Yet it would be a mistake to regard the story line of this stage of Ratzinger's life as centering on the revision of his previous positions. This was also the most creative period of his career as a theologian, re-sulting in the production of significant books that rank among the most impressive theological output of the era. Pride of place goes to his 1968 book *Introduction to Christianity*, a contemporary presentation of Christian faith. The book was no legalistic manual stuffed with rules and regula-tions; it was a meditation on faith that reached into the depths of human experience, a book that dared to walk naked before doubt and disbelief in order to discover the truth of what it means to be a modern Christian. Many found it exhilarating. Another significant title from this period is *Eschatology: Death and Eternal Life* (1977), which Ratzinger himself once called "my most thorough work, and the one I labored over the most strenuously." In it, Ratzinger argues for the need to "detach eschatology from politics," to never construe the Reign of God with some this-worldly social or political order. This, he argues, does not mean disen-gagement from politics, but rather a relativization of politics that sets limits to power and ultimately upends totalitarianism.

ARCHBISHOP OF MUNICH

After relocating to Regensburg to continue his theological career, a new twist came in 1977, when Paul VI named Ratzinger archbishop of Munich and then, just weeks later, made him a cardinal. Suddenly Ratzinger found himself at the pinnacle of the career ladder in the Catholic Church, despite never having served in a chancery, never hav-ing worked in the Vatican, and never having served as a diocesan bishop. It was a daring choice by Paul VI to elevate a thinker rather than a bu-reaucrat; the Pope obviously felt that, given the way the winds were blowing in Western Europe, and especially Germany, the Church had to do more than "business as usual" in order to mount a credible response. Upon his appointment, the future pope chose as his episcopal motto *Cooperatores Veritatis*, "coworkers of the truth," reflecting a concern for objective truth that runs through his thought and career.

The Pope's brief stint as archbishop is of interest because it marks his only direct experience as a pastor prior to being elected the Bishop of Rome in the conclave of 2005. How those years look depends to a great extent upon whom you ask.

As archbishop, Ratzinger played a minor role in the decision by Pope John Paul II to strip Hans Küng, his old colleague from Tübingen, of his license to teach Catholic theology. He also blocked Johann Baptist Metz, another erstwhile colleague, from an appointment at the University of Munich in 1979 (a right he enjoyed under the Bavarian concordat of 1924). Many in the theological community complained that Ratzinger had forgotten his roots, such as famed German Jesuit Karl Rahner, who called the move an "injustice and misuse of power." Some of the priests in the Munich archdiocese also complained that Ratzinger was aloof and did not communicate well with them, although others dispute this. Defenders of Ratzinger recall him as a devoted shepherd, whose actions only made the German press when they had some disciplinary connotation; his gentleness with ordinary believers and his simplicity, they say, remained largely hidden.

As a footnote to the Metz episode, Ratzinger appeared at a 1998 symposium to mark Metz's seventieth birthday. Metz described that appearance in an interview with the *National Catholic Reporter* as "a gesture of reconciliation towards the theological community."

Ratzinger's appointment as a cardinal in 1977 also meant that he was on hand to take part in the two conclaves of 1978, which elected John Paul I and John Paul II. In the interregnum leading to the second conclave of 1978, Ratzinger warned in a newspaper interview against the "Marxist presuppositions" underlying liberation theology in Latin America, which he said opened the door for "ideological struggle." At the same time, he said, the reality of social injustice, coupled with what he termed a "pushy Americanism" demanding conversion to free-market principles, created a real basis for social protest. Some Vaticanologists believe Ratzinger played a role in the election of the cardinal of Krakow, Karol Wojtyla, as John Paul II; prior to both conclaves, Ratzinger made some short lists of *papabili* himself.

In November 1980, Ratzinger was responsible for organizing John Paul II's trip to Munich. Also in 1980, John Paul appointed Ratzinger as the *relator*, or chairman, of the Synod of Bishops on the Family, and in that capacity he won high marks as a listener and synthesizer of the bishops' concerns, despite the fact that in his own speeches at the synod he strenuously defended traditional positions on birth control and other issues of sexual morality. His professorial capacity to bracket off his own views and listen to those of others, coupled with his reputation as a eminent theologian, made it little surprise when John Paul called Ratzinger to Rome in 1981 to take over the Congregation for the Doctrine of the Faith, becoming the first truly first-rate theologian to become the pope's top doctrinal authority since St. Robert Bellarmine in the sixteenth century.

RATZINGER IN THE VATICAN

In many ways, Ratzinger's twenty-four years at the Congregation for the Doctrine of the Faith are so well-documented as to make reviewing them here unnecessary.

Critics remember Ratzinger as the driving force behind some of the most controversial aspects of the pontificate of John Paul II, including the disciplining of theologians such as Fr. Charles Curran, an American moral theologian who advocates a right to public dissent from official Church teaching; Fr. Matthew Fox, an American known for his work on creation spirituality; Sr. Ivone Gebara, a Brazilian whose thinking blends liberation theology with environmental concerns; and Fr. Tissa Balasuriya, a Sri Lankan interested in how Christianity can be expressed through Eastern concepts.

Ratzinger also reined in a series of bishops seen as unacceptably progressive, including Archbishop Raymond Hunthausen of Seattle, Washington, reproached by Rome for his tolerance of ministry to homosexuals and his involvement in progressive political causes, and Bishop Dom Pedro Casaldáliga of Sao Félix, Brazil, criticized for his political engagement beyond the borders of his own diocese.

It was Ratzinger who in the mid-1980s led the Vatican crackdown on liberation theology, a movement in Latin America that sought to align the Roman Catholic Church with progressive movements for social change. Ratzinger saw liberation theology as a European export that amounted to Marxism in another guise, and brought the full force of Vatican authority to stopping it in its tracks.

Ratzinger sought to redefine the nature of bishops' conferences around the world, insisting that they lack teaching authority. That campaign resulted in a 1998 document, *Apostolos Suos*, that some saw as an attack on powerful conferences such as those in the United States and Germany that to some extent acted as counterweights to the Vatican. He also expanded the borders of "infallibility" to include such disparate points as the ban on women's ordination and the invalidity of ordinations in the Anglican Communion under the umbrella of a de facto infallibility as part of the "ordinary and universal magisterium of the Church."

It was Ratzinger who, in a famous 1986 document, defined homosexuality as "a more or less strong tendency ordered toward an intrinsic moral evil." In the 1990s, Ratzinger led a campaign against the theology of religious pluralism, insisting that the traditional teaching of Christ as the lone and unique savior of humanity not be compromised. This effort culminated in the 2001 document *Dominus Iesus*, which asserted that non-Christians are in a "gravely deficient situation" with respect to Christians. The same effort led to critical notifications on the work of two Jesuit theologians, Jesuit Fr. Jacques Dupuis of Belgium, and Fr. Roger Haight of the United States.

Despite Ratzinger's reputation as a stellar theologian, critics also say that sometimes he can be sloppy, relying on misleading assessments by aides and consultors. English Presbyterian writer John Hick, for example, pointed out in 1997 that in a public lecture criticizing his work,

Ratzinger erroneously identified him as an American, and cited page numbers in one of his books that had nothing to do with the matter under discussion. In the Dupuis case, Ratzinger's office prepared a highly critical notification that it asked Dupuis to sign, only to have Dupuis's defenders object that once again the citations were incorrect and the statements attributed to Dupuis were, in fact, nowhere to be found in his book. Ratzinger took the point, and a milder version of the notification was drafted.

This track record means that some in the Catholic theological community, especially on the more liberal wing, are not great Ratzinger admirers. A Jesuit who followed the Dupuis case closely, asked for his thoughts on the possibility of a Ratzinger papacy days before the conclave opened, said tersely: "It fills me with dread."

Ratzinger also has a reputation for making occasionally provocative comments that stir controversy. He once called Buddhism an "auto-erotic spirituality," and in *Salt of the Earth* was critical of Islam: "Nor must we forget that Islam was at the head of the slave traffic and by no means displayed any great regard for the blacks. And above all Islam doesn't make any sort of concession to inculturation," he said. He later added, "One has to have a clear understanding that it is not simply a denomination that can be included in the free realm of a pluralistic society."

Ratzinger has also said on many occasions that the Church of the future may have to be smaller to remain faithful, referring to Christianity's short-term destiny as representing a "creative minority" in a world largely hostile to its message. He has also used the image of the "mustard seed," suggesting a smaller presence that nevertheless carries the capacity for future growth as long as it remains true to itself. Such views have drawn criticism in some quarters for being excessively pessimistic. The English Catholic writer Eamonn Duffy, for example, said in 1985 of Ratzinger's judgment about the contemporary world: "The 'world' is not entirely inhabited by hedonistic bourgeois materialists, any more than it is by abortionists, pornographers or concentration camp commandants. The 'world' is the place where ordinary men and women live and must find their salvation."

Finally, Ratzinger has insisted that his primary responsibility in the doctrinal office is not primarily to make life easy for theologians, but to protect the right of the 1.1 billion Roman Catholics in the world to have the faith presented to them fully and accurately. As he put it in 1997, "Those who, as it were, can't fight back intellectually have to be defended—against intellectual assault on what sustains their life." He has suggested that theological "creativity," as it has come to be understood, may be partly to blame for the decline in Catholic religious practice in some quarters: "Theologians should ponder to what extent they are to blame for the fact that increasing numbers of people seek refuge in narrow or unhealthy forms of religion. When one no longer offers anything but questions and doesn't offer any positive way to faith, such flights are inevitable," he said.

All these positions, and many others, have made Ratzinger a polarizing figure, at least within center-left circles in academia and ecclesiastical life. Fr. Charles Curran, one of Ratzinger's targets for his views on sexual morality and theological dissent, blames Ratzinger for artificially shutting down theological discussion.

"The problem is that he has too readily identified the truth with what the magisterium has taught at a given moment," Curran said in 1999. "The Holy Office cannot have a copyright on what it means to be Catholic."

Yet Ratzinger's fans, and they are many, insist that focusing only on the public controversies associated with his tenure leaves two essential pieces of the picture out of focus: the personal qualities of the man, and the abiding concerns upon which the specific battles he's waged are based.

As for Ratzinger's personal side, those who have worked with him insist that he is not the bruiser that a quick rehearsal of his public record, like the one above, might suggest.

"He is an extraordinarily refined, calm, and open-minded person," said Archbishop William J. Levada of San Francisco, who worked on Ratzinger's Vatican staff in the early 1980s. "He can listen and synthesize a group of people's thought and find much of value in almost anything that is said. He has the uncanny ability to articulate those things we meant but forgot to say," Levada told the *National Catholic Reporter* in February 1999.

That graciousness is reflected in the fact that, as prefect of the doctrinal congregation, Ratzinger on many occasions has accepted invitations to dialogue with intellectuals of other faiths and of none, often in very public settings, and has always come off as open, willing to concede points when they were well articulated and cogent, and never defensive or arrogant. On October 25, 2004, for example, he took part in a colloquium with Italian lay thinker Ernesto Galli della Loggia, a conservative nonbeliever, at Rome's Palazzo Colona. In his opening remarks, Ratzinger called contemporary society "truly ill," and said that humanity's moral capacity has not kept pace with its technological skill. In such a context, he argued, there is an urgent need for religious believers and secularists of goodwill to join forces in an attempt to revivify moral reasoning.

"I've come with this realization of needing to make common cause," Ratzinger said.

During the discussion, Galli della Loggia challenged Ratzinger, objecting to what he called the Church's tendency to blur "life" with "personhood," saying he agreed that an embryo is life but not that it is a person, and not all the same moral categories apply.

Ratzinger readily conceded the point.

"I think a use of the word 'life' that sometimes substitutes 'person' is mistaken," he said. "After all, a plant is life."

At the end of the evening, the audience roundly applauded Ratzinger's stamina and openness, and most scored him the winner of the exchange.

A similar event took place in a jam-packed Roman theater in 2000, when Ratzinger agreed to an exchange with Italian philosopher Paolo Flores d'Arcais, a self-described atheist. Many in the crowd of several hundred people arrived skeptical of the Vatican's "enforcer," but were gradually won over by his charm, quick wit, and willingness to listen to the other party. When Flores drew cheers for suggesting that sometimes nonbelievers have done a better job of living gospel values than believers, Ratzinger said: "I'm satisfied with the applause. It's good for both of us to be self-critical, to reflect anew."

Admirers say Ratzinger's kindness is not just hauled out for public display at this sort of event, but is a fundamental quality of the man. After his election as pope, for example, Ratzinger went by his apartment in the Piazza Leonina to pick up whatever personal effects he wanted to collect. The apartment is on the same floor with the apartments of three other cardinals, and as he left, Pope Benedict rang the doorbells of the other three apartments to thank the startled religious women who act as the household staffs for the cardinals for being such good neighbors during his years in that location. (As a footnote, many of these sisters are Americans, members of the Mercy Sisters of Alma.) Those who know the new pope well say it was a vintage gesture.

The devotion Ratzinger inspires among his staff at the Congregation for the Doctrine of the Faith is also the stuff of legend. When he visited the office shortly after his election, he was accompanied by the secretary of state, Cardinal Angelo Sodano, and the *sostituto*, or "substitute," Archbishop Leonardo Sandri, both men known for maintaining rather formal and distant relationships with subordinates. One staff member at the congregation described the two as "stunned" by the outpouring of affection for the new pope from his former aides; most staffers, when introduced to the Pope, choked back tears. One said he was literally unable to speak when his turn came, and had to content himself with later writing a note to Pope Benedict trying to describe his emotions.

Further, defenders insist, the positions articulated by the Congregation for the Doctrine of the Faith over these twenty-four years are not the personal musings of Joseph Ratzinger, but represent the collective judgment of the staff of the congregation, as well as the other cardinals who are its members. Ratzinger himself made this argument in *Salt of the Earth*: "I would never presume to use the decisions of the Congregation to impose my own theological ideas on the Christian people. . . . I see my role as that of coordinator of a large working group," he said. "When the Cardinals meet, we never make decisions if the consultors aren't in substantial agreement, because we say that if there are markedly different opinions among good theologians, then we can't declare by some higher light, as it were, that only one is right. Only when the advisory team has come to at least a large degree of unanimity, a basic convergence, do we make decisions as well."

This point was made by Washington's Cardinal McCarrick after Pope Benedict's election.

"The Congregation for the Doctrine of the Faith is not just Ratzinger going into his office, closing the door, and writing documents," he said. "Everything he does has to be in continuity with the tradition of the Church."

To some degree, therefore, Ratzinger admirers, including many of the cardinals who elected him pope, believe that he has unfairly shouldered the public blame for a quarter-century for conclusions that virtually any prefect of the doctrinal office would have been obliged to reach. Behind the scenes, they argue, he has sometimes had a moderating effect, such as his widely rumored intervention during the drafting of the 1993 encyclical *Veritatis Splendor* to argue that the Church's teaching on birth control, because it is not directly a matter of divine revelation, cannot be declared formally infallible.

As for Ratzinger's core concerns, which presumably will extend to his new role as Pope Benedict XVI, admirers insist that he has no interest in choking off theological debate simply for the sake of exercising power, or for offending constituencies who may find some of his public pronouncements painful, such as homosexuals or women who feel called to the Catholic priesthood. He is not, they say, by nature a head-knocker.

Instead, they argue, the underlying passion of Ratzinger's life has always been truth. No doctrine, Ratzinger believes, can truly liberate, and no theological discussion is truly free, if it leads human beings into false conceptions of the meaning and purpose of their lives. In that sense, Ratzinger sees no contradiction between doctrinal and pastoral imperatives—the best pastoral service the Church can offer, he believes, is to tell someone the truth. Drawing on his own experience of National Socialism in Germany, Ratzinger argues that he has witnessed the ruin that lies on the other side of wrong ideas, false doctrine. Insisting upon the capacity of the human intellect to attain truth, and that this truth is offered in its fullest form in the Christian gospel, is, he believes, the only secure basis of authentic humanism.

"A lot of people read everything I may say as part of a mechanism that basically wants to keep mankind in tutelage and not as a genuine, honest, intellectual attempt to understand the world and man," Ratzinger said in *Salt of the Earth*.

For this reason, Ratzinger's admirers have long scoffed at characterizations of him as a kind of "control freak."

"I do not believe any credible case could be made for him as an authoritarian," Dominican Fr. Augustine Di Noia told the *National Catholic Reporter* in 1999. At the time, Di Noia was the chief theological adviser for the U.S. bishops conference; later, he would come to Rome to serve as Ratzinger's undersecretary in the Congregation for the Doctrine of the Faith, a position he holds today.

"Faith is not the suppression of intelligence, but its exaltation," Di Noia said in 1999. "The fundamental divide between dissenting or revisionist theologians and the mode of John Paul II and Ratzinger lies along this fault. Ratzinger is stating points which would have been totally noncontroversial even fifty years ago," Di Noia said. On the rare occasions when he has had to rein someone in, Di Noia said, it is because "a clear line in the sand" was crossed.

A FINAL CASUALTY

Just two weeks after Benedict's pontificate began, a final casualty was claimed in the battles fought during his tenure at the Congregation for the Doctrine of the Faith, one last echo of the controversies rehearsed above. Fr. Thomas Reese, S.J., editor of the respected Jesuit-run *America* magazine, resigned after the congregation asked the Jesuit authorities to remove him as editor, capping five years of largely hidden tensions between Ratzinger's office, the Jesuit order, and Reese himself.

Ironically, Reese got the news just days after returning to New York from Rome, where he covered the conclave that elected Ratzinger as Pope Benedict XVI.

Over the course of a five-year exchange between the doctrinal congregation and the Jesuits, the congregation had raised objections to various editorial choices at *America* under Reese's leadership, including:

- An essay exploring moral arguments for the approval of condoms in the context of HIV/AIDS;
- Several critical analyses of the doctrinal congregation's September 2000 document *Dominus Iesus*, on religious pluralism;
- An editorial criticizing what *America* called a lack of due process in the congregation's procedures for the investigation of theologians;
- An essay about homosexual priests;
- A guest essay by Congressman David Obey (D., Wis.), challenging suggestions that the Church should refuse Communion to Catholic politicians who do not vote pro-life.

In each case, defenders note, while these contributions in some respects challenged official Church positions, they were published as part of *America*'s broader coverage of the topic, which always included substantial contributions making the opposing argument.

The formal correspondence about Reese's fate was carried on between the Congregation for the Doctrine of the Faith and the superior general of the Jesuits, Fr. Peter-Hans Kolvenbach of Holland, with the content then relayed to Reese's Jesuit superiors in the United States. Although critics of Reese both in the United States and Rome have occasionally accused him of an "antihierarchical" mentality, supporters noted in their responses to the congregation that over his seven years as editor, *America* routinely published weighty pieces by prominent members of the hierarchy, at one stage including Ratzinger himself.

In February 2002, the Congregation for the Doctrine of the Faith proposed creating a three-member commission of America bishops to act as "censors" for *America*, though in the end this never came to pass. Throughout the back-and-forth discussions, the congregation told the Jesuits that it was acting in response to concerns from bishops in the United States. Whatever the source, the tensions did not diminish, and by early spring of 2005 it was clear that Reese would have to go. A letter requesting that he be removed was dated in mid-March. Observers speculate that had someone other than Ratzinger been elected pope, Reese might have waited to see how policy would develop, but given Ratzinger's victory, Reese believed he saw the handwriting on the wall. He elected to take a sabbatical in California while considering his next move.

Reese's departure will be seen as puzzling in some quarters, given that *America* has long been seen as a moderate, though clearly left-leaning, sophisticated publication that tried to steer between extremes. Perhaps, some speculated, Reese's high profile in the American media as a commentator on Church affairs was a factor in making him a "target," though if so, the intervention seemed destined to be futile. Reese was already widely cited in the press prior to taking over at *America* in 1998, and presumably the notoriety of having been "fired by the new pope" will do little to reduce his visibility. Others concluded that it was *America*'s reputation for intelligent, nuanced commentary that made it a "threat."

Defenders of the Congregation for the Doctrine of the Faith, on the other hand, argued that it is not unreasonable to expect a publication sponsored by a religious order, and with a member of that order as editor, to uphold the teaching of the Church.

Whatever one makes of the debate, it should be emphasized that the pressure for Reese's removal dates from the end of Ratzinger's term at the doctrinal office, and it may be unfair to treat it as a sign of where Benedict's pontificate will go. Further, despite the fact that the buck at the congregation stopped on Ratzinger's desk, it is unclear to what extent he was personally involved in the deliberations surrounding Reese.

Still, the fact that the congregation targeted Reese and *America* will be troubling to some trying to discern where Benedict XVI may want to take the Church. If *America* is not safe, some observers in the Catholic Church will wonder, who is?

A COMPLEX MAN

This, then, is the complex man who has become Pope Benedict XVI: a serious intellectual, an ardent defender of the faith, a man with deep doubts about the health of contemporary culture, willing to use the disciplinary tools of the teaching office when a matter of faith is at stake, but also a man of deep kindness and humility, someone capable of stirring remarkable love and devotion in those close to him, a man with a reputation for being both tough and collegial, erudite yet concerned with the common person. Given these facets of his history and personal character, which sometimes rest in uneasy tension with one another, his promises to be a fascinating pontificate.

Chapter Six:

BATTLING A
"DICTATORSHIP OF RELATIVISM"

Perhaps the most perceptive comment in the immediate aftermath of Pope Benedict's election came from Cardinal Francis George of Chicago, one of the few men in the College of Cardinals who, observers say, can match the new pope in terms of intellectual depth. During a press conference at the North American College the morning after the election, while several other American cardinals shared personal impressions of the new pope and expressed thanks to the media for their positive coverage of the Church, George could not resist plunging deeper in terms of the providential logic for the election of Joseph Ratzinger.

"In 1978, when Karol Wojtyla was elected as Pope John Paul II, the primary challenge to the Catholic Church came from the East, in the form of Soviet communism," George said during the press conference. "Today the most difficult challenge comes from the West, and Benedict XVI is a man who comes from the West, who understands the history and the culture of the West."

What George meant to suggest, it seems, was a kind of parallelism in the historical contexts in which the last two popes took office. In 1978, Karol Wojtyla, this "pope from a far country," was the ideal man to mount a spiritual and cultural resistance to Soviet dictatorship. In 2005, the College of Cardinals has elected a man similarly suited for the struggle against what he himself defined, in his homily at the Mass *pro eligendo papa* the morning the conclave opened, as a "dictatorship of relativism" in the West. If resistance to the Soviets was the defining feature of at least the early stages of the Wojtyla papacy, in other words, could resistance to relativism be the lodestar of Ratzinger's?

George seemed to think so.

"There was a fault line in the Soviet empire that brought it down, that its concern for social justice was corrupted by the suppression of freedom," he said. "In the West, there's also a fault line between concern for personal freedom and the abandonment of objective truth." George said that both contradictions "are not sustainable in the long run." George added that the "time and tempo" with which Pope Benedict's witness against relativism in the West would gather force are not yet clear.

Whether there will be the single dramatic moments that characterized John Paul's moral crusade against the Soviet domination of the East, such as his stirring 1979 return to Poland, is unknowable; relativism is a much more diffuse, amorphous, unsystematic opponent. In the East, Soviet oppression produced explicit political resistance, such as the Solidarity movement, which could be endorsed and assisted by the Pope; in the West, relativism tends to produce ennui and purposelessness rather than organized opposition, which means that the first thing the Pope must do is convince people that there *is* a dictatorship to be resisted, a preliminary challenge John Paul II never faced.

Going into the conclave, many cardinals told the *National Catholic Reporter* that they had identified secular culture, especially the relativistic and post-Christian culture that often dominates western Europe, as a source of special preoccupation. Against the backdrop of that concern, many concluded that Ratzinger was the man with the right life experience and intellectual preparation to take on the challenge. This is not to suggest that Ratzinger's election should be read as an explicit mandate from the cardinals for a war on relativism; most cardinals did not approach things in such specific terms.

Yet thinkers such as George, and, perhaps more importantly, such as Benedict XVI himself, men who believe there are no accidents in history, will strive to descry what God may have had in mind in having things turn out this way. They will want to ask, what role does Benedict's pontificate have in God's cosmic plan? At least in the early stages, the most compelling answer to that question seems to be "To save the West from itself, just as John Paul helped to save the East."

TWO CAUTIONS

This insight, however, can be easily misunderstood if pushed too far in one of two directions. First, it could suggest that Benedict's papacy will have an exclusively European focus, or second, as if the main thrust of his pontificate will be to excoriate the dominant culture. Neither will likely prove to be the case.

Pope Benedict realizes that he is now the pastor of the universal Catholic Church, and that two-thirds of the Catholics in the world today live in the global south. His focus cannot be exclusively on Europe, as important as the recovery of Europe may be for the fate of Catholicism. If he cannot give voice to the experience and aspirations of Catholics from the south, his pontificate will be judged a failure, however much impact he has in Europe and North America. Moreover, Benedict also realizes that however much he may regard the secular West as teetering on the brink of its own dark age, people will not be attracted by a kind of "Taliban Catholicism" that knows only how to condemn or retreat. Fundamentally, he must inspire passion, offering humanity a compelling vision of the beauty that the Gospel can inspire. It is not criticism by which his pontificate will be judged, but its capacity to stir hope.

Still, George's analysis that the redemption of the West is at the heart of the new pope's agenda was echoed by another thoughtful American, Cardinal Francis Stafford, who heads the Apostolic Penitentiary, a Vatican court that deals with matters of conscience.

"The tragedy of Europe is rooted in the eclipse of the Christian identity of individual Europeans and their society as a whole," Stafford said in a later interview. "Unfortunately that is being repeated in the European Union. There is a kind of Christophobia, a fear of Christ, not just a withdrawal from him. . . . Pope Benedict will be able to bring to the people of Europe a new, rediscovered sense of the dignity of what it means to be a child of God— to have been chosen by God in Christ to be his child."

WHY "BENEDICT"?

Popes choose names for different reasons, and they're not always terribly revealing about the kind of pontificate they intend to lead. Sometimes they pick a given name because it's the patron saint of the city they come from, for example, or to honor a special figure in their lives. Sometimes, as in the case of John Paul I and John Paul II, the name is taken to honor one's immediate predecessors. Yet in the case of Benedict XVI, it's clear that the choice of name cuts deeper than that, and unlocks something essential about how he understands the logic of his election.

In the first place, the name is a reference to St. Benedict, the great founder of European monasticism, who built the foundations of a new civilization in an era in which the old order of the Roman Empire was falling apart.

Benedict (480–543) was the son of a Roman noble in Norcia, a small Italian town near Spoleto, and spent his youth in Rome living with his parents and studying. At the age of nineteen or twenty, fully equipped for the contented life of a wealthy patrician, he chose instead to forsake his studies and pursue a life of monastic isolation, fleeing from what he considered the moral licentiousness and aimlessness of fifth-century Rome. He withdrew to the countryside, founding a small community of people who shared his diagnosis of the contemporary situation, and decided to support himself through manual labor. Over the course of time, he became the founder of a monastery and eventually authored his famous "Rule," an outline of the monastic life based on charity, prayer, and moderation, always with an eye toward living basic human virtues suffused with a sense of their supernatural origin and purpose.

When Cardinal Angelo Sodano, the vice-dean of the College of Cardinals, asked Joseph Ratzinger the name by which he would be known, the new pope did not hesitate. Not only did he respond "Benedict," but he was ready with an explanation. As Cardinal George later told the story to the press, the Pope said something like, "Benedict lived at a time when the Roman Empire was collapsing, and he saw the role of the Church as to preserve the best in human culture throughout the centuries. The whole world was crumbling, and Benedict helped ensure that human civilization survived."

In his first General Audience, on Wednesday, April 27, the Pope said of St. Benedict: "He constitutes a fundamental point of reference for the unity of Europe, and a powerful call to the irrefutable Christian roots of European culture and civilization."

The new pope's attachment to St. Benedict is anything but accidental. As a young man in Bavaria aspiring to the Catholic priesthood, Ratzinger once considered joining a Benedictine monastery. For many years, the then-Cardinal Ratzinger took his private annual retreat in the Benedictine Abbey of Scheyern, located between Munich and Regensburg in Bavaria. The memory and model of St. Benedict, and the impact the saint had on his times, has thus long been a part of the new pope's religious imagination and personal spirituality.

Just twenty-four hours before Pope John Paul II died, the man who would take the name of Benedict XVI traveled to Subiaco, Italy, home to a famous Benedictine monastery, to receive an honor from Abbot Mauro Meacci—ironically, called the Premio San Benedetto, or St. Benedict Award. Then-Cardinal Ratzinger delivered a twelve-page speech reflecting on the Benedictine rule and spiritual legacy; preparing this speech on St. Benedict was the last reflective bit of intellectual activity Ratzinger performed before the whirlwind of events that led to his election as pope.

It's worth quoting at length what Ratzinger said on that occasion:

*What we need above all in this moment of history are people
who, through an illuminated and lived faith, render God credible in
this world. The negative testimony of Christians who spoke about
God but lived against Him has obscured the image of God and has
opened the door to disbelief. We need people who keep their gaze
directed at God, learning from there what is true humanity. We
need people whose intellect is illuminated by the light of God and
in whom God opens their heart, so that their intellect can speak to
the intellect of others and their heart can open the hearts of others.
It is only through people who are touched by God that God will be
able to return to the people. We need people like Benedict of
Norcia, who, in a time of dissipation and decadence, sank himself
into the most profound solitude, succeeding, after all the
purifications that he was forced to undergo, in making the light rise
again, returning to found Montecassino, the city on the hill where,
amid all the ruins, he put together the energies from which a new
world was formed. Thus Benedict, like Abraham, became the
father of many peoples. The recommendations to his monks placed
at the end of his rule are indications that demonstrate also to us the
path that leads to the heights, out of the crises and the ruins. "Just
as there is an evil zeal of bitterness which separates from God and
leads to hell, so there is a good zeal which separates from vices and
leads to God and to life everlasting. This zeal, therefore, the
monks should practice with the most fervent love. Thus they should
anticipate one another in honor; most patiently endure one
another's infirmities, whether of body or of character; vie in paying
obedience one to another—no one following what he considers
useful for himself, but rather what benefits another; tender the
charity of brotherhood chastely; fear God in love; love their Abbot
with a sincere and humble charity; prefer nothing whatever to
Christ. And may He bring us all together to life everlasting!"*

From this talk, one draws a keen sense of how Pope Benedict XVI
understands the historical legacy of his namesake. In an era of cultural

turbulence, of "dissipation and decadence," Benedict founded an utterly new kind of community, one based on love and truth, and in so doing kept the true humanism alive in a dark time. By way of analogy, the new pope has long believed that a similar process of intellectual and moral decay is at work in the contemporary West, and that Christianity's mission is once again to preserve an alternative vision of the meaning and purpose of human existence. Just as Benedict challenged the mores of the fifth century by generating a mode of life based on different principles, the new pope believes that Christians today must find ways to order their lives that challenge the dominant relativistic mind-set. Christians must "keep their gaze directed at God," learning from that source what "true humanity" means.

The comparison with the fifth century is not accidental. Though Joseph Ratzinger is too sophisticated a thinker to draw simplistic parallels between the collapse of the Roman Empire and the situation of the West in the early twenty-first century, he is nevertheless frequently struck by the commonalities. In a November 28, 2000, lecture on the contemporary situation in Europe delivered in Berlin, he said: "The comparison with the Roman Empire at twilight imposes itself. [Rome] still functioned as a kind of great historical framework, but in practice it lived off forces that were destined to dissolve it, because in itself it no longer possessed vital energy."

Benedict XVI, as a man eminently aware of the intellectual conversation in the West, certainly knows the classic 1981 work *After Virtue*, by Alasdair MacIntyre, one of the most celebrated works of contemporary philosophy on the cultural right. In it, MacIntyre unpacks this implied parallel between the final decay of the Roman Empire and the contemporary Western situation, and specifically located St. Benedict in this comparison. One of the new pope's aides and admirers suggested that I consult this passage from MacIntyre to contextualize the Pope's choice of name. MacIntyre wrote in 1981:

> *It is always dangerous to draw too precise parallels between*
> *one historical period and another, and among the most misleading*

of such parallels are those which have been drawn between our own age in Europe and North America and the epoch in which the Roman Empire declined into the Dark Ages. Nonetheless certain parallels there are. A crucial turning point in that earlier history occurred when men and women of good will turned aside from the task of shoring up the Roman imperium and ceased to identify the continuation of civility and moral community with the maintenance of that imperium. What they set themselves to achieve instead—often not recognizing fully what they were doing—was the construction of new forms of community within which the moral life could be sustained so that both morality and civility might survive the coming ages of barbarism and darkness. If my account of our moral condition is correct, we ought also to conclude that for some time now we too have reached that turning point. What matters at this stage is the construction of local forms of community within which civility and the intellectual and moral life can be sustained through the new dark ages which are already upon us. And if the tradition of the virtues was able to survive the horrors of the last dark ages, we are not entirely without grounds for hope. This time however the barbarians are not waiting beyond the frontiers; they have already been governing us for quite some time. And it is our lack of consciousness of this that constitutes part of our predicament. We are waiting not for a Godot, but for another—doubtless very different—St. Benedict.

A quarter-century later, MacIntyre has his Benedict.

It's important to stress quickly that Benedict XVI is not quite the cultural pessimist that these passages can suggest. Over the course of his intellectual career, he has identified many positive elements in the contemporary social order that should be defended and built upon, chief among them democracy, and the respect for human rights upon which it is based. Yet Benedict also believes that democracy is dependent for its vitality upon citizens with a sense of moral purpose and attachment to ultimate truths that democracy itself cannot supply, and it is precisely this sense of purpose, this awareness of an objective order that does not depend upon human subjectivity, that relativism saps. "Democratic society lives by energy that it can't produce itself," he said in 1997. "Democracy itself calls for supplementary realities that give the mechanisms their meaning, and then in turn are constructed in such a way that they live up to their own essential task."

St. Benedict's response to the collapse of the moral order in his day was to withdraw from the world, building up communities that could ride out the storm. His monks eventually reemerged in the High Middle Ages as the architects of a new civilization. Pope Benedict XVI has also spoken admiringly about the effort of some Christians today, especially in the "new ecclesial movements," to foster forms of community that have the capacity to transmit a different set of assumptions and values than one imbibes from the broader culture. Yet his exhortation to these communities is not to disengage from the world but to remain engaged with it, so that the life and hope they generate may be offered to all.

Thus Pope Benedict will not call on Catholics to flee for the hills, retreating from the contemporary world in order to construct self-imposed ghettoes. In his April 25 remarks at the Basilica of St. Paul Outside the Walls, Benedict recalled John Paul II's missionary zeal and love for proclaiming the Gospel, and then said: "May the Lord wish to nourish also in me a similar love, so that I will not rest before the urgency of announcing the Gospel in the world of today." In other words, Pope Benedict does not intend to abandon the world, but to challenge it.

At the same time, however, the legendary realism of the new pope means that he is under no illusions about the prospects for short-term conversion of the secular world, and parallel to his work of evangelization, he will also encourage Christian communities to jealously safeguard their identity, making sure they are not assimilated by a secular culture in the developed West that may be on its last historical legs, but, he believes, is still capable of taking large sectors of the Church down with it.

"THE GRAVEST PROBLEM OF OUR TIME"

When Pope Benedict XVI said in his homily on the morning of April 18, the day the conclave of 2005 began, that the West is in the grip of a "dictatorship of relativism," it was not a spur-of-the-moment remark. It was a summary statement of one of the core concerns of his life, and, given that he did not expect or desire to be elected pope, it was also a carefully chosen expression of his own theological legacy. It was, in effect, the final challenge Joseph Ratzinger intended to leave the Roman Catholic Church before he exited the public stage.

Where does the concern with relativism come from?

One of Ratzinger's most developed treatments of the theme came in 1993, in a speech in Hong Kong to the presidents of Asian bishops' conferences and the heads of the doctrinal committees of bishops' conferences in Asia, titled "Christ, Faith, and the Challenge of Cultures." It was a propitious occasion, since Ratzinger had long been concerned that Western philosophical relativism was being "baptized" by Eastern religious agnosticism, resulting in an ideological concoction that packs a tremendous appeal for the modern mind.

Ratzinger began by arguing that relativism is dangerous, in the first place, because it is false. That is, it suggests that objective truth does not exist, or at least it is unattainable by the human mind. This assumption, he warned, turns Christian orthodoxy on its head, which is premised on the idea that God has revealed the truth about the human condition in the person of Jesus Christ, and this truth is valid and binding across time, culture, and personal experience. In that light, he bluntly defined relativism as "the gravest problem of our time."

In effect, Ratzinger warned, relativism obscures the Christian claim that "Jesus of Nazareth is . . . the incarnate meaning of history, the Logos, the self-manifestation of truth itself." Christianity, he argues, rises or falls on this fundamental conviction. Relativism is, therefore, not merely a modern version of ancient heresies such as Monophysitism or Pelegianism, which distort one or another element of the Church's creed; it is, to borrow a phrase, "the mother of all heresies," in that it denies the possibility of objectively binding creedal statements in the first place.

Ratzinger repeated these convictions in a 1996 speech in Mexico City, before the heads of doctrinal commissions from Latin American bishops' conferences. In that context, he said, "Relativism has thus become the central problem for the faith at the present time. . . . It is presented as a position defined positively by the concepts of tolerance and knowledge through dialogue and freedom, concepts which would be limited if the existence of one valid truth for all were affirmed."

A related danger is that relativism deprives Christianity of its missionary impulse, since if truth is relative, then "imposing" a truth on another culture or person becomes an act of colonial domination.

"Christian universalism concretely carried out in mission is no longer the dutiful passing on of a good, namely, truth and love intended for everyone," Ratzinger warned in his Hong Kong address. "Rather, mission becomes the arrogant presumption of a culture which thinks itself superior to the others and so would deprive them of what is good and proper to them." For a religion whose origins lie in the injunction of its founder to "Go forth and make disciples of all the nations," this is, from Ratzinger's point of view, a serious matter indeed.

Further, Pope Benedict believes, relativism postures as an intellectual expression of tolerance and appreciation for diversity, but in reality it opens the door for totalitarianism, by undercutting any basis for asserting that there are moral limits to what secular power can do. "She [the Church] is a basis for freedom precisely because her form is one of communion, which also includes a common binding commitment. Therefore, when I stand up to a dictatorship, I do so not just in my own name as a private individual, but in virtue of an inner strength that transcends my own self and my subjectivity," the new pope has written.

To put the point a different way, it is the Church's insistence on absolute truth, on "truth with a capital T," that makes it insusceptible to being co-opted by alien ideologies, whether National Socialism, Marxism, or free-market capitalism. In typically pithy fashion, Ratzinger once made the point this way: "Where there is no dualism, there is to-talitarianism." By denying the existence of any transcendent truth, and of a supernatural realm in which that truth is grounded, the new pope believes, the West runs the risk of "divinizing" the present, of looking for the Reign of God in the here and now. This was the basic error in Marxism, he argued, mistaking politics for eschatology. Relativism thus encourages a kind of utopian approach to politics, which ultimately, in Ratzinger's view and life experience, leads to Dachau and the gulags.

A related danger is that relativism undercuts respect of human rights by treating rights claims as grounded in social convention rather than transcendent truth. Ratzinger unpacked this point in November 1999, when he was given an honorary *juris doctorate* by the LUMSA School of Law in Rome. In a culture dominated by relativism, Ratzinger warned, law becomes distorted and human rights are in jeopardy.

> *The majority determines what must be regarded as true and*
> *just. In other words, law is exposed to the whim of the majority,*
> *and depends on the awareness of the values of the society at any*
> *given moment, which in turn is determined by a multiplicity of*
> *factors. This is manifested concretely by the progressive*
> *disappearance of the fundamentals of law inspired in the Christian*
> *tradition. Matrimony and family are increasingly less the accepted*
> *form of the statutory community and are substituted by multiple,*
> *even fleeting, and problematic forms of living together. The relation*
> *between man and woman becomes conflictive, as does the relation*
> *between generations. . . . The sense of the sacred no longer has*
> *any meaning for law; respect for God and for that which is sacred*
> *to others is now, with difficulty, regarded as a juridical value; it is*
> *displaced by the allegedly more important value of a limitless liberty*
> *in speech and judgment. Even human life is something that can be*
> *disposed of: abortion and euthanasia are no longer excluded from*
> *juridical ordering. Forms of manipulation of human life are*
> *manifested in the areas of embryo experimentation and transplants,*

in which man arrogates to himself not only the ability to dispose of
life and death, but also of his being and of his development.

In this context, Ratzinger delivered a stirring defense of law based on objective truth, drawing upon his own experience of Nazi Germany.

> *In the so-called years of struggle, law was consciously*
> *castigated and placed in opposition to so-called healthy popular*
> *feeling. The Fuhrer was successively declared the only source of law*
> *and, as a result, absolute power replaced law. The denigration of*
> *law is never in any way at the service of liberty, but is always an*
> *instrument of dictatorship. To eliminate law is to despise man;*
> *where there is no law, there is no liberty.*

In summary form, then, we can say that Pope Benedict XVI believes relativism is "the gravest problem of our time" because it subverts traditional Christian teaching; because it undercuts efforts to bring the gospel to the world; because it fosters utopian political thinking and ultimately totalitarianism; and because it compromises the basis for human rights and leads to abuse of power by the State, even over life and death. Given that diagnosis, one can understand why, for Pope Benedict, the defense of objective truth is not simply a matter of abstract philosophical interest. It is the burning issue of our times, and in an era in which relativism seems to have the upper hand and a social order built on truth is crumbling, it is up to the Church to keep the candle of objective truth burning.

BRINGING DOWN THE "DICTATORSHIP OF RELATIVISM"

As Pope John Paul II took up the struggle against Soviet communism in Eastern Europe, he fought the battle on three fronts. First was the intellectual and cultural dimension, proposing a Christian vision of human life in which God, not the State, was the ultimate arbiter of right and wrong. When he stood in Victory Square in Warsaw in 1979 and thundered, "It is not possible to understand the history of the Polish nation without Christ," it had the effect of flinging down a gauntlet at the totalitarian system. Second was the geopolitical front, collaborating with the Western powers, especially the United States, in trying to exploit the fault lines in the Soviet system. Third was the aim of supporting organized resistance behind the Iron Curtain, above all the Solidarity movement in his native Poland.

Though Pope Benedict may not consciously conceive of his own efforts against the Western "dictatorship of relativism" in such explicitly strategic terms, one can nevertheless expect a similar three-pronged effort during his pontificate.

There will be a teaching thrust, meaning efforts to stimulate conversation about what he sees as the false promises of relativism on the intellectual and cultural front; political interventions intended to remind legislators and others responsible for civic life of the demands of objective truth; and finally, the attempt to encourage forms of "resistance," especially communities that strive to carve out an alternative vision of life rooted in Christian faith.

The aim will be to defeat relativism on its own turf. Contemporary Western secularists believe that only "pluralism," by which they often mean relativism, can adequately guarantee human liberty, by protecting people from the imposition of beliefs and values by others. Pope Benedict will argue that relativism enslaves rather than liberates, because it eviscerates the only genuine basis for human rights, which is the belief that every human being has transcendent value because he or she is a child of God. True liberty, Benedict will insist, flows from ordering one's life on the basis of truth, which is revealed in the person of Jesus Christ.

Further, one can anticipate that it will not take long before this aspect of Pope Benedict XVI's pontificate comes into focus. The Pope will be driven by a special sense of urgency, given that he was seventy-eight years old upon election, and he knows that his time in office is unlikely to be as long as that of his immediate predecessor, John Paul II. In commenting on his selection of the name "Benedict," the new pope reminded the cardinals in the Sistine Chapel that the last man to hold the name, Benedict XV, led a "brief pontificate." Benedict XV's was the third-shortest papacy of the twentieth century, from 1914 to 1922 (only the pontificate of John XXIII, 1958–63, and John Paul I, who reigned just thirty-three days in 1978, were briefer). Hence Benedict XVI is likely to be animated by a sense of "time's winged chariot hurrying near," and will not wait to take up the struggle that everything in his life experience and worldview have prepared him to regard as the reason God did not answer his prayer that someone else be elected.

Teaching

Pope Benedict XVI is perhaps the most accomplished intellectual to be elected pope since Leo XIII in 1878. As Archbishop of Perugia, Cardinal Gioacchino Pecci, who became Leo XIII, was known as the leading thinker in the College of Cardinals. He had written an impressive series of pastoral letters in Perugia that were seen as "dress rehearsals" for his later papal encyclicals. One of his favorite pastimes was composing verse in Latin, and he could recite whole pages of material from the Fathers of the Church, in the original Latin or Greek, from memory. His pontificate blossomed into a moment of great intellectual ferment for the Catholic Church; he launched the tradition of modern Catholic social teaching, met the intellectual assaults of the nineteenth century against religious faith with a ringing defense of Thomism, encouraged scientific biblical research, and founded a number of universities.

Enthusiasts expect the same sort of intellectual flourish under Pope Benedict XVI, a man of potentially even greater learning and refinement. Indeed, some Church insiders gently whisper that it may even be a deeper and more lucid teaching pontificate than that of John Paul II, whose core ideas were electrifying, but whose prose could also sound vague and mystical, sometimes expressed in mountains of dense philosophical verbiage or in ambiguous poetic excurses. The great contribution of John Paul II, some confidants of Benedict XVI believe, was that he created such enormous interest in the papacy that the world will now be paying attention when Pope Benedict speaks. As one Belgian monsignor recently put the point, "John Paul invited everyone to the feast, and now it's up to Benedict to cook the meal."

If Benedict holds to traditional patterns, his first encyclical will be a "programmatic" document, laying out the underlying convictions that will guide his pontificate. John Paul II's 1979 encyclical *Redemptor hominis* did this, sketching out his emphasis on Christ as redeemer, and the evangelical drive that results from that conviction. One would expect Pope Benedict's first encyclical to call the Church to witness to a truth that transcends human subjectivity, not in a spirit of power or domination, but in service to authentic human flourishing. He will insist that living one's life in accord with God's design does not mean sacrificing personal liberty, but realizing one's full potential and reaching a happiness that does not fade. As noted Catholic writer George Weigel put it in *Newsweek*, Pope Benedict will strive "to challenge his fellow Christians to convert their cultures and to rebuild the moral foundations of the free society."

It will not just be in major teaching documents, however, where Pope Benedict XVI enjoins the world to resist the siren song of relativism. One can expect that he will come at the theme again and again in his "ordinary magisterium," meaning in his remarks at General Audiences, in the Sunday Angelus address, in comments to private audiences with various groups, in messages to congresses and other Church meetings, and in the various other forums that a pope has available to him to launch a message. The "beauty of truth," *Veritatis splendor*, can be expected to become the choral refrain of his papacy, the leitmotif around which the various movements of the symphony will pivot.

Every battle is waged with both offensive and defensive strategies, and the teaching aspect of Pope Benedict's reign will mark the offensive dimension of the struggle against relativism. He will try to express his ideas in positive and outward-directed language, confounding expectations of a pontificate largely built on condemnation and lament. At the same time, however, there will be challenging moments, because the Pope will not shrink from marking lines in the sand. Authentic love for humanity, he believes, implies telling people the truth, even if it's not what they want to hear. One can anticipate that Benedict XVI will therefore sometimes be a jarring voice in the cultural conversation, on all manner of issues.

This does not mean he will be dismissed. There is, in fact, a powerful current in the West today of people dissatisfied with the consumerist ethos, frustrated with a lazy "anything goes" morality, and convinced of the hollowness of materialist visions of happiness that so often seduce their children and distort their relationships with friends and family. In that context, Benedict XVI may emerge, even more than John Paul II, as a cultural point of reference regardless of religious affiliation. Given the penetrating quality of his mind, the Pope has the potential to prompt a wide cross-section of men and women to reconsider the premises upon which their lives and careers are based. If he succeeds, his papacy could mark a turning point in the cultural history of the West. That, at least, is the dream of his admirers, which means that the new pope faces a lofty set of expectations indeed.

Politics

Benedict XVI will be forced to confront relativism not just at the level of ideas, but also in what he perceives as its real-world political consequences. In his view, these appear across a wide range of issues, from what he would consider an "assault" on the family in the contemporary West, to a lack of respect for human dignity in wars and the inequities of structural development. In that sense, one can expect Benedict, as John Paul II before him, to energetically exploit the "bully pulpit" of the papacy to try to reshape the international agenda.

This will be, therefore, a very political papacy.

Pope Benedict will first extend, and deepen, John Paul's call for Europe to recover its Christian roots. The first test of the new pope's commitment is likely to come in Spain, where the Socialist government of Jose Luis Rodriguez Zapatero appears determined to press forward with legislation authorizing gay marriage and adoption rights for gay couples. Senior Church leaders in Spain have spoken in strong opposition to these measures, and will look to the new pope for support. The Bishop of Castellon, Juan Antonio Reig Pla, has even called for "civil disobedience," adding, in language that echoes some of the new pope's own theological reflections, that "one has to obey God before man, otherwise it will lead to a totalitarian state."

"If obeying the law comes before conscience, this leads to Auschwitz," said the Archbishop of Barcelona, Ricard Maria Carles, in a similar vein.

Spain remains an overwhelmingly Catholic country, at least as measured by baptismal records, and the continuing vitality of its Catholic roots was on display when John Paul II visited Madrid in May 2003, drawing a boisterous crowd of energetic young Spanish Catholics. Pope Benedict will aim to mobilize those resources in what promises to be a protracted struggle against the social policies of the Spanish government. At least in the early stage of his pontificate, Spain will be on the cultural scene what it was in the military sense in the mid-1930s; the site of a proxy war, where all the forces in the great divide test their weapons and work out strategies.

The vexed question of what to do about pro-choice Catholic politicians will be another test case, especially in the United States, where the dilemma was posed in especially acute form during the presidential candidacy of Senator John Kerry, a Democrat and Catholic who opposes legal restrictions on abortion. In his capacity as the then-prefect of the Congregation for the Doctrine of the Faith, Cardinal Joseph Ratzinger was involved in the debate over how the Church ought to respond to Kerry. Ironically, he was cited both by those who came down in favor of nonconfrontation, arguing that it is wrong to politicize the Eucharist, and those who wanted to cut Kerry off from Communion, insisting that a public figure cannot label himself "Catholic" yet defy core Church teaching.

During the debate in the spring of 2004, Ratzinger prepared a confidential memorandum for the American bishops on the general principles for the reception of Communion. After writing that pastors should attempt "precautionary measures," such as warnings, before denying

Communion to erring politicians, the heart of Ratzinger's memo was the following passage:

> When "these precautionary measures have not had their
> effect or in which they were not possible," and the person in
> question, with obstinate persistence, still presents himself to receive
> the Holy Eucharist, "the minister of Holy Communion must
> refuse to distribute it" (cf. Pontifical Council for Legislative Texts
> Declaration "Holy Communion and Divorced, Civilly Remarried
> Catholics" [2000], nos. 3–4). This decision, properly speaking, is
> not a sanction or a penalty. Nor is the minister of Holy
> Communion passing judgment on the person's subjective guilt, but
> rather is reacting to the person's public unworthiness to receive
> Holy Communion due to an objective situation of sin.

Nevertheless, when the American bishops voted to leave the decision up to each bishop in his diocese, Ratzinger sent a letter to the U.S. bishops declaring their work "very much in harmony" with the guidelines he had issued. In fact, Ratzinger was referring to the general principles laid out in the bishops' document, not necessarily the specific decision they reached on how to implement those principles. At the time of his election as pope, Ratzinger's team at the Congregation for the Doctrine of the Faith was working on a document about the principles underlying the reception of Communion, with the American debate over pro-choice politicians in the background.

One would expect that, in his papacy, Benedict XVI will insist on coherence between the professions of faith of Catholic legislators and their political positions. How he will choose to make this case, and the punitive instruments he might contemplate for those who resist, is still unclear. There is no evidence that Pope Benedict wishes to wage a "holy war," and the episode with the American bishops suggests a capacity to be flexible in deference to the judgment of others, even if he personally feels a matter of principle is at stake. In fact, this episode was cited by some cardinals leading up to the conclave as evidence of a largely unacknowledged capacity on the part of Ratzinger to be collegial, since he publicly supported the judgment of the American bishops despite a somewhat different sensibility as to how things should shake out. It stands in contrast with what happened in Germany in the late 1990s, when Ratzinger compelled the German bishops to abandon a state-funded counseling program for pregnant women, seeing it as unacceptable complicity in a system that led to legalized abortion. He took this action despite a strong consensus among the German bishops, led by Cardinal Karl Lehmann of Mainz, that the Church should remain in the system.

In the end, there is little doubt that Benedict will insist that Church teaching on abortion, homosexuality, stem cell research, and other matters is not merely a matter of internal ecclesiastical discipline, but of defending critical truths about human life and the human family. These truths, he believes, are not just "Catholic," but objectively valid for all times and cultures. One can therefore expect that pro-choice voices within Catholicism, whether belonging to politicians, moral theologians, or reform groups, will find life increasingly difficult on his watch. On these issues, the political thrust of Pope Benedict's papacy will be aligned squarely with what in the United States is known as the "religious right," defending the whole cluster of issues that came to be known during the John Paul II years as a Culture of Life.

At the same time, Pope Benedict's political interests will not be restricted to what wags have sometimes called the "pelvic issues," meaning the matters of sexuality that loom large in the Western press. This will not be a single-issue papacy, as Benedict's vision and ambitions are much broader.

The new pope is also committed to combating a relativistic devaluing of human life in matters of war and peace and the international economic order, especially having listened to one cardinal after another from the global south open his heart on these matters during the General Congregation meetings leading up the 2005 conclave. He struck this note in the explanation of his name inside the conclave itself, associating himself not merely with St. Benedict, but with Benedict XV, "who strove to be a peacemaker in a time of war." The new pope returned to that theme in his first General Audience on Wednesday, April 27. Benedict XV, he said, "was a courageous and authentic prophet of peace and made truly strenuous efforts to avoid the drama of war, and then to limit its nefarious consequences. In his footsteps, I desire to place my ministry at the service of reconciliation and harmony among people and the peoples, profoundly convinced that the great good of peace is above all a gift of God, a fragile and precious gift that must be invoked, safeguarded and constructed day after day with the support of all." The Pope's commitment to that ideal can be glimpsed from his public opposition to both U.S.-led Gulf Wars; the second time around, Ratzinger pointedly observed that the concept of "preemptive war" does not appear in the *Catechism of the Catholic Church*.

Benedict is therefore likely to emerge as an unexpectedly vocal critic of armed conflict, as well as international economic systems that fail to do justice to the world's poor. Observers expecting him to function as a sort of "Chaplain of the Atlantic alliance," softening the Vatican's critique of Western militarism and globalization, are likely to be disappointed. In Pope Benedict, in fact, they will find themselves up against a formidable critic, someone in a position to develop a profound intellectual substructure for viewing the exploitation of the poor as a manifestation of the same disregard for truth that leads to exploitation of unborn children or embryonic life. His work on behalf of social justice will be rooted not merely in pious sentiment or good-heartedness, but a deep conviction that such witness is of a piece with his broader project of reawakening the West to a truth that surpasses its own convenience.

Alternative Communities

Benedict XVI knows very well that hundreds of years of Western history cannot be reversed in the blink of an eye, and that in the short term the "dictatorship of relativism" is unlikely to crumble. For that reason, like St. Benedict before him, the new Pope will see preserving islands of alternative modes of living as an essential strategy, places where the Christian vision of human existence can be lived integrally and passionately, a sort of "mustard seed" that, in a different cultural moment, can sprout and produce renewal, just as Benedictine monasticism helped lay the groundwork for the High Middle Ages. Pope Benedict is fond of Toynbee's insight that the destiny of a society always depends on its "creative minorities," and in some respects he sees the role of Christianity in the present historical moment as representing precisely such a minority.

In a 1986 article in the theological journal *Communio*, the new pope wrote that "the word 'subculture' should not frighten us," and recommended building "islands of spiritual concentration."

Ratzinger has long been aware of, and sympathetic to, efforts to carve out such islands. One example is the Community of St. John, a group founded in 1945 by the famed Swiss theologian Hans Urs von Balthasar, whom Ratzinger regards as something of a mentor, and mystic Adrienne von Speyr. The community was recognized as a secular institute of diocesan right in 2000, but it is an international organization in the sense of having members outside Switzerland, albeit not many. Sources say the Community of St. John numbers perhaps sixty members all told, divided into three branches of laymen, lay/women, and diocesan priests. In the United States, there are perhaps four or five members. It is admittedly tiny, but it offers an example of creative attempts to envision new models of life that can keep the flame of Christian humanism lit.

In general, Benedict's papacy is likely to continue the policy of John Paul II of supporting the so-called new movements in the Catholic Church, such as the Focolare, Neocatechumenate, Sant'Egidio, L'Arche, and the wide range of other groups that have flowered in the period after the Second Vatican Council. As a pragmatist, Pope Benedict is aware of the criticism of these groups. He knows that they are capable of exaggeration, of disconnecting themselves from the broader Church, of a kind of uncritical "cult of personality" around their founders. He will encourage them to mature and to deepen their intellectual and theological foundations. At the same time, however, he will see them as precious models of community based on truth.

In 1997's *Salt of the Earth*, Ratzinger said: "One can always raise objections to individual movements such as the Neo-catechumenate or the Focolarini, but whatever else you may say, we can observe innovative things happening there." In 1984's *The Ratzinger Report*, he was enthusiastic: "What is hopeful at the level of the universal Church—and that is happening right in the heart of the crisis of the Church in the Western world—is the rise of new movements, which nobody had planned and which nobody has called into being, that have sprung spontaneously from the inner vitality of the faith itself. What is manifested in them—albeit subdued—is something like a Pentecostal season in the Church."

Despite the consummately rational character of the Pope's mind, he is also a supporter of more emotional forms of Christian expression, such as the charismatic movement.

"It is evidence of hope, a positive sign of the times, a gift of God to our age. It is a rediscovery of the joy and wealth of prayer over against theories and practices which had become increasingly ossified and shriveled as a result of secularized rationalism," he said in *The Ratzinger Report*.

At the same time, the traditionalist side of Pope Benedict's personality means that he will be conscious of what some established religious communities in the Church, such as the Benedictines, Franciscans, and Jesuits, took as a neglect of religious life under John Paul II at the expense of the new movements. In their more bitter moments, men and women religious sometimes felt as if John Paul had given up on them, deciding that the future belonged to the movements. Pope Benedict, who chose to name himself after the founder of monasticism, will see a genuine renewal of religious life as an important ambition of his papacy. This may mean some uncomfortable moments for the more progressive communities, who may have a different conception of religious life, stressing social engagement and dialogue with modernity, but at least they will not have the same sense of neglect. Pope Benedict will see religious orders as precious laboratories in which life based on objective truth can be held up to a secular, relativized world, as a reminder of what the human spirit can accomplish when it is in alignment with God's plan.

While this activity of teaching, staking out political positions, and fostering new forms of life may sometimes appear disjointed and episodic as they pop up on the cultural radar screen, it will all be of a piece with a deep current of conviction in Pope Benedict XVI—that God has revealed a set of truths about human life and destiny, that the Church is enjoined to safeguard and propound those truths, and that societies that defy them cannot endure. Benedict XVI's papacy will rise or fall based on his success in persuading the rest of the world that he's right.

EUROPE

Though Pope Benedict's efforts to stem the relativistic tide will unfold worldwide, the front lines of the struggle, and the place where his success or failure will be gauged, is Europe. He is a product of the European intellectual tradition, Europe is historically the cradle of Christian culture, it is still the primary center of institutional and pastoral energy in the Catholic Church, and, in the words of one senior Vatican official, "Europe is simply too big to fail." Addressing the demoralization and "ecclesiastical winter" in western Europe, and the cultural crisis that Pope Benedict believes lies underneath these phenomena, will be the most crucial challenge he faces at the start of his papacy.

The first task will be rousing Europe from its dogmatic slumber, reminding it that Christianity is at the root of its cultural identity. This effort, for example, is the context in which his August 2004 comments about the admission of Turkey to the European Union must be understood. In an interview with the French paper *Le Figaro*, Ratzinger said: "Throughout history Turkey has always represented a different continent, always in contrast with Europe." He warned that taking Turkey into Europe would lead to a flattening out of cultural characteristics on both sides.

"It would be a mistake to make the two continents the same, it would mean losing the richness of their differences and giving up culture in return for advantages in the economic field," he said.

In some quarters, Ratzinger's words were interpreted as an anti-

Islamic broadside, and they helped to account for a somewhat lukewarm response from some Islamic leaders to his election as Benedict XVI. Yet to understand the comments, they have to be seen in the context of his views about Europe. If the cultural project of Europe is inextricably tied to its Christian origins, as Pope Benedict believes, anything that further obscures those origins is unhelpful. His opposition to Turkey is not about keeping Muslims out, as he sees it, but about keeping Christian identity in.

Pope Benedict has laid out his understanding of Europe in a variety of different venues, most recently in a small book entitled *Europe: Its Foundations Today and Tomorrow*, published in Italian in 2004 by San Paolo. The book collects essays and lectures then-Cardinal Joseph Ratzinger has given on Europe over recent years.

What emerges, in the first place, is the Pope's clear conviction that "Europe" is a cultural and historical concept before a geographic one. In the era of Charlemagne, the Pope writes, the word "Europe" expressed both a political reality, meaning a group of states that formed a new Roman Empire, but also a mission—preserving the best of antique culture, and carrying it forward into history. Ironically, Benedict writes, at its moment of supreme triumph—when, in a globalized world, the languages and science of Europe have become the culture of the globe—Europe itself seems oddly hollowed out, "paralyzed in a certain sense by a crisis of its circulatory system, a crisis that puts its life at risk, relying on transplants that cannot but eliminate its identity."

There is in Europe today, the Pope writes, a striking lack of hunger for the future. This ennui is best expressed in declining fertility rates, as children come to be seen not as investments in the future but a risk to the present, threats to take away personal liberty or material prosperity. Europe, in effect, has preserved the forms of its Carolingian self-understanding, but has lost its sense of mission.

The Pope then examines two different models for understanding what the future might hold. The first is that of Spengler, who argues that there is a natural life-cycle to civilizations—they are born, they grow, and they die. From this point of view, European civilization in the cultural sense of the term is in its old age, and sooner or later death is inevitable. The other model is that of Toynbee, who argues that if a culture is undergoing spiritual crisis, it can be healed by a new injection of moral purpose. That, the Pope argued, is the reading the Church should embrace, seeing itself as a source of rejuvenation for Europe, even if in the short term there seems precious little interest in what the Church has to offer.

Benedict XVI's strategy for Europe, therefore, is likely to be twofold.

On the one hand, he will relentlessly remind Europe that the values it touts on the world stage—democracy, human rights, pluralism, tolerance—are rooted in its Christian heritage, and ultimately unsustainable without that basis.

On the other, he will work to ensure that the Catholic Church and the communities within it maintain their identity, that they do not assimilate to the broader secular mentality, that they do not, in biblical language, become like "salt that has lost its flavor." In order to function as a "creative minority," Christianity must practice the "politics of identity," preserving its own language, practices, and belief systems, its markers of difference in a rapidly homogenizing world. The redemption of Europe is a long-term affair, from the Pope's point of view, and one important contribution Catholicism can make is to foster vital cells of ecclesiastical life, not too numerous but alive with faith and passion, where the faith is transmitted fully and without compromise.

In a Vatican conference on new movements sponsored by the Pontifical Council for the Laity on June 16, 1999, then-Cardinal Joseph Ratzinger laid out this vision with typical lucidity and bluntness.

"Even when we are a minority, our priority is the message," he said. "In the West, the statistics reveal a reduction in the number of believers; we are living in a time of apostasy of the faith, while the identity between the European-American culture and Christian culture has almost dissolved. The challenge today is not to allow the faith to withdraw into closed groups, but to have it enlighten everyone and speak to everyone.

If we go back to the Church of the first centuries, the Christians were few, but they caught people's attention because they were not a closed group. They carried a general challenge to all which touched all. Today we also have a universal mission: to make present the real answer to the demand of a life that corresponds to the Creator."

Pope Benedict will strive to be a man of joy and compassion, especially for Europeans, whom he believes are often mired in aimlessness and a loss of confidence in their own future. Yet being Catholic will increasingly mean being different, especially as measured against the dominant culture of secular Europe. That transition will be a jolt to a swath of Catholic life in Europe and elsewhere. Make no mistake: As far as Catholic identity goes, this pontificate will have teeth.

THE UNITED STATES

Benedict XVI's political approach to the United States, in the main, is likely to closely resemble that of Pope John Paul II, with the same intriguing mix of admiration and ambivalence.

To begin with, Benedict is the first pope in the history of the Catholic Church ever to have been an American prisoner of war. In the final months of World War II, the eighteen-year-old Ratzinger deserted from the Germany army, where he had been a decidedly unenthusiastic draftee, but was flagged by American troops as a potential combatant. He was held for a few weeks in a camp in Ulm, Germany, and released on June 19, 1945, hitchhiking a ride home to resume seminary studies in Bavaria. As a sign of the healing of historical wounds, Ratzinger was Pope John Paul II's delegate to the commemoration of the seventieth anniversary of the D-Day invasion of Normandy, held in June 2004.

There is no indication whatsoever that the Pope's youthful experience left any bitterness about the United States, and in the aftermath of his election, reaction from the American government was largely, if not overwhelmingly, positive. President George Bush tapped his brother Jeb

Bush, governor of Florida, to head the American delegation to the new pope's inaugural Mass. During an April 23 press conference at the American embassy to Italy, Governor Bush expressed confidence that Benedict XVI and the United States would enjoy positive relations.

"President Bush met with John Paul II three times, and attended his funeral," Governor Bush said. "This is more than symbolism. It reflects the importance of the Holy See as a moral voice in world affairs. The president looks forward to the same relationship with Benedict XVI, in advancing social justice, freedom, and democracy around the world."

The governor said he expected Benedict XVI to be an especially important voice on issues of life.

"How we value life, how we appreciate life, how we strengthen family life," he said, ticking off areas where he felt the new pope's leadership would be helpful. "In some ways, we seem to have lost our way about respect for the fundamental values that keep the country from falling apart."

Bush located this point in the context of the Terry Schiavo case, expressing the hope that the new pope would issue a forceful reminder that "all people have dignity, that God treats us all equally." He described both abortion and end-of-life issues as areas where he expected Benedict XVI to make a positive contribution to contemporary political debate. In these areas, the policies of Benedict XVI will largely be in alignment with those of the political right in the United States, so Bush is probably correct to expect harmony between the Vatican and the White House—and where Benedict is an ally, he's likely to be a forceful one.

Such questions, however, hardly exhaust the range of political judgments a pope is called upon to make. On other issues, such as the war on terrorism, the death penalty, economic development, and the extent to which the culture of the United States ought to set the global tone, Benedict's policies will likely be more ambivalent with respect to American interests.

On the war in Iraq, for example, then-Cardinal Ratzinger took a measured position. On the one hand, he said that John Paul's opposition to the war was not a matter of faith, bolstering the position of some American Catholics who saw the conflict as an instance of just war. In a November 2002 interview with the respected Italian magazine *30 Giorni*, he said: "The Pope has not proposed the [antiwar] position as the doctrine of the Church, but as the appeal of a conscience illuminated by the faith. . . . This is a position of Christian realism which, without dogmatism, considers the facts of the situation while focusing on the dignity of the human person as a value worthy of great respect."

Yet Ratzinger was personally unstinting in his criticism of the conflict. Speaking at a conference in Trieste in September 2002, he was asked if the war could be justified. "In this situation certainly not," he replied. "There is the United Nations. It is the authority that should make the decisive choice. The choice must be made by the community of peoples, not a single power. The fact that the United Nations is seeking a way to avoid the war seems to me to demonstrate with sufficient proof that the damages which would result [from the war] are greater than the values it would seek to save."

Ratzinger also criticized the Bush doctrine of preemptive war. "The concept of preemptive war does not appear in the *Catechism*," he said. "One cannot simply say that the *Catechism* does not legitimate war, but it's true that the *Catechism* has developed a doctrine such that, on the one hand, there may be values and populations to defend in certain circumstances, but on the other, it proposes a very precise doctrine on the limits of these possibilities." Later, when Baghdad fell in April 2003, Ratzinger expressed gratitude that the outcome was not as violent as might have been expected. Still, he said, opposition to the war was the correct stance; "Resistance to the war, to this threat of destruction, was the right thing to do," he said.

The position staked out by Ratzinger in 2003 echoed views he expressed in 1991, during the First Gulf War, when he was likewise critical of the American invasion of Iraq. In an interview on Vatican Radio in 1991 after the American bombing campaign had begun, Ratzinger argued that given the nature of contemporary weaponry, both conventional and nuclear, it was difficult to imagine that any modern war could truly be termed "just."

All these comments suggest the potential for disagreement with the United States over future uses of force.

Some observers may have anticipated, given his background in the battles against liberation theology in the 1980s, that Pope Benedict will soften John Paul II's critique of social injustice that sometimes made neo-conservatives and free-marketeers in the United States uncomfortable. In fact, there's little evidence to support such a hypothesis. It's true that Ratzinger rejected what he saw as the attempt of liberation theology to erect the Reign of God in the here and now, along with what he regarded as its uncritical adoption of the concept of class struggle, but he also insisted that Christians must be concerned with social equity. In a 1986 document from the Congregation for the Doctrine of the Faith on authentic liberation, entitled *Libertatis conscientia*, Ratzinger wrote: "The evil inequities and oppression of every kind which afflict millions of men and women today openly contradict Christ's Gospel, and cannot leave the conscience of any Christian indifferent." As pope, Benedict will likely continue his predecessor's advocacy for a more just international economic system, in ways that will not always square neatly with American political and commercial interests.

In addition, the new pope has occasionally expressed reservations about the values he sees operative in America's international conduct. In an interview with Munich's *Süddeutsche Zeitung* in October 1978, shortly before the conclave that elected John Paul II, for example, Ratzinger said that underlying the liberation theology movement was a legitimate protest against social injustice, as well as what he termed a "pushy Americanism," by which he meant the free-trade capitalist ideology of the United States.

In a 2000 lecture in Berlin, Ratzinger returned to the theme, asserting that "certain milieus in the United States are aggressively promoting the Protestantization of Latin America, and therefore the dissolution of the Catholic Church, in the interest of forming free churches, out of the conviction that the Catholic Church is not capable of guaranteeing a stable political and economic system, and for that reason is incapable of fostering the education of nations, while the model of free churches will render possible a moral consensus and a democratic formation of the public will similar to that in the United States." The language is somewhat dense, but what Ratzinger meant is that, in his view, certain forces in the United States do not see Catholicism as compatible with the free-market, consumerist social systems, and hence are trying to subvert Latin America's Catholic identity.

The point is not whether Pope Benedict is correct, but rather to observe that his judgments about the United States are, like those of his predecessor, to some extent ambivalent. When it comes to America, therefore, the policies of Benedict's papacy may be more unpredictable than some anticipate, and no one should expect that he will always be a reliable moral apologist for American policy.

THE AMERICAN CHURCH

As far as the American Catholic Church, the new pope's most extended commentary came in 1997's *Salt of the Earth*. It's worth quoting at length what he had to say:

Q: In the United States, a large number of bishops intend to answer the Roman Church in the future blow for blow, as they say, with polemical writings of their own. [The reference was to a group of American bishops who in the mid-1990s announced plans to press Rome for certain reforms.]

A: The number is not large, thirty bishops at most. Then too, I have spoken with one of the main leaders, and he stressed that they have been completely misinterpreted. We're good Catholics, loyal to the Pope, he said, we just want to introduce better methods. I have read the writings in question very carefully, and I also said that I was fully in agreement with a whole series of things they mention, whereas I thought other things were rather dubious. I would say that there is no really out-and-out anti-Roman mood in the American episcopal conference. It has a certain breadth, which is also a good thing. There are only a few among them who are perhaps really somewhat extreme. But my impression is, after the fifteen years I have been here, that Rome and the United States have learned to get along much better. On the whole, we have a very good relationship with the American bishops' conference. It's a conference with great intellectual and religious capacity, with many outstanding pastors who are making an important contribution to the development of doctrine in the universal church. Its officers visit us here twice each year, and we have a very cordial relationship.

Q: Can the Church in North America profit from the religious awakening that is in the offing there?

A: Yes, I think so. Although we ought not to read too much into certain events and mass demonstrations of Catholicism, they do show that young people in search of religion feel they can have a home in the Catholic Church and that also the Pope is a reference point and a religious leader for them. Tensions have really eased in the last fifteen years, and there have been a lot of positive new developments. In America there is not only a movement of conversions among Anglican priests but also a completely new relationship to the Evangelicals, who were formerly the sharpest critics of the Catholic Church. At the Cairo and Beijing conferences a very interesting closeness between Evangelicals and Catholics developed, simply because they see that Catholicism doesn't, as they have thought until now, threaten the Bible and overlay it with some kind of papal domination, but that it is a guarantee that the Bible will be taken seriously. These new rapprochements won't lead to reunions anytime soon, but they show that Catholicism is once again an "American" possibility.

Q: What might be spurring on the new religiosity in America?

A: There are undoubtedly many factors, which I can't analyze because

I have so little knowledge of America. But there is a commitment
to morality and a desire for religion. In addition, there is a protest
against the predominance of modern media culture. Even what
Hillary Clinton has said—"Turn off the television, don't put up
with it anymore"—shows that there is a broad current that says we
no longer want simply to submit ourselves to this culture."

In his Berlin lecture of 2000, Ratzinger again commented on
American Catholicism:

> Today the Catholic Church is the largest religious community
> in the United States, and in its faith life it stands decisively on the
> side of Catholic identity. Yet [American] Catholics with regard to
> the relationship between faith and politics have inherited the
> tradition of the free churches, in the sense that precisely a church
> not confused with the state best guarantees the moral foundations
> for all, so much so that the promotion of the democratic ideal seems
> like a moral duty profoundly consistent with the faith.

Finally, in the 2002 book-length interview *God and the World*,
Ratzinger said that American Catholicism "has today become a decisive
force in the context of the global Church," because it has "the courage
to consecrate all of existence to the faith, drawing from it the courage
and the strength to place oneself at the service of others. It's a Church
with a great educational and health care system, with an enormous social responsibility." He praised American Catholics for having found a
"way of life" that is "nourished by Catholic values, and not just drunk
on American culture," and lauded the capacity of the American Catholic
Church to "speak up in a mute world."

The comments are suggestive on a variety of levels, revealing a man
who concedes that he doesn't know the United States well, regards the
relationship between Rome and the American bishops as fundamentally
healthy, and detects some very positive trends in terms of American religiosity, especially the new climate between Catholics and conservative

Protestants, and the growing self-confidence of the American Catholic Church. He seems genuinely eager to work collegially with the bishops, and even the bishops' conference. Yet the Pope also worries that the "free church" tradition has rendered democracy so obvious an ideal that American Catholics sometimes struggle to arrive at a proper understanding of the nature of the Church. (In that sense, his concerns echo the famous dictum of Cardinal Francis George, who once said that American Catholics are denominationally Catholic but psychologically Protestant.)

Pope Benedict does not seem to take office with a special "agenda" for American Catholicism, but rather a cautious yet open stance. He's appreciative of the breadth of the American Catholic experience, yet with concerns about both the Church and broader culture. Given his concern with the impact of America's Protestant heritage on the religious psychology of U.S. Catholics, he may appoint a number of "Catholic identity" bishops, men who will approach issues from a classically Catholic cultural worldview, challenging what is considered obvious and normal from within a democratic framework. Such appointments may fuel a gap between the expectations of some "Main Street" American Catholics and their leaders, marking a tension that Pope Benedict will have to navigate. At the same time, anyone who expects Pope Benedict to simply echo the positions and rhetoric of the American Catholic right, or for that matter any of the other blocks of opinion on the American Catholic scene, is likely in for a paradigm shift. The Pope's outlook is too complex to justify any such expectation.

Chapter Seven:

CHANGING THE CULTURE OF THE CHURCH

When Cardinal Jorge Medina Estevez stepped out onto the central balcony of St. Peter's Basilica on the evening of Tuesday, April 19, to reveal the name of the new pope, several monsignors from the Secretariat of State were positioned on a balcony outside their offices awaiting the announcement. Curiously, as soon as Medina said "Ratzinger," several of them turned around and went back inside. In the ever-cynical environment of ecclesiastical Rome, a joke quickly made the rounds about what they were doing: polishing their résumés.

Though there's little evidence that Pope Benedict intends to conduct an immediate purge of the Roman Curia—indeed, one of his first steps was to confirm the heads of Vatican offices in their previous positions, albeit "for the time being"—most observers, including many of the cardinals who voted for him, expect a shake-up, and not in the terribly distant future. As evidence of this conviction, I relayed the joke above about officials in the Secretariat of State to one cardinal the day after the conclave, and with a twinkle in his eye, he looked at me and said, "That's probably right."

A reform of the Roman Curia, from Benedict's point of view, assuming it comes, will not be an end in itself. It will be the first step toward a larger transformation of the culture inside the Roman Catholic

Church, away from a system that mimics the bureaucratic patterns and psychology of secular institutions, toward a more evangelical and distinctively "Catholic" model of self-organization, asking at all times whether a particular structure or institution still promotes an alternative vision of life, or whether it has outlived its usefulness.

This attention to the internal dynamics of the Church will be another of the subtle differences between Pope Benedict and John Paul II. At age seventy-eight, nobody expects Pope Benedict to travel as much as his predecessor, or to spend as much time conducting mega-events in St. Peter's Square. Benedict is expected to be more attentive to the internal nuts and bolts of governance, making sure that the pastoral and intellectual impulses of his papacy are translated into structural reality so they endure. In that fashion, many believe Pope Benedict will leave behind a Church that is leaner, streamlined, and more focused on core objectives. Given his reputation for doing his homework, many also anticipate a greater climate of accountability at all levels of Church life, a sense that somebody in the home office is paying attention. This shift should have consequences, to take one application, for how Rome responds to situations such as the sexual abuse crisis in the United States.

One aspect of John Paul's outward-directed papacy that is unlikely to be repeated under Pope Benedict, for example, is his record-making pace of beatifications and canonizations: 1,338 beatifications and 482 canonizations all told, more than all previous popes combined. In 1989, then-Cardinal Ratzinger, at a conference held in San Rocco di Seregno outside Milan, wondered aloud if too many people were being raised to the altar "who don't really have much to say to the great multitude of believers." Italian headlines soon blared that Ratzinger had charged there were "too many saints" on John Paul's watch, which brought the following clarification from Ratzinger in the pages of *30 Giorni*:

> *I've never affirmed that there are too many saints in the*
> *Church. That would be an absurdity, because the Church can*
> *never have too many saints. . . . The number of saints, thanks be*
> *to God, is innumerably greater than that group of figures singled*

out for canonization. The question I raised, whether there has been too dense a series of canonizations, referred only to this second group. . . . In reality, I said that up to recently this problem didn't exist, but now it needs to be addressed. This affirmation, which is very cautious, presupposes the consideration that every canonization is inevitably a choice in favor of a priority. . . . It seems legitimate to me to ask if the priorities in vigor at the present shouldn't be revised with new accentuations, in order to place before the eyes of Christianity those figures who more than everyone else render the Holy Church visible, amid many doubts about its holiness.

While the cardinal's language is measured, it seems reasonably fair to imagine that, on his watch, the standards for beatification and canonization will become more stringent—one element of a general "tightening up" that many anticipate.

After almost twenty-seven years in which everyone realized that the Pope was not terribly interested in matters of internal administration, a new wind is blowing in Rome. Though it has yet to gather strength, most forecasts suggest it will generate a number of ecclesiastical tsunamis before it fades.

POPE BENEDICT AND BUREAUCRACIES

One of the ironies of politics within Roman Catholicism is that on the issue of the distribution of power, positions are aligned in the exact inverse of secular politics in the United States. In America, conservatives tend to be the advocates of States' rights, while the liberals support a strong central government, on the grounds that they generally trust federal officials in Washington more than local legislators in Mississippi or Oklahoma to uphold their values. In the Catholic Church, however, it is the liberals who favor decentralization, while the conservatives support strong central authority, because conservatives generally have more faith in the traditionalism of Rome than in bishops' conferences in places such as Germany or the United States.

Because of this dynamic, Cardinal Joseph Ratzinger has sometimes been styled as a champion of big ecclesiastical government, because he has repeatedly made the case for strong central authority in the papacy. This is a serious misreading of his position. In the popular mind it may be difficult to distinguish the pope and the Vatican, but seen from Rome these are two different institutions, and Ratzinger's theological belief in the Roman pontiff's "supreme, full, immediate and universal ordinary power," to use the language of the *Code of Canon Law*, does not translate into affection for a massive ecclesiastical infrastructure in the Vatican or elsewhere. Indeed, like most classic conservatives, Pope Benedict has a natural skepticism about bureaucracies, seeing them as too prone to become self-justifying and self-perpetuating, taking on logics and agendas that often are inimical to the ends they were originally intended to serve.

None of this should suggest that the Vatican is especially top-heavy on bureaucracy. A staff of some 2,700 people in the Roman Curia oversees the affairs of some 1.1 billion Catholics worldwide, which upon a moment's reflection is a rather staggering indication of efficiency. Management guru Peter Drucker once calculated that if the same ratio were to be applied to the U.S. government, something on the order of 500 people would be on the federal payroll. That fact led Drucker to list the Catholic Church as one of the three most efficient organizations in history, alongside General Motors and the Prussian Army.

All the same, however well-oiled an organization may be, there is always the danger of overinstitutionalization, a kind of subtle shift in priorities that comes to regard maintenance of the apparatus itself as the greatest good. This risk has long been a preoccupation of the new pope.

"What the Church needs in order to respond to the needs of man in every age is holiness, not management," he said in *The Ratzinger Report*. "The Church, I shall never tire of repeating it, needs saints more than functionaries."

He expanded the point in *Salt of the Earth*.

"The great churches of the Christian countries are perhaps also suffering on account of their own over-institutionalization, of their institutional power, of the pressure of their own history. The living simplicity of the faith has been lost to view in this situation. Being a Christian means simply belonging to a large apparatus and knowing in one way or another that there are countless moral prescriptions and difficult dogmas. . . . The flame that really enkindles can't, you might say, burn through because of the excess of ash covering it."

In his 1988 work *A New Song for the Lord,* then-Cardinal Ratzinger was even more explicit: "In the past two decades an excessive amount of institutionalization has come about in the Church, which is alarming," he said. "Future reforms should therefore aim not at the creation of yet more institutions, but at their reduction."

All this suggests that Pope Benedict XVI, while certainly enough of a realist to understand that the Church cannot survive without an institutional dimension, is also keenly aware of the danger that institutions can sometimes get in the way of evangelization and pastoral care, and can stifle rather than foster the kind of alternative models of fully Christian life he wants the Church to offer, especially in the West, where the Church sometimes too often takes its cues from the cult of management in corporate and political life.

At the 1985 Synod of Bishops, devoted to assessing the implementation of the Second Vatican Council twenty years after its formal close, then-Cardinal Ratzinger struck many of these notes in a much-discussed speech on the synod floor. For many, he said, the Church has the image of "a great multinational" with a self-preoccupation that can never make it "the object of love" it should be. It is "a sad spectacle," he warned, if "we are concerned only with ourselves and church structures." Such an attitude, he said, will drive people elsewhere for religion.

Moreover, Benedict XVI is skeptical that the mere fact of creating or expanding allegedly representative bodies within the Church, such as pastoral councils or lay boards, will result in more collaborative governance. In at least some cases, he believes, these bodies simply end up imposing the views of a determined minority on the life of the Church, without making the Church more sensitive to the actual concerns and needs of the entire "People of God."

"The Soviet Union began like that," he argued in *Salt of the Earth*. "The 'base' was supposed to decide things via the councils; all were supposed to take an active part in governing. This allegedly direct democracy, dubbed 'people's democracy,' which was contrasted with representative (parliamentary) democracy became, in reality, simply a lie. It would be no different in a Church made up of such councils."

Benedict XVI's papacy is therefore likely to be one where ecclesiastical institutions, and the personnel who serve them, will be reviewed, at all levels, with respect to the broader aims the Church should serve. By and large one should not expect the creation of new structures or institutions, but rather an attempt to foster a more robust Catholic spirit, and a critical eye toward the possibility that existing bureaucracy may actually stifle rather than promote life according to Gospel principles.

CURIAL REFORM

At first blush, Joseph Ratzinger may seem an odd choice to lead a reform of the Roman Curia, since he has been at the pinnacle of power in that system himself for almost a quarter-century. On the eve of his election a veteran observer of the Roman scene, Fr. Gino Belleri, director of Libreria Leoniana, argued before a packed audience at the Centro Russia Ecumenica on the Borgo Pio, just behind the Vatican, that it would be a mistake to elect Ratzinger. After so many years in office, Belleri asked rhetorically, "What does he have left to give the Church?"

Yet talking to several cardinals after the conclave had ended, it was clear that many of them indeed expect their new pope to lead an overhaul of the system in which he has lived and worked for twenty-five years. Their argument boils down to this: To reform the Curia you have to know it from inside, and on that count, no one fits the bill like Ratzinger. Further, as already noted, the cardinals came to see Ratzinger as a different sort of curial figure, a man who came into the system as a cardinal, and hence someone who does not have the same careerist debts as prelates who rose up through the Vatican's standard pathways.

"Ratzinger has always managed to stay above the fray in the Curia," one cardinal told me after the election. "The Congregation for the Doctrine of the Faith on his watch was never a political office. His relationship with the Pope was substantial, so he didn't have to worry about access. He was never seen as the quintessential curial cardinal."

"A number of residential bishops are frustrated with the Curia," this cardinal said. "They saw Ratzinger as someone who can take it in hand, and not be party to one section or the other. He knows the difficulties. There is attention needed, and he can give it."

This cardinal confirmed that such thinking "was in my mind" when he cast his own ballot for Ratzinger.

Moreover, several cardinals confirmed that Ratzinger's support in the conclave of 2005 was by no means exclusively, or even primarily, dependent upon other curial cardinals. The election of Benedict XVI was not a vote for the status quo with respect to curial patterns of governance. One of the main advocates of Ratzinger's election, Cardinal Christoph Schönborn of Vienna, for example, is not a curial figure.

So what does curial reform mean to the cardinals who elected Benedict XVI?

First of all, as one put it, it means "fewer bureaucrats and more experts." To be blunt, it means more people like Ratzinger himself in key Vatican positions, people who have the subject-area background to understand in depth the issues to which they are called upon to respond.

Ratzinger was an outstanding figure in his field, but the same cannot necessarily be said for other prefects and presidents of curial offices. At present, for example, the Congregation for Catholic Education is headed by a man who has never been an educator, the Council for Health Care is run by someone with no medical background, the Congregation for the Propagation of the Faith is led by a man with no missionary experience, and the Congregation for Divine Worship and the Discipline of the Sacraments is presided over by a man with no background in liturgy. None of this is to say that, taken individually, these men are ineffective administrators; some people praise the work that Cardinal Francis Arinze has done at the Congregation for Worship, for example, arguing that his goodwill and openness compensate for his lack of background. Moreover, some Vatican officials, schooled in neo-Thomist thought, are skeptical of the very idea of a cult of "experts" who know the price of everything and the value of nothing. Technical expertise, they insist, is less important in administering the Church than being sure that the imaginations and instincts of the people in charge are shaped by the culture of Roman Catholicism, rather than by that of whatever discipline or secular pursuit they represent.

At the same time, however, there has long been frustration among many bishops that it's difficult to have meaningful discussions with some Vatican officials who are in over their heads, and who sometimes seem to make decisions on the basis of personal ties of loyalty, or simple bureaucratic reasoning, rather than a genuine grasp of the issues at stake. This is what makes dealing with Ratzinger refreshing, they say, because at least he has done the homework and understands the material. As pope, Benedict XVI is expected to appoint more men of substance to head these Vatican offices, so that decisions will become better reasoned, more objective, and more grounded in the real issues at stake rather than extraneous institutional considerations. Under Benedict XVI, being a graduate of the Accademia, the Vatican's elite school for diplomats near the Piazza Minerva will no longer function as a quasi-automatic entitlement to hold almost any job in the Holy See.

The first sign that Pope Benedict may move quickly in this regard came on April 21, just two days after his election, when he confirmed the cardinals and archbishops currently in charge of the various offices of the Vatican, but did so *donec aliter provideatur*, roughly meaning "for the time being." In other words, the new pope put people on notice that these are not five-year appointments, and that change may be in the offing.

"At first, I heard that he had reconfirmed everyone for a year," one cardinal said the next day. "I thought, 'No, that's not good, it ties his hands.' Then when I heard it was *donec aliter provideatur*, I thought, 'Good, now he can move.'"

Second, curial reform under Benedict XVI may mean shrinking certain Vatican offices, eliminating some, consolidating others, and reducing the workforce of still others. It would not be surprising if certain offices of the "post–Vatican II curia," meaning the councils that sprouted under Paul VI, were to be reexamined under Benedict XVI. Is a Pontifical Council for Migrants and Refugees, for example, necessary as a self-standing dicastery (the Vatican term for an office of the Roman Curia); and if it is, why not a separate office for other constituencies, such as a Pontifical Council for the Unemployed or a Pontifical Council for Expatriates? Is the Pontifical Council for the Family essential, given that many of the issues with which it deals already fall under the purview of the Congregation for the Doctrine of the Faith? Given Pope Benedict's aversion to bureaucracies that become self-justifying, it's conceivable that the need for some of these dicasteries will be examined anew.

None of this should call into question the positive contributions often made by these dicasteries, or the personal dedication of the people who staff them. The point, rather, would be to take a hard-headed look at whether these contributions could be performed more efficiently, with less danger of duplication of resources or working at cross-purposes, under another arrangement. Pope Benedict's desire will be that the Curia have the bare minimum of structures necessary in order to accomplish its core purposes.

One department that will certainly not be eliminated, but may have its wings clipped, is the Secretariat of State, styled by Paul VI as a kind of "super-dicastery" that plays a coordinating role among all the others. Under Paul VI and John Paul II, in virtually every area of Church life other than doctrine, work from the other dicasteries had to move through the Secretariat of State before it could get to the pope. This was something of a reversal of curial tradition, since historically the doctrinal office (known before Vatican II as the Holy Office) was considered *la suprema*, meaning first among equals in the Vatican power structure.

The ascendancy of the Secretariat of State was long seen by critics as a triumph of bureaucracy over content, and no doubt there will be a subtle, but real, shifting of power back to the Congregation for the Doctrine of the Faith under Pope Benedict XVI. The Secretariat of State's second section, which handles relations with states and diplomatic matters, seems relatively insulated from the impact of such shifts, but the first section, which deals primarily with internal church governance, may see some reduction in both size and influence.

The new Pope may also want to consolidate the Vatican's communications operation, since one reason for the perception of conflicting messages is because there is no single office responsible for press relations. Under John Paul II, the Vatican Press Office under Navarro-Valls was responsible for relations with the print media, while the Pontifical Council for Social Communications under American Archbishop John Foley dealt with television and radio. In addition, Vatican Radio is in some sense too the "voice of the Pope." The result was sometimes duplication of efforts and mixed signals, and Benedict XVI may well ask if the work of these various offices could be better coordinated.

Finally, curial reform under Pope Benedict XVI will mean a Vatican less likely to speak with different voices, operating with greater coordination and internal focus. The days when officials such as Cardinal Renato Martino, president of the Pontifical Council for Justice and Peace, could walk into the Vatican Press Office and condemn U.S. forces for treating the captured Saddam Hussein "like a cow," then, when world headlines blared "Vatican blasts Americans," insist he had been expressing only a personal opinion, will likely draw to a close. Similarly, public clashes between cardinals, such as the dispute between Cardinal Alfonso Lopez Trujillo, president of the Pontifical Council for the Family, and Cardinal Javier Lozano Barragan, president of the Pontifical Council for Health Care, over whether married couples may ethically use condoms to prevent the spread of disease, will also likely be brought under a greater degree of control. Even relatively trivial incidents of disarray, such as the embarrassing flap over whether the Pope did or did not say "it is as it was" with respect to the Mel Gibson film *The Passion of the*

Christ, will be less likely to recur. Pope Benedict will try to ensure that the Catholic faithful are clear about the positions of the Holy See, especially when they brush up against a question of the faith.

This does not mean Pope Benedict will appoint only yes-men and choke off internal debate. In fact, if he surrounds himself with experts, men who are well-trained and creative thinkers themselves, the internal diversity of the Vatican will, if anything, increase. Moreover, Ratzinger is not expected to deny Vatican officials the opportunity to express themselves in a personal capacity. The one request he made of John Paul II when he was asked to head the doctrinal office was that he be allowed to continue publishing his own theological material, a condition John Paul readily accepted. The Pope honored that pledge, despite occasional grumbling that it was difficult to distinguish when Ratzinger was another voice in the theological conversation, and when he was speaking as the Pope's doctrinal czar. Having requested that freedom for himself, Pope Benedict will be unlikely to refuse it to his aides.

At the same time, however, he will expect those aides to be prudent in choosing the time and place for those expressions, and to avoid provocative comments that will create confusion about what the Holy See is trying to express, especially on matters of faith and morals. The expectation, in other words, is that there will be greater discipline within the Roman Curia, with fewer impressions of disarray or working at cross-purposes.

In general, then, the cardinals who elected Pope Benedict XVI expect him to transform the culture of the Roman Curia, making it more responsive to the concerns of local bishops by virtue of the fact that real experts will be making decisions, not civil servants whose main interest sometimes seems to be reminding people who's in charge. Decisions will be driven by argument, not by power plays. Further, they expect a more focused Curia, potentially a smaller one, which provides clearer direction to the bishops and to the wider world. The hope is that the relationship between day-to-day operations in the Vatican and the pastoral vision of the papacy will be less distant than it sometimes was under John Paul II, that the Pope's own desire to be collegial and to make decisions on the basis of real doctrinal and pastoral concerns will be reflected in the day-to-day operating style of the bureaucracy that serves him.

It is not mere speculation to anticipate moves in this direction from the new Pope. In September 1990, at an annual Comunione e Liberazione convention in Rimini, then-Cardinal Ratzinger addressed explicitly the subject of curial reform:

> *After the Council we created many new structures, many councils at different levels, and we're still creating them. . . . We have to be aware that these structures remain secondary things, of help with respect to the primary thing, and must be ready to eventually disappear, not substituting themselves, so to speak, for the Church. In this sense I've suggested an examination of conscience that could also profitably be extended to the Roman Curia, in the sense of evaluating whether all the dicasteries that exist today are really necessary. Following the Council we've already had two reforms of the Curia, so a third shouldn't be ruled out.*

This will not be, it should be noted, the kind of curial reform that some progressive Catholics in various parts of the world have long desired, meaning formally stripping power from the Vatican and transferring it to national bishops' conferences and local dioceses. The new pope has said many times that a strong center of authority in Rome is essential to maintaining the unity of the Church, and that in an age of instant communications, it's naïve to think that problems can remain "local" for very long. Pope Benedict, in that sense, is unlikely to deconstruct the powers of the papacy. Yet in the exercise of those powers, the cardinals who elected him expect him to be more collegial, and more reliant on good advice, than was sometimes the case under John Paul II, whose evangelical passion for encounter with the world often left him dependent upon "the system" at home.

"Reform of the Curia cannot be done without renewal of collegiality among the bishops," one European cardinal said after Pope

Benedict's election. "In electing Ratzinger, we didn't think he would be unfair in listening to the real concerns that people have."

As a cautionary note, it should be said that more than one pope has come into office with the desire of shaking things up inside the Vatican, only to find the system remarkably durable and resistant to change. The extent to which these hopes for Pope Benedict's impact will be realized remain to be seen. For now, however, the important point is to understand that by electing a "curial cardinal," the conclave of 2005 was not thereby endorsing "business as usual." In fact, the cardinals elected the one man whom they felt could get his hands around the Roman Curia to ensure that John Paul's pastoral approach, and now presumably his own, are better reflected in the way the sausage is ground in Rome.

APPOINTMENT OF BISHOPS

As part of his willingness to leave routine governance in the hands of aides, John Paul II only occasionally took a strong personal interest in the appointment of bishops. As a general matter, he would tap the first name on the *terna*, a list of three recommendations, presented to him by the Congregation for Bishops. Only in a few well-documented cases did he set aside the *terna* to make another selection; this was the case, for example, with Cardinal Edward Egan of New York, whom John Paul II had known as a judge on the Roman Rota who worked closely with him on the revision of the *Code of Canon Law* in 1983. The Pope's willingness to rely largely on the system meant that the appointment of bishops was handled in the first instance by the nuncio, or the papal ambassador, in most countries, and then by the Congregation for Bishops, which, since September 2000, has itself been headed by a product of the papal diplomatic corps, Cardinal Giovanni Battista Re.

Allowing Vatican diplomats to handle the selection of bishops, according to some critics, has meant that diplomatic criteria have been the dominant ones, which by and large have meant "safe" appointments. As a result, some Church officials believe that the quality of bishops appointed during John Paul's papacy has been rather low, with a large number of "gray" figures—reliable administrators and good pastors, but too often lacking imagination, creativity, and personal vision. Evidence of the point, some believe, can be found in the College of Cardinals itself. As noted in an earlier chapter, the short supply of truly outstanding figures in the College of Cardinals was one of the factors that made Joseph Ratzinger's election to the papacy seem such an obvious choice to many of the electors.

"The bishops appointed by John Paul II are generally very good pastors with good hearts, but they lack brains from time to time," said Cardinal Godfried Danneels of Belgium in an interview shortly before the April 18 conclave. "His nominations have been good shepherds, with a profound empathy for people, much more than thirty years ago," Danneels said. "Yet if you compare the college of bishops today with fifty or a hundred years ago, the intellectual strength of the episcopacy is much lower. The intellectual standard for bishops has declined."

One cause of this, Danneels said, is that under John Paul II, too many canon lawyers and church bureaucrats were appointed to the episcopacy and not enough theologians.

"They don't make theologians bishops anymore," he said. "The result is that you don't have many bishops who have an active life of the mind."

Danneels conceded that the vocations crisis, especially in Europe, is part of the problem, since there is often not a large corps of talented young priest-theologians in many places from whom bishops could be drawn. Still, he argued, in virtually every diocese, such candidates could be found; the problem, he insisted, is that under John Paul, such candidates were generally not desired.

One expectation among the cardinals who elected Pope Benedict XVI is that he will be more attentive to the appointment of bishops, reviewing the case files and intervening when necessary, especially in the critical early months, so that the nomination process learns to take its cues from him. They also believe he will be more likely to appoint bishops of substance, men of genuine intellectual curiosity and depth. This does not mean that anyone expects Benedict XVI to appoint theological liberals to key positions, but rather that being solid on matters of doctrine will become a necessary, not a sufficient, condition to be named a bishop. Beyond doctrinal orthodoxy, the electors expect the new pope to also look for creativity, imagination, and learning. This would be true especially of appointments to major archdioceses and positions in the Roman Curia, so that the College of Cardinals becomes more truly a collection of the "best and brightest" in the leadership of the Roman Catholic Church.

In that sense, some cardinals compare the kind of appointments they expect from Pope Benedict to those made in the era of Pope Pius XII. Although Pius XII was in most regards a theological conservative, he made a series of impressive appointments of men who did not necessarily share his views on every particular: Julius Döpfner in Munich, Josef Frings in Cologne, Franz König in Vienna, Giacomo Lercaro in Bologna, Bernard Alfrink in Holland, and Giovanni Battista Montini in Milan, who would later become Paul VI. All were men of genuine learning; Montini, for example, is said to have moved ninety cases of books with him to Milan from Rome. They were men of substance, who later become the architects of the Second Vatican Council precisely because they had the depth and independence of judgment to make decisions for themselves. Pope Benedict XVI, in the eyes of many of the cardinals who voted for him, can be expected to make similarly well-considered and thoughtful appointments to the episcopacy, identifying candidates on the basis of objective criteria, and looking for the best rather than the safest candidate.

One indication of Pope Benedict's capacity for sound judgment about bishops' appointments came in 1985, when the long-serving Cardinal Franz König stepped down in Vienna, Austria. At the time, Pope John Paul II's personal secretary, then-Monsignor Stanislaw Dziwisz, informed the Congregation for Bishops that the Pope had Auxiliary Bishop Kurt Krenn of Vienna in mind as König's successor. Krenn was known even then as not only sharply conservative but, at least in the minds of some, as an isolated and unstable figure. When John Paul had appointed Krenn as an auxiliary in Vienna with special responsibility for cultural affairs, the choice was ridiculed after Krenn admitted on national television that he could not name a single living Austrian artist, painter, poet, sculptor, novelist, musician, or scientist. Later he became the bishop of Sankt Pölten, and within the Austrian bishops' conference Krenn developed a reputation as pugnacious, difficult, and somewhat erratic. In 2004, Krenn would have to resign in disgrace as bishop of Sankt Pölten when photos of seminarians and staff members in sexually provocative poses were published in an Austrian magazine, and one of his seminarians was found to have a computer brimming with images of child pornography.

According to reports in the Austrian press, it was Ratzinger who blocked Krenn's elevation to the cardinal's post in 1985, persuading John Paul not to make the appointment. Austrian journalist Norbert Stanzel reported the intervention in his 1999 biography of Krenn, *Die Geisel Gottes* ("The Scourge of God"). Krenn had studied under Ratzinger at Tübingen in 1965, and the two were colleagues on the theology faculty at Regensburg during the 1970s. Sources told Stanzel that Ratzinger had strong personal reservations about Krenn. Though Stanzel does not spell out what they were, it's not hard to guess; Ratzinger knew that Krenn would be a disaster in a high-profile forum such as Vienna, and, in effect, saved the Pope from himself. It is the kind of sober, objective judgment that many cardinals expect him to bring to bear on a broad scale.

For the United States, this aspect of Benedict's papacy could be especially important, given that four of the seven residential cardinals in the country are within two years of retirement age, if they have not already reached it. That suggests Pope Benedict will be in a position to make a series of appointments in the coming months that will shape the Catholic Church in the United States for years to come.

BISHOPS' CONFERENCES

As the head of the Congregation for the Doctrine of the Faith, then-Cardinal Joseph Ratzinger led a reevaluation of the nature and purpose of bishops' conferences that resulted in the 1998 papal document *Apostolos Suos*. In effect, it held that episcopal conferences have no theological status of their own, and hence have no authority to teach unless they do so unanimously—that is, drawing on the individual authority of each member bishop, or with the prior approval of the Holy See. The point, as Ratzinger and others saw it, was to clarify that a conference is an administrative organism, not a theological reality; each bishop, by himself, is the vicar of Christ in his diocese, and cannot dislodge his responsibility onto a bureaucratic structure. *Apostolos Suos* built on Ratzinger's long-standing concern that the expanding size and scale of conferences around the world, especially in places such as the United States and Germany, risked creating a situation in which majority votes and the agendas of ecclesiastical bureaucrats, rather than decisions made in conscience by bishops, would set the tone in the life of the Church.

"It is a matter of safeguarding the very nature of the Catholic Church, which is based on an episcopal structure and not on a kind of federation of national churches," he said in *The Ratzinger Report*. "The national level is not an ecclesial dimension."

To some extent, this wariness about conferences reflected his larger concern with bureaucracies, which in his view tend to flatten and institutionalize the creativity and boldness of individual leaders. He saw this, he felt, in the way the German Catholic Church responded to the rise of the Nazi movement.

"The really powerful documents against National Socialism were those that came from individual courageous bishops," he said in 1985. "The documents of the conference, on the contrary, were often rather wan and too weak with respect to what the tragedy called for."

Aidan Nichols, in his 1987 study *The Theology of Joseph Ratzinger*, argued that part of the cardinal's ambivalence about conferences can be traced to the theology of the *Volk* developed by some German Protestants who became apologists for National Socialism. The danger, Ratzinger felt, is that of allowing an element of nationalism to creep into the Church's self-understanding and theological reflection, so that a conference comes to see itself as a sort of mediator between the universal

Church and the Church in a given nation. Taken to an extreme, this could produce a distorted sense of the universality of Roman Catholicism, whereby "American Catholicism" or "Brazilian Catholicism" end up as distinct religious groupings, rather than local manifestations of the one, universal Church.

Finally, Ratzinger has also been concerned that the bishops could find themselves manipulated by forces bent on co-opting the conference in favor of particular aims.

"In many episcopal conferences, the group spirit and perhaps even the wish for a quiet, peaceful life or conformism lead the majority to accept the positions of active minorities bent upon pursuing clear goals," he said.

None of these reservations means that Pope Benedict will shut down bishops' conferences around the world, or refuse to meet with their officers. On the contrary, he can be expected to maintain cordial relations with the officers of national conferences, most of whom he already knows and is accustomed to seeing on a regular basis. In the early 1990s, Ratzinger made a series of trips to various parts of the world to meet with the heads of doctrinal commissions of the various bishops' conferences in those regions, and the Congregation for the Doctrine of the Faith instituted regular dialogues with the staff and officers of the bishops' conferences. The new pope thus brings a history of what he regards as largely positive contacts with bishops' conferences, and he will doubtless want that to continue.

"Above all, our contacts with the bishops' conferences have led to greater mutual understanding and have also helped the bishops to a common view of their task, in common among themselves and in common with Rome," he said in *Salt of the Earth*.

At the same time, however, Pope Benedict will strive to ensure that what he hears in these dialogues with episcopal conferences is truly the voice of the bishops, and not that of a class of ecclesiastical apparatchiks. Further, the fact that a bishops' conference has adopted a given position by a majority vote will likely count for less in Benedict's papacy when he has to make decisions about policies for a given nation or region.

Given his skepticism about the inner dynamics of bureaucratic structures, this will not be a pope who defers to the judgments of conferences when he believes important matters of faith or church discipline are at stake.

Equally importantly, Pope Benedict will encourage bishops to take personal responsibility for the internal deliberations within conferences, so that the work is truly that of bishops and not a class of "experts" whose own judgments and instincts end up dominating the conference's work. The Pope is therefore likely to encourage bishops, especially those in countries with powerful and well-funded conferences, to review their structures and systems to be sure that they truly serve evangelical rather than bureaucratic ends. In that sense, many conferences may be likely to undergo the same review and winnowing that many expect for the Roman Curia. The new pope may be skeptical of new structures—such as the National Review Board, set up in the United States to respond to the sexual abuse crisis—which he believes run the risk of relieving bishops of the personal responsibility for making difficult decisions.

The overall thrust of Benedict's papacy in this regard will be to emphasize the direct responsibility of bishops to teach, sanctify and govern, and to take personal responsibility for these choices rather than shifting that responsibility onto staffs or structures, and to encourage Catholics to think of themselves as members of the universal Church first, so that other markers of identity—race, nationality, class—become relative and secondary. In the inevitable tension between the local and the universal Church, Pope Benedict is decidedly a man of the universal, and will not want to see institutional structures at varying levels confuse Catholics about their primordial membership by virtue of baptism in the one, holy, Catholic and apostolic Church.

ECCLESIASTICAL INSTITUTIONS

One of the longest-running controversies in the United States during John Paul's papacy came over Catholic colleges and universities. In his August 15, 1990, document *Ex Corde Ecclesiae*, the Pope encouraged

Church-affiliated colleges to revitalize their Catholic-Christian identity, ensuring that the values of Roman Catholicism, and not secular academia, set the tone. The point was not that Catholic universities shouldn't strive to meet the highest secular standards of excellence, but that beyond these measures, they should foster authentic Catholic belief and practice, and ensure that Gospel principles are reflected in curriculum, instructional method, and every other facet of institutional life. To a great extent, John Paul had the United States specifically in mind, where critics charged that some of the nation's premier Catholic institutions had unacceptably compromised their religious identity. A debate at the Jesuit-run Georgetown University over whether it is appropriate to display crucifixes in classrooms was often cited as a classic case in point. Fr. James Burtchaell's much-discussed 1998 book, *The Dying of the Light*, was for some a wake-up call on the issue.

The most controversial provision of *Ex Corde* required Catholic theologians to receive a *mandatum*, or license, from their local bishop, certifying their orthodoxy. After years of resistance, including strong resistance from the leadership of Catholic colleges and universities in the United States, the U.S. bishops finally approved norms in 1999 that gave the Vatican most of what it wanted. The decade-long controversy had the effect of forcing many colleges and universities to confront anew what it means to call themselves "Catholic," but at the same time it deepened a climate of resentment and mistrust between bishops and theologians in some cases, and resulted in the impression that Rome and elements of the American hierarchy wanted to squelch academic freedom on Catholic campuses. Some prominent Catholic theologians publicly refused to request a *mandatum*, and many others just quietly let it drop.

Under Pope Benedict, such a protracted struggle over the preservation of Catholic institutions would be less likely. The Holy See will be hesitant to expend resources to keep nominal control over institutions perceived as already lost to secularism. The new pope has on many occasions made the argument that it is a mistake for the Catholic Church to attempt to preserve a sprawling network of institutions if those institutions are no longer motivated by a strong sense of Catholic identity. Quality, not quantity, will be this pope's watchword. The Church's reason for existence, from his point of view, is not to operate more schools or hospitals than anyone else, but to ensure that in whatever the Church does do, a mode of life is fostered that allows the Gospel to shine through, showing the world what a life based on Christian principles looks like. Better to have one college that does this convincingly, from Benedict's point of view, than ten that are muddled and compromised, bringing the Church into disrepute.

In part, this insight also reflects the Pope's experience of German Catholicism during the era of National Socialism. In his memoir, *Milestones*, Ratzinger reflected on the German church's struggle to hold on to its schools under the Nazis.

"It dawned on me that, with their insistence on preserving institutions, [the bishops] in part misread the reality," Ratzinger wrote. "Merely to guarantee institutions is useless if there are no people to support those institutions from inner conviction."

In fact, the new pope observed, by the 1930s, the older generation staffing most Catholic schools was rabidly anticlerical, reflecting the "away from Rome" mood of German Catholicism of the late nineteenth and early twentieth centuries. The young generation, meanwhile, was infected with the ideology of National Socialism, and the consequent hostility to systems of thought that did not arise from German soil. Thus the overwhelming majority of those working inside the Catholic school system did not share the core principles the system was supposed to foster, and yet the German Catholic bishops fought titanic battles to maintain their control over the schools, preserving the fiction that they were still "Catholic."

"So in these cases," Ratzinger has written of those struggles, "it was inane to insist on an institutionally guaranteed Christianity."

The new pope's conviction is that sometimes the best thing the Church can do under such a set of circumstances is to let an institution go, recognizing that once its vital link with the faith is severed, clinging to it merely fosters the impression that the Church is interested in possessing institutions for their own sake. In other words, it too often gives people the impression that institutional Christianity is primarily about wealth, power, and social prestige, rather than the ideals it professes. Under some circumstances, Ratzinger has argued, it's better to become smaller and less socially significant, in order to remain faithful.

He laid out this view in *Salt of the Earth*: "Once the Church has acquired some good or position, she inclines to defend it. The capacity for self-moderation and self-pruning is not adequately developed," he said. "It's precisely the fact that the Church clings to the institutional structure when nothing really stands behind it any longer that brings the Church into disrepute."

The same point applies also to other institutions, such as hospitals and hospices, social service agencies, youth programs, and all the other structural expressions of the Church's ministries. The important thing, from Pope Benedict's point of view, is not to be the ecclesiastical equivalent of McDonald's, with a franchise on every corner. The key is to make sure that those institutions the Church does operate are animated by an integral, uncompromised sense of Catholic identity.

The likelihood, therefore, is that the battles waged under John Paul II over the *Ex Corde* issue, for example, will not recur in the pontificate of Benedict XVI. The new pope will be inclined not to waste energy defending the nominal Catholic identity of institutions that have already, in his view, severed meaningful ties to the Church. His inclination would to be to let these institutions go, concentrating instead on expressions of authentic ecclesial life, which may not be too numerous, but which in his view keep the Catholic vision of human life alive.

THE SEXUAL ABUSE CRISIS

When the *Boston Globe* broke a story on January 6, 2002, about Cardinal Bernard Law's inaction regarding accusations of sexual abuse against a former Boston priest Fr. John Geoghan, it triggered what would eventually become the deepest crisis in the history of American Catholicism.

Revelations that bishops had been aware of charges of sexual abuse against priests and yet left them in active ministry, in some cases transferring them to new assignments without notifying anyone of their past, generated wide indignation both at the grass roots of the Catholic Church and in the American press. The white-hot period of the scandal faded after 2003, but many dioceses around the country, including major urban dioceses such as Los Angeles, continue today to face potentially crippling litigation related to these episodes.

In the early stages of the crisis, a number of Vatican officials expressed skepticism both about the true dimensions of the scandal and the motives of lawyers and journalists for resurrecting cases that often lay decades in the past. While these officials no doubt intended to come to the defense of the American Church, in many ways the public statements proved unhelpful, creating an impression of a hierarchy "in denial" about the seriousness of the problem and engaging in the typical cover-the-wagons pattern of response that many critics felt had generated the crisis in the first place.

Among the senior Vatican aides making such statements was then-Cardinal Joseph Ratzinger. His most explosive statement came during an appearance in Murcia, Spain, on November 30, 2002, at a congress titled "Christ: Way, Truth and Life," at the Catholic University of St. Anthony. Ratzinger was asked, "This past year has been difficult for Catholics, given the space dedicated by the media to scandals attributed to priests. There is talk of a campaign against the Church. What do you think?"

"In the Church, priests also are sinners," Ratzinger replied. "But I am personally convinced that the constant presence in the press of the sins of Catholic priests, especially in the United States, is a planned campaign, as the percentage of these offenses among priests is not higher than in other categories, and perhaps it is even lower. In the United States, there is constant news on this topic, but less than one percent of priests are guilty of acts of this type. The constant presence of these news items does not correspond to the objectivity of the information or to the statistical objectivity of the facts. Therefore, one comes to the conclusion that it is intentional, manipulated, that there is a desire to discredit the Church."

Many took the comments as an attempt to minimize the crisis and to blame the media for exaggerating its contours. In hindsight, Ratzinger had relied on misleading data about the percentage of priests against whom credible accusations had been made; a study commissioned by the U.S. bishops from the John Jay College of Criminal Justice in New York that was released in February 2004, a year and a half after Ratzinger's speech, found that in the period between 1950 and 2002, 4.3 percent of diocesan priests and 2.5 percent of religious order priests faced at least one accusation of sexual abuse. Ratzinger had based his November 2002 comment on an earlier estimate given by Philip Jenkins, an American Catholic writer, who drew on a study of accusations against priests in the Archdiocese of Chicago in a period well before the current crisis began.

In the aftermath of these comments, some American Catholics, especially the victims of sexual abuse and their advocates, styled Ratzinger as merely another bishop with his head in the sand about the reality of the crisis, unwilling or unable to take steps to address it. In fact, however, Ratzinger was by that time already getting "up to speed" on the American situation. In May 2001, John Paul II had entrusted his office with the juridical responsibility for processing accusations against priests. Under the weight of the evidence he reviewed, Ratzinger seems to have developed a new appreciation for the gravity of the situation, and the need for a firm response from church authority.

There are two tribunals in the Congregation for the Doctrine of the Faith that examined the cases, with the Promoter of Justice, Monsignor Charles Scicluna from Malta, in charge of coordinating this process. Under Scicluna's leadership, by November 2004 the congregation had responded to more than 500 of the 750 cases submitted, an astounding turn-around given normal Vatican work rhythms. Among other things, this makes the new pope one of the few churchmen anywhere in the world, including in the United States, to have read the files of virtually every Catholic priest ever credibly accused of sexual abuse in recent decades, giving him a familiarity with the contours of the problem that virtually no other figure in the Catholic Church can claim.

Ratzinger has also learned something about the crisis from being the target of a lawsuit, in this case one filed in the 127th District Court of Harris County, Texas. Three alleged victims of sexual abuse in the United States ("John Does I, II and III") sued Ratzinger on the grounds that he acted outside of his authority when he sent a letter to Catholic bishops around the world in May 2001, subjecting accusations of sexual abuse against priests to secrecy and the authority of his office. On March 25, 2005, attorneys representing Ratzinger filed papers in a federal court indicating that Ratzinger had acted as Prefect of the Congregation for the Doctrine of the Faith, and as such enjoys sovereign immunity. The filing came just eight days before Ratzinger was elected pope.

This experience seems to have had an effect in the mode of response to the crisis from the congregation. Of the five-hundred-plus cases Ratzinger's office had dealt with as of fall 2004, the majority were returned to the local bishop authorizing immediate action against the accused priest. In a more limited number of cases, the congregation has asked for a canonical trial, and in a few cases the congregation has ordered the priest reinstated. This marks something of a reversal from the initial insistence from Vatican officials, Ratzinger included, that in most instances accused priests deserved the right to canonical trial. Having actually sifted through the evidence, however, Scicluna and Ratzinger drew the conclusion that in many instances the proof is so overwhelming that immediate action is justified.

The new pope's sensitivity to the question can be glimpsed from an exchange on the subject with Cardinal Francis George of Chicago, which George described during a postconclave session with the press at the North American College.

Two days before the opening of the conclave, George said he had a conversation with Ratzinger about the American sex abuse norms, in light of the fact that the Vatican will shortly have to make a decision about whether to reauthorize those norms, which were initially approved for a provisional two-year period. George said he wanted to discuss with Ratzinger the arguments for leaving the norms, the heart of which is the "one strike" policy by which priests are removed from ministry for life for even one act of sexual abuse of a minor, more or less as they are. George asked if Ratzinger had any questions. Ratzinger, according to George, showed "a good grasp of the situation."

Forty-eight hours later, Ratzinger was the pope. As George kissed his hand, Pope Benedict XVI made a point of telling him, in English, that he remembered the conversation the two men had had about the sexual abuse norms, and would attend to it. George said he hoped survivors' groups would be "reassured" by the Pope's comment. He also said he has "reason to believe" that the new pope will extend the American norms as they are.

Aside from this direct experience of the crisis, there are two other factors in Pope Benedict's background that dispose him to react aggressively to the sexual abuse crisis. First, he has a high theology of the priesthood, and seeing it tarred through the abuse of children by priests is deeply shocking; second, Pope Benedict also has a keen sense of the bishop's role as governor, and will be inclined to foster a stronger sense of accountability for the administrative dimension of the bishop's task. Under Benedict's papacy, Rome's engagement on the issue is likely to be swifter and more aggressive. There will be a clear sense that someone in Rome is paying attention.

Finally, two responses to the sexual abuse crisis that were already under way prior to Benedict XVI's election are likely to get an emphatic boost from the new pope.

First, an apostolic visitation of American seminaries is currently being organized, and the Pope will want to see this process taken seriously. He has a keen sense of the need for attention to priestly formation, especially the presentation of doctrine in seminary education and the kind of spiritual and personal disciplines seminary life fosters. The Pope is therefore likely to take a strong personal interest in the outcome of this process.

Second, the Congregation for Catholic Education has, for some time, been preparing a document on the admission of homosexuals to seminaries. The document was close to publication under John Paul II, and will now rest in the new pope's hands. Though Pope Benedict will want to hear the views of the American bishops on the question, the document seems destined for eventual publication, especially given then-Cardinal Ratzinger's unambiguous conviction, expressed in a 1986 document of the Congregation for the Doctrine of the Faith, that homosexuality is an "objective disorder" that implies an inclination to sin. This does not mean that Benedict XVI sees the sexual abuse crisis as a "homosexual" issue. It does mean, however, that in the general review of seminary policies occasioned by the crisis, this looms as one point where the Pope may support a tightening of discipline that he and others regard as a matter of fidelity to the priest's capacity to stand "*in persona Cristo*, "in the person of Christ."

CULTURE SHOCK

Pope Benedict XVI is not going to turn the Catholic Church on its ear overnight, nor is he going to launch a purge to get rid of "undesirables." Despite the fevered imaginations of some parties on all sides of ecclesiastical debates, Benedict's leadership will almost certainly be more measured, more moderate, and more collaborative, than most are expecting.

"My real program of governance is not to do my own will, not to pursue my own ideas, but to listen, together with the whole church, to the word and the will of the Lord, to be guided by Him, so that He himself will lead the Church at this hour of our history," Pope Benedict said in his homily during his inaugural Mass.

At the same time, however, over the arc of his papacy, one can expect a gradual evolution in the culture of the Catholic Church.

- "Evangelization" will be defined less in terms of mass events or numerical expansion, and more in terms of the Church's capacity to inspire passion for living an authentically Christian life, however sociologically insignificant the number of people with this vocation may be.

- "Ministry" will be defined less in terms of a profusion of programs and services that secular agencies can also offer, and more in terms of direct pastoral activity, celebration of the sacraments, and preaching of the Gospel.
- "Collaboration" will be seen less as a matter of creating or expanding the structural dimension of the Church, through councils and boards, and more as immersion in the spiritual, liturgical, and ministerial activity of the Church, resulting, at least in theory, in a naturally reciprocal relationship between pastors and people.
- "Catholicity," meaning the markers of Catholic identity, will be defined less in terms of institutional affiliation, external indicators, or a general "feeling" of identification with the Catholic tradition, and more in terms of the interior life, belief, and practice associated with a given activity. In effect, this may mean that over time, fewer activities come to be seen as specifically "Catholic."
- "Episcopacy" will be understood less by way of analogy to the manager of large corporate structure, and more in terms of the role played by the early apostles of being the chief teacher, overseer, and liturgical leader of a local Church.

The net result, if Benedict XVI's vision succeeds, will be a less sprawling form of Roman Catholicism, one more distinct from the culture that surrounds it, clearer on its own identity and purpose. The measure will not be how much activity the Church generates, but how much faith. As judged by the usual standards of secular success, it may seem smaller and less powerful, but, in the Pope's mind, it will be more *alive*. In effect, Pope Benedict XVI adumbrated this vision in his homily at his April 24 inaugural Mass: "The Church is alive!" he insisted time and again, in a refrain that was both a propositional sentence and a statement of aspiration. It will be fanning the flames of that life that forms the heart of Benedict XVI's agenda for the Catholic Church.

Chapter Eight:

SURPRISES AND CHALLENGES

Despite persistent media images as a "conservative" pope, John Paul II was in many ways the least traditional pope of modern times. Over the course of a quarter-century, he redefined the nature and the style of the papal office, making it a more evangelical and less managerial position. He did all manner of things that popes weren't supposed to do, like saying he was sorry (more than fifty times, all told), beatifying and canonizing at a dizzying rate, and breaking the old model that the world comes to the pope by traveling the equivalent of three and one-third times the distance between the earth and the moon. Until the very end, he remained a pope of surprise, always capable of upending business as usual.

This capacity to do the unexpected came across in matters large and small. On the eve of his trip to Greece in 2001, for example, I was interviewed on Greek state television about whether the Pope would apologize for the Fourth Crusade, which resulted in the sack of Constantinople and hardened anti-Latin feelings among the Christians of the East.

"You shouldn't expect it," I said in response. "Though John Paul has apologized for different historical episodes such as the Galileo case, these are always controversial moves that have to be well-prepared theologically. A pope doesn't simply offer an apology off the cuff."

Those comments were broadcast on Greek television screens just before John Paul sat down with Archbishop Christodoulos of Athens on the Acropolis on May 4, 2001, and offered precisely the apology I had confidently predicted he would not utter.

A similar scene played out in Toronto in 2002, when John Paul II arrived for World Youth Day. By that stage, the Pope's Parkinson's disease and other ailments had rendered him effectively unable to move. As I walked down the rear stairway of the papal plane and across the tarmac, I got a call on my cell phone from a producer at CNN asking if the Pope would walk down the front stairs under his own power, as a show of resolve.

"Are you kidding?" I said. "He can't do it. It's not going to happen."

The producer then suggested I look over my right shoulder to the main stairwell, where John Paul had just begun to do what I had once again predicted he could not, and would not, do.

A POPE OF SURPRISES

If John Paul II was a consummate man of surprise, at first blush his successor seems a man cut from a more conservative, traditionalist cloth, less likely to dazzle the world with unpredictable flourishes. Yet it is precisely the rigidity of those expectations, the popular sense that one knows exactly what Joseph Ratzinger will do now that he holds the top job in Roman Catholicism, which may actually transform him, too, into a "pope of surprises," though perhaps not quite in the same world-shaking way as John Paul II.

The reality is that one cannot draw a straight line from Cardinal Joseph Ratzinger's service as the prefect of the Congregation for the Doctrine of the Faith and his new role as Supreme Pontiff. An erudite and spiritual man, Pope Benedict XVI understands that he is playing a new role, that his prime task is less defending the faith than inspiring it, and that this calls on him to think and act in new ways. Whatever people's expectations, their hopes or fears about the pontificate of Benedict XVI, the new pope may well confound them all.

Public Image

For one thing, Pope Benedict XVI will not come across as the dour, pessimistic figure that many associate with his years as the head of the Vatican's doctrinal office. As already noted, this is a man with an impish sense of humor, a reservoir of grace in interpersonal situations, and a genuine appreciation for beauty and the arts. He will be a much more positive, upbeat public figure than many expect. Despite his somewhat gloomy diagnosis of the contemporary situation, Pope Benedict XVI is a happy man, and this will become clear as the world gets to know him.

Benedict XVI will also be someone to whom the world pays attention. Whatever people make of his doctrinal views or his cultural criticism, everyone understands that given the force of his intellect, he is a figure of whom one must take account. When he speaks, he will not do so in empty platitudes or superficial formula that come off as simplistic sermonizing; he will cut to the quick, sparking debate, generating conversation, making headlines. Heads of state and other VIPs will seek his counsel, will invoke his words and take note of his teachings. He will be a forceful participant in moral and political debates. In the language of street politics, he will be a "player."

His pontificate will not be a repeat of the final years of Pope Paul VI, when the "Hamlet pope" retreated into a self-imposed exile. Benedict XVI will be a consequential public voice, a leader who will inspire pride among Catholics who want their pope to be taken seriously. That heft will generate enthusiasm when he travels and during public events in Rome, and although no one expects that Benedict will have the same populist magic associated with John Paul II, he will nevertheless generate surprisingly large and enthusiastic crowds, startling many who expect a drop-off in the drawing power of the papacy.

Benedict will also make a special point of reaching out to the young, again surprising those who regarded the outreach under John Paul II as an unrepeatable feature of his papacy. The new pope struck this very note in the homily at his inaugural Mass. Addressing young people, Benedict quoted from John Paul's own installation Mass on October 22, 1978: "Be not afraid of Christ!" Boisterous cheers erupted. "Yes, open the doors to Christ," he said, continuing John Paul's words, which have become something of a motto.

For Benedict, this is not simply a matter of fidelity to the pastoral approach of the Pope he served, though that in itself would be a weighty consideration. It is also consistent with his deep desire to encourage the formation of islands of Christian life in contrast with the dominant culture. He realizes that it is far easier to entice young people to disengage themselves from the dominant ethos than adults, who are often less open to significant change in worldview and lifestyle. To be the "Benedict" of his era, the man who marked out a new path as an old order fell apart, the Pope realizes that he must establish a rapport with the young.

Pope Benedict has another advantage as a public figure that has been underappreciated: his remarkable command of languages. When he addresses groups from various parts of the world, he will be able to do so in their own language, and not just working from a prepared text, but making the impromptu comments and off-the-cuff quips that cement a pope's bond with his audience. His fluency is not just a matter of grammar and syntax, but it reflects the extent to which he grasps the cultural and intellectual forces that have shaped different parts of the world. He will be able to draw upon that fluency as he crafts his messages. In that sense, while Benedict XVI may never attain the moniker of Great Communicator, by which John Paul II was known, he will nevertheless be surprisingly effective.

Finally, it is still unclear to what extent Pope Benedict's reputation as an "enforcer" will follow him to the Apostolic Palace. The very name "Ratzinger" strikes terror in some quarters, and progressive-minded Catholics received his election as an omen of dark days ahead. Such reactions are perhaps not entirely exaggerated, as the Pope has previously suggested that the Church may need to become smaller to remain true to itself, and no doubt some elements on the liberal wing of Catholicism are part of what he has in mind in terms of potential downsizing. In

September 2003, Raymond Arroyo of the Eternal Word Television Network asked then-Cardinal Ratzinger if his vision of the future meant "smaller numbers." He replied:

> *Smaller numbers, I think. But from these small numbers we will have a radiation of joy in the world. And so, it's an attraction, as it was in the old Church. Even when Constantine made Christianity the public religion, there was a small number at this time; but it was clear, this is the future. . . . And so, I would say, if we have young people really with the joy of the faith and this radiation of this joy of the faith, this will show to the world, "Even if I cannot share it, even if I cannot convert it at this moment, here is the way to live for tomorrow."*

Yet Pope Benedict has not given any indication that he intends to artificially force a contraction by drumming people out willy-nilly, the episode involving Fr. Thomas Reese notwithstanding. Immediately after his election was announced on April 19, some Catholic conservatives began talking about the great crackdown to come, but the very choice of the Pope's name might have given them pause. Benedict XV, to whose memory the new pope explicitly linked himself, was the man who brought the antimodernist crackdown under Pius X to a halt, saying that elaborate loyalty oaths were not necessary. Benedict XV said instead that it was enough for one to say, "Christian is my name, Catholic my last name." He was seen as a pacifier and reconciler after years of bruising intra-Church battles.

Whether Benedict XVI will be inspired by the same moderate, healing impulse remains to be seen. No doubt he will be resolute if matters of faith are at stake, but to date there are no signs of any great putsch. Ironically, it may turn out to be the self-appointed members of the "orthodoxy police" who are most disappointed in Pope Benedict's reign, given their high expectations.

None of this should obscure the reality that Pope Benedict will lead a decisive pontificate, which will include some difficult moments. He

will discipline theologians, intervene to correct pastoral practices he believes have gone astray, and issue challenging documents that will generate controversy and, in some quarters, pain. Some will see this as fueling
polarization in the Church, others as the price that must be paid for fidelity. The point, however, is that causing division will not be the aim
of his pontificate, and perhaps not its most memorable feature.

Ecumenism

Traditionally, in Church politics, those most passionately in favor of ecumenism, or the search for unity among the various Christian denominations, have been liberals for whom doctrinal disputes have never been
as important as the basic sense that in order to credibly preach the
Gospel, Christianity must demonstrate love and reconciliation. Conservatives, on the other hand, sometimes worry that ecumenism means
glossing over important markers of identity, in effect sacrificing truth for
good intentions.

Cardinal Juan Luis Cipriani of Lima, Peru, one of the world's two
Opus Dei cardinals and a classic Catholic conservative, offered an example of these reservations about ecumenical dialogue in a June 2004 interview at his residence in Lima.

"[Other Christians] are blocked on the primacy of Peter," Cipriani
said. "But that's a matter of divine will, it's not just a question of moving cards around. It's of a divine nature . . . there's one Peter. It was not
Peter and Paul, it was Peter. I understand that some people would like
to continue on very aggressively with this movement [ecumenism], but
I am a little bit worried that it will take a high cost on the Church. So I
will not agree with people who think that way."

On the basis of this sort of analysis, which many Church-watchers
associate with Pope Benedict, the early consensus was that his election
would, on the whole, slow down Catholicism's ecumenical outreach.
Pope Benedict XVI has been at pains to say this is not so, committing
himself to the search for "full Christian unity" in his first message as
pope, in the Mass he celebrated in the Sistine Chapel with the cardinals
on the morning of April 20. Yet many observers have taken this as the

sort of proforma statement that new popes always make, and fear that as the substance of the pontificate begins to unfold, ecumenical dialogue may take a backseat.

In truth, however, the new pope is a committed ecumenist, even if his realism means that he is not terribly sanguine about the prospects for swift progress toward full structural unity.

Benedict XVI can be expected to press especially forcefully on the dialogue with the Eastern Orthodox, in particular the Russian Orthodox Church. In part, this is because he believes the Orthodox have an important role to play in his project of stirring the Christian identity of Europe. In part, too, it is because the Orthodox tend to be more theologically conservative than many of the Protestant churches of the West, so there is greater common ground on some issues. Finally, Pope Benedict is a keen student of the liturgy, and a great admirer of the liturgical traditions of Eastern Christianity.

In a 1986 work called *Seek That Which Is Above*, then-Cardinal Ratzinger said that "Rome's single condition for intercommunion should be to accept the teachings of the first millennium on the primacy of the Pope." Neither the Catholic nor the Orthodox side, he said, should view subsequent developments as heretical. This point has long been advanced by the Orthodox themselves as the sine qua non of reunion, and is sure to be well received among Eastern theologians and bishops.

Reflecting this background, reaction within the Orthodox world to the election of Benedict XVI has been remarkably positive.

Patriarch Alexei II, the head of the Russian Orthodox Church, for example, told the Moscow daily *Kommersant* on April 27 that Benedict has a "powerful intellect," and he praised the new pontiff's record for strenuously defending traditional Christian values.

"The entire Christian world, including the Orthodox one, respects him," Alexei said. "Without doubt theological differences exist [between Catholics and Orthodox]. But as far as his views on modern society, secularization and religious relativism are concerned, our points of view are very similar."

Alexei held open the possibility of a meeting with Benedict XVI, something that he would never permit with John Paul II.

"My meeting with the new representative of the Roman Catholic Church will depend on his approach to the Russian Orthodox Church, on how much willingness, wisdom and tact he shows in attempting to resolve the existing problems," Alexei told *Kommersant*. "If it happens, our meeting must demonstrate to Christians and to the whole world that our relations have changed for the better, that the difficulties of recent years have been overcome."

In light of this opening, Pope Benedict XVI may be in a position to realize the most cherished of all John Paul II's unfulfilled dreams: a trip to Moscow, to herald a new era in relations between Eastern and Western Christianity.

In his first Sunday Angelus address from the window of the papal apartments overlooking St. Peter's Square, Benedict XVI's thoughts went out to the Orthodox, noting that this day, May 1, marked their celebration of Easter.

"From my heart, I hope that the celebration of Easter will be for them a choral prayer of faith and praise to He who is our common Lord, and who calls us to pursue decisively the path toward full communion," the Pope said.

Benedict will not, however, forget the Churches of the West. As head of the Congregation for the Doctrine of the Faith, Cardinal Joseph Ratzinger in 1999 was responsible for rescuing the *Joint Declaration on the Doctrine of Justification*, an agreement signed by the Vatican and the Lutheran World Federation declaring the fifteenth-century dispute over whether salvation came by faith alone, or also through works, largely resolved. The heart of the agreement was this key sentence: "By grace alone, in faith in Christ's saving work and not because of any merit on our part, we are accepted by God and receive the Holy Spirit, who renews our hearts while equipping us and calling us to good works."

As noted earlier, Pope Benedict is enthusiastic about the growing rapprochement in the United States and elsewhere between conservative

Evangelical Christians and the Roman Catholic Church, an ecumenical flowering he will want to pursue.

The new pope's background is a bit more mixed with respect to Anglicanism. In July 1998, Pope John Paul II issued *Ad Tuendam Fidem*, a document adding penalties to canon law for dissent from certain kinds of Church teaching. Ratzinger penned a commentary offering a series of doctrines as examples of this category of teaching, which included Pope Leo XIII's 1896 document *Apostolicae Curae* that declared Anglican ordinations to the priesthood to be "absolutely null and utterly void," meaning, in effect, that priests in the Anglican Communion aren't really priests. That statement produced deep irritation among many Anglicans. More recently, the decision by Episcopalians in the United States to consecrate an openly gay bishop exacerbated Ratzinger's reservations about the future of the dialogue with Anglicans, since it seemed to him like a backward step on a core matter of moral teaching.

On the other hand, the new pope has shown interest in factions within Anglicanism striving to defend a more traditional interpretation of doctrine and church discipline. On October 8, 2003, Ratzinger sent a letter to 2,700 dissident Episcopalians meeting in Dallas, assuring them of his "heartfelt prayers."

"The significance of your meeting is sensed far beyond [Texas]," he wrote. "In the Church of Christ, there is a unity in truth and a communion of grace which transcend the borders of any nation." The conservative Episcopalians at the meeting, who opposed the consecration of the gay bishop, greeted the letter with a standing ovation. Some critics on both sides of the Anglican/Catholic divide criticized Ratzinger for meddling in the internal affairs of another denomination, but he wanted to encourage fellow Christians striving to resist the relativistic tide.

Pope Benedict the pragmatist understands that with the Churches of the West, especially the more liberal, "mainline" Protestant denominations, reunion is unlikely in the near term. He will strive to deepen theological dialogue with these bodies and seek to make common cause on the social and cultural front, but at the same time one imagines that he might entertain some potentially provocative steps from which his predecessor shrank. It's possible to imagine, for example, Pope Benedict expanding the "Anglican use" provision for members of the Anglican Communion who wish to join the Roman Catholic Church while preserving their own liturgical and devotional traditions. (In 1980, the Congregation for the Doctrine of the Faith under then-Cardinal Joseph Ratzinger approved a "pastoral provision" for Episcopalian clergy and laity entering the Catholic Church in the United States.) He may even entertain the idea of creating special Church structures, such as prelatures or apostolic administrations, for dissident Anglicans or Evangelicals who desire union with Rome but who require special pastoral care.

The leadership of those denominations might be scandalized by such moves, seeing it as a "divide and conquer" strategy on the part of the Roman Catholic Church. Ecumenical experts on the Catholic side will urge the Pope to practice caution. Benedict XVI, however, has never been a man to be hamstrung by diplomatic logic, and if he sees a pastoral and doctrinal exigency, he will act. Benedict XVI will always be polite, but one expects that his will be an ecumenism of truth, as he sees it, not of good manners.

Social Justice

Speaking with one American cardinal the day after the conclave ended, I asked what he expected to be the distinguishing features of Benedict XVI's papacy. He immediately said "secularism, those issues," almost dismissively, as if it were obvious that Pope Benedict could be expected to engage the crisis of truth in the West. Then, however, he came quickly to the point that interested him: "He will also carry forward the social thinking of John Paul II on the north/south divide."

As noted earlier, this is perhaps a surprising claim for a man remembered as the chief opponent of liberation theology in the 1980s, a movement that sought precisely to place Roman Catholicism on the side of the poor in north/south debates. Yet this cardinal insisted that Pope Benedict will not retreat from the Church's "preferential option for the poor."

"He's very aware of the growing inequality of resources, education, health care, and the spread of disease such as HIV/AIDS, which plague the developing world," the cardinal said. "This man is very committed to that agenda."

"I had breakfast with him on Tuesday morning, before the balloting resumed," the cardinal said. "He talked about the situation in Asia and Africa . . . he brought it up himself. He said he had been moved listening to bishops from the south. He said that John Paul himself said the issue of the future for the Church was no longer the East/West divide, but the north/south divide."

In his programmatic speech just twenty-four hours later, after celebrating Mass in the Sistine Chapel, the new pope indeed committed himself and the Church to pursuing "authentic social development," meaning a better deal for the world's poor. Perhaps just as decisively, he pledged continuity with the pontificate of John Paul II, and the former pope was a tireless champion of economic justice. As a final, somewhat more political consideration, Pope Benedict knows that many Catholics in the developing world were hoping for a pope from the south, precisely because they felt such a pope would give voice to their struggles and aspirations. Benedict will not want these Catholics, who today represent two-thirds of the Catholics in the entire world, to feel that the election of a European means the Church will be insensitive to their concerns.

There are intriguing hints in Pope Benedict's personal background of a largely unacknowledged social consciousness. In 2003, for example, he was part of an effort with Deutsche Bank to launch a new credit card, the "Hope 2000 Card," styled as an "ethical card." A percentage of all purchases made on the card are destined to help needy children around the world. Benedict XVI is also the first pope to enter office as a declared organ donor. In the late 1990s, a debate arose among some Catholic ethicists about the conditions under which organ transplantation is licit. On February 3, 1999, Ratzinger himself acknowledged that he was enrolled in an association of organ donors, and carries with him at all times a card indicating that he had authorized the use of his organs after his death.

"To offer, spontaneously, parts of one's body for someone who needs them is an act of great love," Ratzinger said then. "It's a gracious act of affection, of availability for others." It will be interesting to see, when the time comes, if his wishes are still honored. The worldwide impact from the example of organ donation by a pope could be remarkable indeed.

This sort of hidden activism may help explain the surprising sensitivity to issues of debt, poverty, and underdevelopment many cardinals from the south detected in then-Cardinal Ratzinger during the interregnum.

The Pope's social concerns touch not just questions of poverty and development, but also war and peace. In explaining his choice of name to the cardinals inside the conclave, he invoked the memory of Benedict XV, whom he described as a "man of peace in a time of war." In his first General Audience on April 27, he returned to the theme, referring to Benedict XV as "that courageous prophet of peace, who guided the Church through turbulent times of war," adding, "In his footsteps, I place my ministry in the service of reconciliation and harmony between peoples." In that light, one can expect Benedict XVI to emerge, as did John Paul II before him, as an apostle of peace on the global stage, and perhaps an inconvenient one for politicians accustomed to invoking the Church's moral stature on other questions.

Collegiality

A large part of the reason that conclave handicappers held back from declaring Cardinal Joseph Ratzinger a shoo-in for pope was because so many of the cardinals heading into the election described "collegiality," meaning a less authoritarian, more participatory style of governance in the Catholic Church, as a top concern. The oft-cited lament among Catholic bishops, and even some cardinals, is that under Pope John Paul II, his minions treated them like "glorified altar boys." In the minds of many analysts, that more or less ruled out Ratzinger, who had been at the pinnacle of power in Rome for twenty-four years, and thus, in the public discussion, was seen as a principal architect of the very system of

Roman absolutism that some cardinals were saying they wanted to deconstruct.

What never occurred to most observers is that a solid majority of cardinals could see Joseph Ratzinger as the *solution to*, not the *cause of*, a lack of collegiality in the governing structures of the Church. In fact, however, that's how many cardinals saw things. Essentially, they felt, if anyone can change the way the Vatican does business, it's Ratzinger.

"The vision that some have of the Holy Father as not being a man of dialogue is skewed," Cardinal Theodore McCarrick of Washington, D.C., said. "Sometimes when people don't get the answers they want, they feel they weren't listened to. But that's not been our experience."

Over and over, cardinals insisted that in their personal interaction with Ratzinger at the Congregation for the Doctrine of the Faith, he had been patient, solicitous, always open to reasonable argument—a way of doing business, many of them wryly noted, not always associated with some of his colleagues. The cardinals said they fully expect that style to flower in his papacy.

How might Pope Benedict act collegially?

First, he will continue the meetings of Synods of Bishops, but try to infuse them with more of what Cardinal Godfried Danneels of Belgium calls "a culture of debate," in which participants have a more open-ended and thorough opportunity to talk through issues and present the Pope with candid advice. When Benedict XVI confirmed that he wanted the already scheduled October synod on the Eucharist to go ahead, it was taken as a positive signal in this regard. While many bishops expressed frustration with the way the Synod functioned under John Paul II, with weeks devoted to aimless speech-making and little real opportunity for a clash of ideas, with the conclusions generally determined well in advance, they still see the Synod as the best vehicle for collegial consultation currently available to the Church.

"The Synod doesn't need to have deliberative powers if there's a real culture of debate," Danneels said in a preconclave interview. "If there is a real consensus among bishops on a given point, and the Pope hears it, he will feel himself bound to act on it."

Second, Benedict XVI will likely seek other opportunities for the members of the College of Cardinals to interact with one another, aside from formal settings of consistories when new cardinals are created. One of the great frustrations voiced by cardinals during the interregnum was that they didn't know one another well, and many expressed a desire to meet, at least in subgroups, on a more regular basis. Benedict XVI will doubtless try to find such opportunities.

"He wants to be collegial," McCarrick said of the new pope the morning after his election. "He wants the advice of the cardinals, and of the other bishops. He'll look for it in the Synods and on other occasions."

Third, Benedict XVI is expected to bring to the papacy the same approach he had as prefect of the Congregation for the Doctrine of the Faith, which is a willingness to talk matters through with bishops and other figures involved, and to wrestle objectively with the substantive issues involved before reaching a judgment. This doesn't mean that he'll satisfy all parties, and not everyone concurs that his tenure at the doctrinal congregation was always distinguished by such a collaborative style. Nevertheless, in comparison to other dicasteries, most cardinals seemed to feel they got a better deal with Ratzinger than virtually anywhere else.

As already noted, all this amounts to collegiality within the context of strong papal authority. No one expects Pope Benedict to authorize the election of bishops by local churches, or to give up oversight of liturgical translation in favor of regional or national translation bodies, or to surrender the notion that the Vatican has the right to launch a doctrinal investigation of a theologian. At the level of principle, his will remain a papacy unapologetic about its sweeping claims to the "Power of the Keys." Benedict has never been a man who believes that structural reform is the answer to revitalizing the Church, and least of all on questions of papal authority.

It is in how he chooses to exercise that authority, however, that many cardinals appear to expect a surprise. They expect to be consulted, listened to, and heard to a greater extent than has been the case in the recent past. No doubt Pope Benedict will listen; it will be fascinating to watch what he does with what he hears.

CHALLENGES

When a new pope is elected, there is a natural desire among most Catholics to support him, to give him the benefit of the doubt, so that in the early stages most criticism gets smothered under the cry of "give him a chance." This period of goodwill strikes most people as a healthy thing, and Benedict XVI is presently reaping its benefits. At the same time, however, despite the overwhelming support for the Pope in the broader Catholic community, or at least the willingness to wait before making judgments, one should not be in denial about the fact that Pope Benedict, given his history and reputation, faces challenges to win over some elements of his own flock.

If Benedict is to be the leader of the entire Roman Catholic Church, and not just its conservative wing, there are two groups particularly at the outset of his pontificate that he will need to reassure: Catholic theologians in the developed world, and progressive Catholic women. Both often feel that they were specially targeted by then-Cardinal Joseph Ratzinger in the Congregation for the Doctrine of the Faith, and both approach his papacy with a palpable heaviness of heart.

Professional Theologians

The theological community in the Catholic Church is not homogeneous, and there are many Catholic theologians who celebrated Ratzinger's election as an endorsement of a more "orthodox" standard. A large swath of the professional theological world, however, especially in the United States and western Europe, already feels that the climate of "thought control" was excessive under the pontificate of John Paul II, and is leery about where things may go under Pope Benedict.

These apprehensions have deep roots. In 1985, for example, in an interview with the *New York Times*, the respected Catholic theologian David Tracy, of the University of Chicago was critical of then-Cardinal Joseph Ratzinger.

"The problem for many of us," he said, "is that Cardinal Ratzinger seems to be conducting a campaign to impose a particular theology upon the universal Church and upon all theologians. It won't work."

Though it's been twenty years since Tracy spoke, such attitudes have not visibly softened. In February 2005, responding to a critical notification from Ratzinger's office that barred Jesuit Fr. Roger Haight from teaching as a Catholic theologian because of doctrinally suspect claims made in his 1999 book *Jesus: Symbol of God*, the board of directors of the Catholic Theological Society of America complained:

> *Ironically, rather than promote greater criticism of the book, the Congregation's intervention will most likely discourage debates over the book, effectively stifling further criticism and undermining our ability as Catholic theologians to openly critique our colleagues. In short, the Congregation's intervention in this case gravely threatens the very process of serious, systematic, internal criticism which the Congregation and the bishops have long been encouraging among theologians. While this process of internal critique can never replace the proper teaching and disciplinary roles of the Magisterium, the intervention of the Magisterium should be a last resort, reserved for situations where this process has clearly failed.*

In response to this sort of critique, Ratzinger has himself occasionally been acerbic.

"This is His Church, and not a laboratory for theologians," he snapped in 1997.

Jesuit Fr. Thomas Reese, well before he resigned as editor of *America* magazine under pressure from Ratzinger, said that the relationship between theologians and Church authorities was at the lowest ebb in Church history during the Ratzinger years than in any era since the Reformation in the fifteenth century. Even Ratzinger admirers such as Michael Waldstein, an Austrian theologian who taught at the University of Notre Dame in the 1990s, said he observed a striking degree of alienation.

"It's a really unfortunate thing that a high level of irritation among many academic theologians has developed," Waldstein said. "I saw it when I was at Notre Dame. It would have helped a lot if Ratzinger had reached out more."

This, then, marks one of the first challenges of Benedict's pontificate: a gesture of reconciliation with the mainstream Catholic theological community, a way of showing that he still respects the guild and wants its support as the main lines of his papacy take shape.

The Pope might consider, for example, inviting one of the main associations of the Catholic theologians in Europe or North America, such as the Catholic Theological Society of America, for an audience in the Vatican. Certainly, he would not shrink from using the opportunity to issue a challenge to theologians to take their Catholic identity seriously. At the same time, it would be a chance to say that he wants to listen as well as to teach. No one understands the essential role of theological debate in the life of the Church better than Pope Benedict XVI, and such an event would be an opportunity to assure theologians who may have different ideas on some issues that they will remain part of the conversation, however challenging and uncomfortable that conversation may sometimes become.

Another step that would be received as reassuring by many in the theological community would be to appoint at least one or two theologians known for moderate views, while still robustly orthodox, to the International Theological Commission, the advisory body to the Congregation for the Doctrine of the Faith. That, too, would be taken as a welcome sign that the new pope wants to reach out, especially since the commission has been criticized over the years for representing a fairly narrow band of theological opinion.

Progressive Catholic Women

In the wake of Joseph Ratzinger's election as Pope Benedict XVI, few constituencies in the Church felt more demoralized than Catholic women who dream of what they term a more "inclusive" Church, one in which the "voice of women" is heard with more regularity and effect. This group includes, but is by no means limited to, women who support a change in the teaching restricting sacramental priesthood to men. Even Catholic women who steer clear of the ordination issue, however, often feel that the Church as presently structured and administered does not do a good job of listening to women's concerns, and they see little in Ratzinger's life and career that suggests things will be different on his watch.

Over the years, the new pope has repeatedly expressed concern with what he sees as an exaggerated form of the feminist movement, even within the Roman Catholic Church.

"What radical feminism—at times, even that which asserts that it is based on Christianity—is not prepared to accept is precisely this: the exemplary, universal, unchangeable relationship between Christ and the Father. . . . I am, in fact, convinced that what feminism promotes in its radical form is no longer the Christianity that we know; it is another religion," he said in *The Ratzinger Report*. In a 1988 news conference at a conference on biblical scholarship in New York, Ratzinger critiqued feminist exegetes: "Whatever else one may say about them, [they] do not even claim to be interested in understanding the text itself in the manner in which it was originally intended. . . . They are no longer interested in ascertaining the truth, but only in whatever will serve their own particular agendas."

Neither do such views represent a dated expression of opinion. As recently as May 31, 2004, the Congregation for the Doctrine of the Faith, the Vatican's chief doctrinal agency, put out a "Letter to the Bishops of the Catholic Church on the Collaboration of Men and Women in the Church and in the World." The letter criticized tendencies in modern thought that create an "opposition between men and women, in which the identity and role of one are emphasized to the disadvantage of the other, leading to harmful confusion regarding the human person, which has its most immediate and lethal effects in the structure of the family." The document cited "radical feminism" as the source of this confusion.

Many Catholic feminists were immediately critical. Benedictine Sr. Joan Chittister charged that the document "demonstrates a basic lack of understanding about feminism, feminist theory and feminist development," and that "both the terms used and the theory appealed to in the argument is pitiably out of date and embarrassingly partial in its analysis of the nature of feminism." Her reaction offers in microcosm a version of the frequent alienation between the Catholic Church and many educated, emancipated women.

Obviously, not all Catholic women reacted in the same way. Many appreciate what they regard as the support for a "new feminism," sometimes called a "Christian feminism," in the John Paul II/Ratzinger years, which endorses the struggle for women's emancipation in the social and political spheres but without devaluing their traditional roles as wives and mothers. In this circle of thought, the new pope has been well-received.

Yet among Catholic women more persuaded by Chittister, a Benedictine sister, than by Benedict himself, there is enormous apprehension about what the new papacy may mean. (As a footnote to the above, in the immediate aftermath of Benedict's election, Chittister, who was in Rome, came across as unfailingly positive, stressing that she wanted to give the Pope a chance.) This group, representing a considerable cross-section of women's opinion in the Catholic Church, especially in the developed world, will have to be persuaded that the Pope is genuinely interested in their experiences and perspectives.

To some extent, of course, no pope can satisfy everyone, and anyone who expects Pope Benedict to ordain women or revise Church teaching on matters of abortion or birth control is living in a fool's paradise. If the only way to have a genuine dialogue with progressive Catholic women is to put those issues on the table, then it's a futile enterprise.

Yet most observers, including most women, acknowledge that the ordination issue is not the only, and perhaps not even the most important, way to phrase the debate over women's role in the Catholic Church. Women can certainly play meaningful roles in Roman Catholicism without being ordained; the confusion arises because historically, priesthood has been the gateway to power in the Church, but it does not have to be so. The priesthood is supposed to be about service, not power, and in fact there are opportunities for laity to exercise managerial and administrative authority that are not dependent upon sacramental ordination.

Here the new pope might agree.

"If I see the Church only under the aspect of power, then it follows that everyone who doesn't hold an office is ipso facto oppressed. And then the question of, for example, women's ordination, as an issue of power, becomes imperative, for everyone has to be able to have power," he said in *Salt of the Earth*.

If Pope Benedict elects to reach out to this sector of opinion, one move he might consider is to invite a group such as the International Union of Superiors General, the main umbrella group for women's religious congregations, to a Vatican audience. Like a session with theologians, this would afford the Pope a chance to make a goodwill gesture. There would be a certain element of risk involved, for it's not entirely clear how some of the women religious might react. In November 2004, when the IUSG and its male counterpart, the USG, organized a world congress on consecrated life, an audience with the Pope was originally on the schedule. At the last minute it had to be scrubbed, which was just as well, because some of the women religious had discussed boycotting the audience because of the deep alienation they felt under the papacy of John Paul II. One hopes that in the early stages of Benedict's reign, if the Pope were to reach out in this way, the reaction would be more generous.

Another gesture would be to extend the precedent set by John Paul II of appointing women to superior-level positions in the Vatican. John Paul named Salesian Sr. Enrica Rosana as undersecretary in the Congregation for the Institutes of Consecrated Life and the Societies of

Apostolic Life, the first woman ever to hold such a high position in the Roman Curia. There would be some precedent for Pope Benedict to follow suit, since for many years one of his collaborators at the Congregation for the Doctrine of the Faith was a woman, a Belgian named Marie Hendrickx. She presented the Pope's Apostolic exhortation "On the Dignity of Women" to the press in 1988, and supervised the theological preparation of some of the Pope's letters. Hendrickx gained a fleeting fame in January 2001 when she published an article in *L'Osservatore Romano* criticizing unnecessary cruelty to animals, citing specifically the modern food industry. She also questioned the moral legitimacy of bullfighting.

Of course, those with deep concerns about the place of women in the Catholic Church will be looking, over the long run, for more than token symbolism and good manners. Yet one of the miracles of Catholicism is the deep desire that Catholics have to hope; usually all it takes from authority to win back public trust is the most minimal gesture of reconciliation and understanding. A man of Pope Benedict's personal charm and sincere humility will, if he wishes, certainly be able to come up with something.

SUMMARY

The papacy of Pope Benedict XVI, 265th Supreme Pontiff of the Roman Catholic Church, promises to be the stuff of high drama. It will be driven by deep ideas, fueled by a sense of limited time and much work to do, and, perhaps, scarred by conflict inside the Church and misunderstanding without. Despite following a pontiff many believe will one day be remembered as John Paul the Great, Benedict XVI has, in some ways, an even better point of departure for greatness. He has a deeper theological and cultural preparation, a greater grasp of the dynamics of ecclesiastical governance, and an immediate international stature that it took John Paul II years to cultivate.

The peculiar drama of this pontificate is that Benedict XVI could spend that capital in so many different ways, that one can imagine such a riot of different outcomes and scenarios. Benedict could steer Catholicism into a more defensive, insular stance, persuaded that the "dictatorship of relativism" he described on the morning of the conclave is, at present, impregnable. He could cede to the desires of some of his most ardent admirers, and preside over a winnowing within the Church, a time of purification intended to eliminate once and for all dissenters and "cafeteria Catholics." Like any attempt at surgical prophylaxis, he might deem it necessary, but in the short run it would make the Church bleed.

Or, Benedict could succeed in his teaching mission to stir anew in Europe and beyond a love affair with Truth, leading to a cultural Renaissance on a grand scale. In the mode of "only Nixon could go to China," he could engineer a cultural change within the Catholic Church that deemphasizes structures in favor of mission, power in favor of love. With a gentle touch and one of his generation's best minds, he could in-spire a reawakening of the Catholic intellectual and artistic tradition, based on his own conviction that "A theologian who does not love art, poetry, music and nature can be dangerous. Blindness and deafness toward the beautiful are not incidental; they necessarily are reflected in his theology."

Every new pontificate stirs a sense of new possibilities, and few in recent memory feel as full of portent at the outset as that of Benedict XVI. Whatever the broader world may conclude about having a seventy-eight-year-old conservative German on the Throne of Peter, anyone who understands this man must intuit that there are days of great adventure, and potentially deep angst, ahead.

Will the Pope have the time to realize the epic potential before him?

Only God knows the answer. By 1998, when John Paul II was seventy-eight years old, he was already well into the winter of his life; his long, slow decline had been visibly under way for some years. How long it will be before the twilight begins to gather around Benedict XVI is anyone's guess. In September 1991, he suffered a cerebral hemorrhage that temporarily affected his left field of vision, but there is no indication that it left lingering difficulties. In August 1992, he cut his head after slipping in the bathroom during a vacation in the Italian Alps, once again without permanent consequences. In comments immediately after the conclave, Cardinal Francis George of Chicago said that two years ago the Pope seemed to experience some "difficulties," but had come back from that and "seems strong now."

The papacy, of course, weighs on a man in special ways, and Benedict's reserves of strength may be depleted quickly under its unimaginable burdens. After hearing of the result of the conclave, Benedict's own brother was dismayed: "At age seventy-eight, it's not good to take on such a job which challenges the entire person and the physical and mental existence," Georg Ratzinger, eighty-one, said. The elder Ratzinger was said to have initially sat shocked in front of his television screen in Regensburg after the announcement was made, unable to process what had just happened. Then, ever the Ratzingerian realist, he said simply: "At an age when you approach eighty, it's no longer guaranteed that one is able to work and get up the next day."

Indeed.

And yet . . . and yet, given the inner fire that still lights those piercing eyes of Joseph Ratzinger, one imagines that he will nevertheless get up, day after day, for whatever time divine providence allots him, putting his indelible mark on the Catholic Church and on history. No one who has read this Pope, who has spoken with this Pope, no one who understands the depth of his thought and the gravity of the crisis he believes stands before him, can fail to see that his papacy will be marked by the spirit of Chicago architect Daniel Burnham: "Make no small plans," Burnham said. "They have no magic to stir men's blood."

Benedict XVI, whatever else history may eventually say of him, will not preside over a pontificate of small plans.